UNIVERSITY OF NORTH CAROLINA AT CHAPEL HILL

DEPARTMENT OF ROMANCE LANGUAGES

NORTH CAROLINA STUDIES
IN THE ROMANCE LANGUAGES AND LITERATURES

Founder: URBAN TIGNER HOLMES
Editor: STIRLING HAIG

Distributed by:

UNIVERSITY OF NORTH CAROLINA PRESS

CHAPEL HILL
North Carolina 27514
U.S.A.

NORTH CAROLINA STUDIES IN THE
ROMANCE LANGUAGES AND LITERATURES
Number 221

THE *VIE DE SAINT ALEXIS*
IN THE TWELFTH AND THIRTEENTH CENTURIES:

AN EDITION AND COMMENTARY

THE *VIE DE SAINT ALEXIS*
IN THE TWELFTH AND THIRTEENTH CENTURIES:

AN EDITION AND COMMENTARY

BY

ALISON GODDARD ELLIOTT

CHAPEL HILL

NORTH CAROLINA STUDIES IN THE ROMANCE
LANGUAGES AND LITERATURES
U.N.C. DEPARTMENT OF ROMANCE LANGUAGES
1983

Library of Congress Cataloging in Publication Data

Vie de saint Alexis.
  The Vie de saint Alexis in the Twelfth and Thirteenth centuries.

  (North Carolina studies in the Romance languages and literatures;
no. 221.)
  Includes text in Old French of two versions of La vie de saint
Alexis: "C'est li roumans de Saint Alessin [S]" and "Vers d'Alexis [M2]."
  English and Old French.
  Bibliography: p. 201.
  Includes indexes.
  1. Alexius, Saint — Legends. 2. Vie de saint Alexis. 3. Alexius,
Saint — Legends — History and criticism. 4. French poetry — To 1500.
5. French poetry — To 1500 — History and criticism. I. Elliott, Alison
Goddard. II. Title. III. Series.

PQ1424.A5 1983   841'.1   83-17389
ISBN 0-8078-9225-4

I. S. B. N. 0-8078-9225-4

DEPÓSITO LEGAL: V. 2.820 - 1983   I. S. B. N. 84-499-6764-3

ARTES GRÁFICAS SOLER, S. A. - LA OLIVERETA, 28 - VALENCIA (18) - 1983

dedicated to

David Rockwell Goddard and Katharine Evans Goddard

PREFACE

It is customary to think of the scholar as a worker in splendid isolation, the inhabitant of the fabled ivory tower. In many respects nothing could be further from the truth. In preparing this edition of two versions of the *Vie de saint Alexis* I owe much to many. The work grew out of my thesis on the relationship between hagiography and epic, and I must thank all those who helped me with that arduous task, above all Joseph J. Duggan without whose erudition and sense of humor — both equally precious — I would have labored with far more pain and less joy. Financial support is as necessary as moral, and I gratefully express my thanks to the American Philosophical Society and the American Council of Learned Societies for grants which enabled me to check the manuscripts in Paris and Carlisle during the summers of 1978 and 1979. Thanks is due as well to Brown University for assistance in meeting publication costs. And finally my gratitude to those who have aided in the preparation of the final copy: to Richard Damon of the Brown University Computer Center who designed the sophisticated computer-generated concordances which facilitated my task, and to Charles Segal and David Buehler who read the manuscript with care and compassion; I owe a particular debt to Suzanne Fleischman for her meticulous and scholarly reading. The errors remain my own, but their number would be substantially greater were it not for the aid of my friends and colleagues.

TABLE OF CONTENTS

INTRODUCTION

I

HISTORY OF THE TEXT

Discussions of the Old French *Vie de saint Alexis* have concerned themselves almost exclusively with the earliest version, the Hildesheim manuscript *(L)*. As a result, little attention has been paid to the later treatments of this poem. The story of Alexis was, however, a popular one; there exist a number of retellings of his life. Some are independent versifications, in Latin and Old French, of the Latin *vita*.[1] The present study is limited to those versions united by a common error. In these poems the saint spends seventeen years in a city named "Alsis,"[2] while in the Latin *vita* and versifications made directly from it, the name of this city is Edessa.[3] All members of the "Alsis-family" of manuscripts are related, but the nature of their interdependence, although usually unquestioned, turns out to be easier to assume than to define in precise terms.

---

[1] For example, "Duxit Romanus vir nobilis Eufemianus," published by Wagner, 1964, and "Eufemianus erat, ceu lectio sacra revelat" (Wagner, 1965). Also "Praestans magnatis, summae vir nobilitatis," attributed to Marbod of Rennes, *Acta Sanctorum* 31, 254 ff. For Old French, see the version of *Alexis* in dodecasyllabic laisses published by Stebbens, 1974, and that in octosyllabic couplets published by Paris, 1879.

[2] The origin of this name remains puzzling. Rohlfs (1963) suggests that *Al* = the Arabic definite article, while *Sis* is an ancient Cilician town. See also Pächt, 1960.

[3] Other vernacular poems give "Rohais," the common name for Edessa in many medieval texts (cf. the octosyllabic poem [Paris, 1879]: "Devant que il vint a Edesse, / Une cité bien renomée / Qui ore est Rohès apelée" [304-306]).

The manuscripts in question are the following:

L   (Lamspringe), now at Hildesheim, XII. c.
Anglo-Norman, the MS most probably copied down
circa 1120.[4]

V   Vatican, Cod. Vat. lat. 5334 (fo. 125), XII. c.
Published by Pio Rajna in 1929, who dated the MS
to 1140-1160. *V* begins in the middle of 425*L*, and
continues to the end of the poem, with some omissions.[5] It is the work of a continental scribe.[6]

A   (Ashburnham), Paris, B. N. 4503, XII. c.
Probably dating to the end of the century.[7]

P¹ Paris, B. N., fr. 19525, XIII. c.
The work of a continental scribe. *P¹* contains 580
lines.

P² Manchester, The John Rylands Library, XIII. c.
Published by R. Fawtier and E. C. Fawtier-Jones,
1923. *P²*, written by an Anglo-Norman scribe in the
second half of the 13th century, contains only
strophes 1-35.

S   Paris, B. N. 12471, XIII. c.
The work of a continental scribe who reveals some
northeastern traits; published by Gaston Paris in
1872, and in the present edition.

M¹ (= *Ma*) Paris, B. N. 1553, XIII-XIV. c.
Published by Gaston Paris in 1872 and Danièle Gatto-
Pyko in 1973. The dialect is Picard-Walloon.

M² (= *Mb*) Carlisle, the Cathedral Library, XIII. c.
Copied by a continental (Picard) scribe; not published *in toto* prior to this edition.[8]

Q   A group of seven manuscripts in rhymed quatrains.
XIV. c.
Published by Léopold Pannier in 1872.[9]

---

[4] Pächt, 1960, p. 278.
[5] It lacks lines 450, 452, and 603, as well as strophes 87, 108, 109,
and 110.
[6] Burgundian, according to Segre (1974); see also Stimm, 1963, 325ff.
Wilmotte (1940) considers that the dialect shows Walloon traits.
[7] Delisle, 1891, p. 663; Waters, 1928, p. xii. *A* and *P¹* are cited from
the diplomatic edition of Foerster and Koschwitz, 1911, 6th ed., 1921.
[8] The variants of *M²* were published by Paris (*Romania*, 1888), and,
following him, by Gatto-Pyko in her 1973 dissertation. Both transcriptions,
however, are marred by inaccuracies.
[9] Pannier's edition is a composite of six MSS. Paul Meyer, 1901,
p. 300, lists another MS from the first half of the XVth c., not known

Pater deus ingenite.
A rhythmical Latin poem, studied and published most recently by Manfred Sprissler (1966). The poem dates to the XI. c.

Of these manuscripts, unquestioned pride of place has been accorded to the Hildesheim manuscript, recommended by its early date, the carefulness of its scribe, its formal perfection. Recently, however, several voices have been raised challenging *L*'s supremacy. Hans Sckommodau, followed by Robertson and Carr, [10] have championed the cause of the Ashburnham manuscript, *A,* in spite of its negligent scribe. Critical opinion has almost entirely neglected the two versions of the poem in laisses, *S* and *M,* not to mention that in quatrains *(Q).*

Previous investigations of the *Alexis* manuscripts have yielded two facts significant here. 1) The Hildesheim manuscript is the earliest, copied not later than 1123. [11] The version which it contains, however, is somewhat older than the actual manuscript, having been dated by Gaston Paris on linguistic grounds to the mid-eleventh century. [12] 2) It is not possible to construct a *stemma codicum* for those manuscripts which reproduce the Hildesheim version with varying degrees of fidelity, that is, for *L, A, P,* and *V.* [13]

---

to Pannier. B. Munk Olsen (1963) tentatively identifies the *remanieur* with Jehan de Saint-Quentin.

[10] Sckommodau, 1954; Robertson, 1970; Carr, 1976; also Elliott, 1980. For a helpful survey, with full bibliography, of the quarrel between Sckommodau and Laugsberg over the merits of *L* and *A,* see Goose, 1960.

[11] Pächt, 1960.

[12] For the language of the poem, see Ewert, 1966, p. 355. Sckommodau, 1963, has suggested that the poem was composed at the time of the First Crusade (1096-99); he sees in the work's ethos a reflection of the Cathar heresy. Mölk (1978), p. 342, also proposes a date towards the end of the eleventh century on the grounds that "Deus pater ingenite" must precede the Hildesheim poem. Jean Rychner (1977) opposes this last view, writing, "La comparaison des textes entraîne, me semble-t-il, la conclusion que le poème latin est une adaptation abrégée de la chanson française" (p. 82). I find Rychner's argument convincing.

[13] Storey, 1968, p. 29 (and see below). All possible combinations of MSS occur (line numbers are those of *L*): *VL* against *AP,* 481; *VP* against *AL,* 495; *VAP* against *L,* 493; *VPL* against *A,* 511; *VAL* against *P,* 525. For valuable and detailed analyses of the whole MSS tradition, together with an assessment of Lachmannian textual criticism as applied to the *Alexis*-tradition, see Contini, 1968, 1970, 1971.

To account for the *Alexis* manuscript tradition, we must assume either that scribal freedom was so great as to render traditional methods of textual criticism frustrating at the best, misleading and misguided at the worst; or that we are dealing with an exceptional degree of contamination. Yet another possibility is textual criticism on the part of the medieval scribes, but the manuscripts are scattered — some continental, others Anglo-Norman — so this seems less likely. What remains is to postulate the critical equivalent of the "tip of the iceberg." The *Vie de saint Alexis* was, we know, a popular work; we have, I believe, only a fraction of the versions of the tale once in existence, some of which probably circulated in written copies while others may have been transmitted orally.

In some respects, the *Alexis* tradition may best be viewed when the manuscripts are considered in reverse chronological order. Therefore this study will begin with *S* and *M* before taking up the more thorny question of the Hildesheim manuscript. One reason for this seemingly perverse behavior is that these later manuscripts are less revered than is *L*, and it is easier, therefore, to approach them with an open mind. In fact, I shall suggest that in some ways the traditional equation of earliest with best is not always justified. Nevertheless, whatever their ultimate value may be, these later manuscripts — *posteriores* but not necessarily *deteriores* — are of considerable interest.

Manuscript S. The oldest of the so-called "interpolated" versions of *L*, *S* has passed virtually unnoticed since its publication by Gaston Paris in 1872; for example, in the index to the first ten years of *Romania* (1872-1881), all references to *Alexis* are to the Hildesheim manuscript, and the reviews of Paris' edition concern themselves solely with this version. [14] Paris dated the work, on the basis of Alexis' voyage to be baptized in the Jordan river, to a period prior to the fall of Jerusalem in 1187 (see the textual note to line 341). The poem incorporates a substantial portion of *L* (about 525 lines), embedded into a 1331-line poem of 136 laisses in assonance. Although Paris occasionally utilized its readings in his critical edition of *L*, other textual critics have

---

[14] E. g., the long review of Boucherie, 1874.

not followed his precedent. Storey, for example, dismisses it, writing: "Ce manuscrit, de la main d'un copiste français très negligent, nous présente une version renouvelée du poème et considérablement augmentée."[15]

S is contained in a thirteenth-century vellum manuscript labelled "Recueil de Poesies," measuring 265 millimeters in length by 190 millimeters in width. The volume consists of two manuscripts bound together; the first (to fol. 120v) includes such edifying pieces as the "Dit des Sages" (fol. 1r), the "Dit du Corps" (fol. 7v), "De l'Unicorne" (fol. 24r) and "Caton en roman" (fol. 110r).[16] Our poem is the eleventh, occupying folios 51v through 73v. It is rubricated, "C'est li roumans de saint Alessin," and is accompanied by a miniature depicting the wedding.[17] The work is written in a single column in a clear hand.

Manuscript M: M*[18] appears to be a reworking of a poem similar to S into rhyming laisses. Gaston Paris wrote of M^1 (= Ma):

> L'auteur de notre rédaction rimée a eu sous les yeux un manuscrit de la version interpolée; le fait est clair. Toutefois ce manuscrit différait assez sensiblement du nôtre.[19]

M^1 has been twice edited, first by Maréchal in Gaston Paris' 1872 critical edition of all the Alexis manuscripts known to him, and then by Danièle Gatto-Pyko in her 1973 Florida State University Dissertation. M^2 has not been previously edited although its variants (in rather inaccurate transcriptions) have been published by

---

[15] Storey, 1968, p. 30.

[16] For a full description of the contents, see Paris' edition, pp. 207-19. The works are labeled on the flyleaf in a considerably later hand.

[17] Not, as Gaston Paris claims, "orné d'une miniature représentant Alexis mort, entouré du pape et des empereurs suppliants" (p. 6). The illumination is correctly described on p. 213.

[18] A note on terminology: Throughout this study, M^1 refers to Ma in Paris' edition, M^2 to Mb. Gatto-Pyko, in her edition, changed the sigla to M^1 and M^2. S* is used to refer to a hypothetical version similar to but not identical with S, M* to the hypothetical exemplar of M^1 (Paris) and M^2 (Carlisle); the siglum will be used to refer to readings common to both MSS. When a quoted line occurs in more than one MS, identical except for orthography or other minor variations, the text is that of the first MS listed.

[19] Paris, 1872, p. 265.

both Paris and Gatto-Pyko.[20] These poems, however, have been little valued. Storey states of M^1, "Manuscrit français mal copié et sans grand intérêt"; and comments even more laconically on M^2 (= *Mb*): "Version rimée de *Ma.*"[21]

The manuscript belonging to the Chapter Library of Carlisle Cathedral which contains M^2 was described by R. Fawtier and E. C. Fawtier Jones in *Romania,* 1924. This work, a collection of hagiographic legends and edifying tales, is in reality three manuscripts bound into a single volume. Manuscript *B*, to utilize the Fawtiers' terminology, begins at folio 112r with the "Vers d'Alexis." The Fawtiers date this section of the manuscript to the second half of the thirteenth century, and identify the dialect of the works contained in it as Picard. One other work is common to both *Alexis* manuscripts edited here, the "Dit de l'Unicorne" (fol. 24r, Paris; fol. 134r, Carlisle, where it directly follows the "Vers d'Alexis").[22] A single scribe is responsible for both works in the Carlisle manuscript, and he continued the "Dit de l'Unicorne" in the same gathering occupied by *Alexis*. The Carlisle manuscript is small, 169 by 125 millimeters. The hand which copied *Alexis* is good. The beginning of the poem is decorated with drawings of two fish, the first blue and the second red. Each laisse is indicated by capitals, alternately in red and blue, some flourished. Nothing is known of the manuscript's provenance.

M^1 and M^2 differ more than Storey's brief summary would indicate. The most obvious difference is length, M^1 containing 1376 lines, and M^2 only 1093. Length, however, does not necessarily imply completeness or preferability. The arts of *abbreviatio* and *amplificatio* were both taught in the rhetorical schools, and both techniques may exist in a single work. The poet shortens those portions of his tale which he finds confusing, uninteresting, or

---

[20] Giving the variants of M^2 in an appendix, Gatto-Pyko (1973) follows the editions of Gaston Paris (*Romania* 1888) and Foerster and Koschwitz (1911), writing, "le dit manuscrit étant inaccessible de nos jours" (p. 31). In fact the microfilm of this manuscript was made on 2 January 1969.

[21] Storey, 1968, p. 30. Both versions are in rhyme.

[22] For a full list of contents, with opening and closing lines, see the Fawtiers' 1924 study. For the "Dit de l'Unicorne et du serpent," consult Jauss (1970), VI: 2, 4036; the text of this work in the Carlisle manuscript differs from that published by Jubinal.

irrelevant, while lengthening others which appeal to him or which he feels need further clarification.

Because of its greater length and certain formal advantages, M^1 has been considered the *manuscrit de base,* and M^2 has remained unedited. Yet in spite of some deficiencies, M^2 is a valuable manuscript, preserving a number or readings preferable on several counts to those of M^1. It appears to be older and closer to S (see the textual notes).

Manuscript Q: Q, edited by Léopold Pannier in Gaston Paris' 1872 edition of *Alexis,* is a family of seven manuscripts. While I cannot here explore at length the rendition of the Alexis-legend presented by this family, its readings can aid in assessing the later tradition, and are particularly relevant to a discussion of M. A few words, therefore, are in order. The poem needs re-editing [23] for Pannier's edition is a composite of the six manuscripts known to him. Without a more reliable edition, it is difficult to determine with precision the place of this version in the later *Alexis*-tradition; it appears, however, to be closer to M^2 than to M^1 omitting, as does M^2, the soul's *planctus* which Alexis quotes in M^1 on his wedding night. This version does suggest that M^1 and M^2 were not the only representatives of the M-*family,* for in some respects Q is more closely affiliated with S than are M^1 or M^2. On occasion Q seems to have access to the tradition now represented by L (see the textual notes to S 399, M^2 1002). Q's rendition of the legend is romantic. The treatment of the bride is sentimentalized, recalling, for example, the development afforded to Aude in the later *Roland* tradition. The poet seems obsessed with the division of the wedding ring, describing this incident in loving detail and returning to it later in his tale (it is the only possession Alexis retains in exile).

Crucial to any understanding of the *Alexis*-manuscript tradition as a whole is a determination of the exact nature of the debt owed by S to $LAPV$. Gaston Paris, writing before the studies of Milman Parry and others increased our knowledge of oral poetry, assumed that the Hildesheim manuscript, "le texte primitif," represented the written exemplar of S, "le texte remanié." Moreover, according

---

[23] In her thesis Gatto-Pyko says she intends to prepare a new edition.

to Paris, the author of *S* modified his exemplar no more significantly than did the author of *A:*

> Le mot de *renouvellement* n'est pas tout à fait juste pour
> désigner le travail que nous a conservé le ms. S. L'auteur
> de ce travail, en effet, n'a pas modifié l'ancien poème;
> il en a respecté les assonances et, en général, le langage,
> ou du moins il ne l'a pas plus modifié que ne l'aurait fait
> un scribe contemporain, que ne l'a fait par exemple l'au-
> teur du ms. A de son original. [24]

More recently Cesare Segre, echoing Gaston Paris' opinion that
the author of *S* did not modify his text, used the statement of the
French scholar, now raised to the status of "fact," as a corner-
stone in an argument which employs the tradition of the *Alexis*
manuscripts — which Segre considers wholly clerical, and therefore
purely written, — to cast doubt upon the oral transmission of the
various versions of the *Chanson de Roland*. Of manuscript *S* Segre
writes:

> Elle a été obtenue soit en gonflant les strophes originaires
> avec de nouveaux vers, soit en ajoutant des laisses com-
> posées *ex novo*. Je soulignerai seulement deux faits: 1) le
> remanieur a effectué des additions mais il n'a pas apporté
> de modifications textuelles: pour ce qui concerne les vers
> qui remontent à la version en strophes, S est un manuscrit
> qui mérite toute notre confiance; 2) les additions exploi-
> tent, souvent en alternance avec les vers de la version
> originale, tous les procedés des laisses similaires. [25]

Since the faithful reproduction of an exemplar *without significant
textual modification* implies written rather than oral transmission,
Segre draws the following conclusion concerning the transmission
of the *chanson de geste* in general:

> Si ce type de remaniement, *fait sans doute sur des textes
> écrits,* a tous les caractères des remaniements des *chan-
> sons de geste*, il n'y a aucune raison de prétendre pour

---

[24] Paris, 1872, p. 199 (author's italics).
[25] Segre, 1974, p. 311. Paris, like Segre, considered *S* a reliable repre-
sentative of the "original poem," and his text of the eleventh-century
version utilizes a considerable number of readings found only in *S*.

ces dernières une transmission orale, au moins jusqu'à
preuve du contraire. [26]

As far as the versions of *Alexis* are concerned, Segre's reasoning
is valid: if *S* incorporates the text of *L* without textual modification, then *S* indubitably belongs to the written tradition despite any
evidence we may have concerning the procedures of oral style
incorporated in it. A careful examination of the texts in question,
however, raises considerable doubt about both Gaston Paris' statement that the author of *S* modified his exemplar no more than did
the author of *A*, and Segre's remark, "le remanieur... n'a pas
apporté de modifications textuelles."

To highlight what he perceived as the close textual relationship
between *L* and *S*, in his edition Paris printed those lines which he
considered additions to "le texte primitif" in italic type and "le
texte primitif" *(L)* itself in roman. Using these type faces as a guide,
we would conclude that *S* omits seventy lines found in *L* and adds
807 new lines, but that the remaining 550 lines reproduce "le texte
primitif" faithfully (these numbers based on Paris' edition, not on
the manuscript). On only one occasion did Paris indicate a change
at the caesura from the new version to "le texte primitif" *("s'il
estoit sers*, jou le feroie franc," *S* 751; compare *L* 227, "Kil me
guardrat, jo l'en fereie franc!"), although there are in fact many
instances where one hemistich of *S* reflects a reading also found
in *L* while the other does not. Of the 550 lines in Paris' edition
which appear to reproduce faithfully the earlier version, twenty-
four represent conjectures by Paris on the basis of *L* (four, 758-61,
added from *L* without any indication in the text or apparatus), and
must be omitted from our comparisons since we cannot determine
with precision their exact wording or indeed whether they were
actually contained in the original version of *S*. The 525 lines (525
and a half if we include 751) available in *S* for comparison with
L should offer no more significant textual modification of *L* than
does *A*, according to Paris and Segre.

Let us consider a line-by-line comparison of strophe 12 (laisse
13). In case of no major variation between *LAP*, the spelling is

---

[26] Segre, 1974, p. 312 (emphasis added).

that of *L*: [27] lines added by *S*, following the convention established by Paris, are in italics, while those differences which I consider significant are in boldface type. [28]

L	Cum veit le lit esguardat la pulcela
AP	Quant vit le lit esguarda la pulcele
S	**Sains Alessins** esgarda la pucele
	Assés i ardent et candoiles et lanternes;
	Mout la vit gente et couvoiteuse et bele.

LA	Dunc li remembret de sun seinor celeste
P	Si lui menbre de sun seignor celeste
S	**Ses oels en torne vers** le signour celestre

L	Que plus ad cher que tut aveir terrestre
A	Que plus ad chier que tute rien terrestre
P	Kil plus a cier que tote **honor** terrestre
S	**Qu'il amoit plus** que nule riens terreste

L	E Deus dist il cum fort pecet m'apresset
AP	E Deus dist il si grant pechiet m'apresse
S	**Elas dist il** com fors pechiés m'apresse

L	Se or ne m'en fui mult criem que ne t'em perde
A	Se or ne m'en fui or criem que tei en perde
P	Se ore ne m'en fui mult criem que ne me perde
S	S'or nen m'en **vois** jou crien que ne te perde

In this case the claim that *S* offers no more substantial modification to the text of *L* than does *A* proves false; in all five lines, the first hemistich of *S* differs sufficiently that it would not be considered a formulaic repetition of *L*; the second hemistich phrases are more similar, their stability perhaps insured by the assonance. In the first two lines, the new reading found in *S* ex-

---

[27] The text of *LAP* is here taken from the diplomatic edition of Foerster and Koschwitz (1911). I have, however, observed modern word divisions. Citations of *L* for manuscript comparison are from this edition, for literary discussion, from the edition of Storey.

[28] In general "major" alterations involve the use of different nouns, verbs, adjectives or adverbs (for the latter those used for their denotative value, not as filler). For a similar MS comparison based on hemistich (formulaic) differences, see the edition of *Gui de Nanteuil* by McCormack (1970).

presses a new idea, and in three it paraphrases the content of *L*. On the other hand, the versions offered by *L*, *A*, and *P* differ by only a single word, and the substitution is frequently a synonym or near synonym of the reading in *L*.

Let us consider another example, strophe 14 (laisse 16), to which no lines are added by *S*. Gaston Paris' text leads one to believe that *S* reproduces *L* faithfully since all five lines are printed in roman type.

LA	Oz mei pulcele celui tien ad espus
P	Oz tu pucele celui tieng a espous
S	**Bele dist il** celui trai a espous [29]
LAPS	Ki nus raens[t] de sun sanc precius
L	An ices secle nen at parfit amor
AP	En cest siecle nen ad parfit amur
S	Car en cest siecle nen a parfite amour
LP	La vithe est fragile n'i ad durable honur
A	La vie est fragile ni ad durable amur
S	**A mout grant joie s'asamblent peceour**
LAP	Cesta lethece revert a grant tristur
S	**Mais il desoivrent a doel et a** tristour

Of these five lines, only the second reveals no textual modification at all in *S*: the first contains a new first hemistich, the third offers a minor variation, and the last two state entirely new ideas. Furthermore, unlike the reading *amur* found in *A* in the fourth line of the strophe, none of the variants in *S* can be plausibly accounted for by scribal error. Examples of divergent readings such as these can be found in nearly every strophe. *S* is hardly a faithful copy of *L*; it more closely resembles what we would expect to find in a text which was recalled from memory instead of copied word for word.

In the first one hundred lines of *L* which are included in *S* (*L* 100 = *S* 393), there are twenty-five first hemistichs unique to *S*, twenty-four unique second hemistichs, and thirteen other lines

---

[29] G.P.'s edition reads "tien a espous."

differing in at least one significant word. In the same one hundred lines, *A* gives six different first-hemistich readings and five second, as well as twelve changes involving a single word. Therefore the claim that *S* represents a tradition no more independent than does *A* is incorrect. Indeed, an analysis of hemistich differences in seventy-five strophes (the first twenty-five and the last fifty), reveals that *L, A,* and *P* agree against *S* sixty-three times, while in the same seventy-five strophes *A* disagrees with *L* forty-nine times. In close to 50 % of the 525 lines available for comparison in *L* and *S, S* introduces significant textual modifications.

The notes accompanying the texts of *S* and *M²* reveal the complexity of the manuscript tradition as far as these two works are concerned. In general, *M²* appears more closely related to *S* than is *M¹*, but it is not a direct descendant of that manuscript. Similarly, *Q* reflects *SM²* more frequently than *M¹*. The complicated filiations, however, strongly suggest that there were more versions in circulation than we now possess. In particular, the concentration of dodecasyllabic lines (see below) in *M²* points to the possibility of the existence of a poem in that meter, perhaps in assonance. In all later versions, the ending of the poem is particularly curtailed, although each manuscript omits different details. For the final laisses of *M²*, the poet neglected to alter the original assonances to rhyme, indicating his ultimate dependence upon a version in assonance similar to, but not identical with, *S*.

Gaston Paris, writing before the discovery of *V* (or of *M²*), had postulated two manuscript families, *LA* and *PS*. Yet closer examination indicates either that the scribes of the *Alexis* tradition were particularly negligent or that the tradition is considerably more complicated than it appears at first glance. Considering the same seventy-five strophes mentioned above, and again counting only textual modifications major enough that the hemistichs in question would not be counted as formulaic repetitions of one another,[30] we find the following: *APS* unite against *L* nineteen times: *LAS* combine against *P* sixteen times; and *LPS* agree against *A* nineteen

---

[30] It is not a question here of determining if phrases are formulaic or not. But the criteria used to do so also provide a convenient (and consistent) means of checking whether or not the differences between a pair of lines are major or minor. See above, n. 28.

times. In the Hildesheim version as a whole, on nine occasions all manuscripts contain different first hemistichs, [31] and on six other occasions all hemistichs but one are different. [32] In five lines all second hemistichs differ. [33] The textual critic who hopes to construct a manuscript stemma must soon admit defeat or else posit an unprecedented degree of contamination. The practical difficulties surrounding the copying of a medieval manuscript make less plausible the hypothesis that the scribe, unlike the modern critic, had access to a number of exemplars from which he constructed his version. [34] Furthermore, the manuscripts of *Alexis* change filiation within the strophe and the line (cf. 7:2, 92:2, 92:3 115:5). To give only one example, consider 34:5 (*S* 527):

L	Ço li cumandet, apele l'ume Deu
A	Ce dist l'ymagene, fai venir l'ume Deu
P	Ceo li cunmande, fai venir l'umme Dei
S	Çou dist l'ymaige, apele l'oume Dé

In the first hemistich $S = A$ and $P = L$, but in the second $S = L$ and $A = P$.

These examples of divergent readings do not represent exceptional cases. In a thirty-line section, strophes 78-83 (in *S* beginning at laisse 96, line 1137) there are major differences between *S* and *LAP* in fourteen lines (a total of seventeen different hemistichs), and considerable discrepancy among the other manuscripts as well. In three cases (1140, 1160, 1170) the divergent readings of *S* represent the introduction of new ideas not found in any other manuscript, and on five occasions *S* expresses the same ideas but uses entirely different words (1137, 1143, 1156, 1157, 1168).

---

[31] Lines 8:5, 15:5, 36:1, 87:5, 106:4, 112:3, 113:3, 115:3, 118:3.
[32] Lines 16:1, 33:3, 96:1, 100:5, 101:5, 115:5.
[33] Lines 28:5, 33:4, 80:3, 80:5, 90:3; on four occasions three out of four manuscripts offer different second hemistichs — 9.3, 88:1, 107:4, 118:2.
[34] Concerning the later MSS, only for the scribes of *Q* might one posit a reading knowledge of *L*, since *Q* reverts to that manuscript's order of strophes in the family's laments for Alexis. Uitti, 1973, p. 55, suggests that the scribe of *A* might have compared his model with the Latin *vita* and tried "somewhat clumsily" to make the ending of the vernacular poem correspond with the Latin version; for another explanation of the ending of *A*, see Elliott (1980).

Therefore in each of the six strophes, *S* at least twice presents a major textual modification.

If we select another thirty-line passage for which we have the testimony of *V* as well, strophes 96-101, we find the same disagreement. There are no lines added to this section by any manuscript, although eleven of the thirty lines are missing from *S* and two from *A*. In this passage only two lines (96:4 and 99:4) reveal no significant difference among the manuscripts. Only *L* and *P* agree more frequently than they disagree; twice *V* offers readings which seem to be garbled versions of *A* (97:3-4 and 99:2-3) but *A* and *V* disagree twenty-five times in the thirty lines. Only eight lines have similar first hemistichs and only four similar second hemistichs. Yet another comparison of thirty lines (strophes 36-41) turns up only five lines containing no significant differences in any manuscript.

I have selected thirty-line segments of *Alexis* for analysis because there is readily available a thirty-line passage from the *Prise d'Orenge* (laisse IV in MS A^1) for which Blanche Katz prints the versions offered by all eight manuscripts.[35] Of this *chanson de geste* the four manuscripts of the *A*-family and the two of the *B*-family are presumed to be written copies of an exemplar identified as *x*.[36] The filiation of manuscripts *C* and *D* is more complex; Claude Régnier writes of *D:* "Remaniement indépendant, mélange curieux de leçons anciennes et d'interpolations souvent absurdes, cette copie donne l'impression d'une version archaïque reconstituée de mémoire."[37] *A* and *B*, then, can best be accounted for by written transmission, *D*, and perhaps *C*, by oral transmission.

A comparison of all eight manuscripts of the *Prise d'Orenge* reveals that the least stable element is line order; if this factor is discounted, and lines are compared with their equivalents, no matter where found within the laisse, the following results emerge:

in general:

1) there are only two lines identical in all manuscripts[38]

---

[35] Katz, 1947.
[36] Madeleine Tyssens, 1967, p. 34.
[37] Régnier, 1966, p. 28.
[38] The first line and *ABC*10, *D*11.

2) within the A-family only one line (5) reveals any significant difference among the MSS.

3) there are no significant differences within the B-family

between the A-family and B-family:

1) eighteen of the thirty lines are the same

2) eight lines differ in only one word

3) four lines contain major differences

among A, B, and C there are only three lines in common [39]

among A, B, and D there are only four lines in common [40]

Therefore the degree of consensus between the A-family and the B-family of manuscripts of the *Prise d'Orenge* in laisse IV is similar to that found for *Alexis L* and *Alexis P* in the thirty lines of strophes 96-101, in which there are twenty-three cases of agreement as opposed to eleven disagreements. In all other cases the readings found in the *Alexis* manuscript differ far more than do those of the A- and B-families of the *Prise*, although the degree of variance found is less than that between, for example, D and A. These findings, coupled with the impossibility of constructing a stemma suggests that we are dealing at the very least with memorial transcription if not with outright oral composition. If the *Alexis*-poems are conceived as belonging to a purely clerical milieu, one which owes nothing to the activity of jongleurs, [41] transcription from memory provides an implausible hypothesis. But if at least some of the versions, and S in particular, are jongleuresque creations, memorial transmission would be the expected mode of reproduction.

---

[39] Lines 1, 3, and AB17, D19.

[40] AB14, D16; A31, B30, D28; AB19, D13; AB9, D8.

[41] The view of Segre (1974) and Mölk (1978).

II

LITERARY ANALYSIS

1. The Sinning Saint: *Alexis S*

Literary as well as textual discussions of the *Vie de saint Alexis* have been almost universally restricted to the Hildesheim manuscript. [42] The implication is that the later versions 1) are uninteresting and 2) lack independence. [43] John Fox characterizes the later versions as "more tedious" than the Hildesheim poem, and finds the greater length of S a "rather ominous change in itself." He continues:

> The author's aim was evidently to put flesh on the bare bones of the original. Not for nothing has the title been changed to *Le Roman de Saint Alexis*. Attempts made to introduce picturesque effects and vivid details have resulted in a loss of concentration of aesthetic purpose and have introduced a note utterly foreign to the ascetic spirit of the legend. [44]

Jessie Crosland, one of the first scholars to refer to S, did so in terms which practically ensured its subsequent neglect, as she wrote of its "clumsy efforts to be just to both sides:" [45]

> There is no need to point out the difference in tone between the eleventh- and twelfth-century poems — the one

---

[42] Exceptions are Robertson (1970) and Maddox (1973), who discuss A as a separate entity. Johnson and Cazelles (1979) give a plot outline of S (which they call *Alexis II*) in the appendix to their study of twelfth-century hagiography; their discussion, however, concentrates on the earlier version.

For a cogent discussion of the neglect of hagiography in general and of later texts in specific, see Dembowski, 1976.

[43] So, for example, Charles Stebbins, in his article, "Une étude comparative des trois grandes versions en vers de la *Vie de saint Alexis* conservées en vieux français" (1978), wholly ignores S and M although they would have lent strong support to his careful demonstration of the greater interest in the saint's humanity evinced by the thirteenth-century version Stebbins analyzes.

[44] Fox, 1974, pp. 29, 32.

[45] Crosland, 1956, p. 10.

sincere and deeply religious in spite of its poetic form, the other didactic and superficial (in its added parts) and clearly adapted to meet a popular demand. [46]

With the statement that S is influenced by "popular demand" there is no question: [47] that the term should imply inferiority is another matter. Crosland's charge, "didactic and superficial," is for the most part unwarranted. There are indeed didactic passages in S, but they are not extensive, [48] nor was the modern antipathy to didacticism shared by medieval audiences. The changes introduced by the S-poet alter somewhat the message conveyed by the saint's life but do not trivialize it. In fact they reveal this poet's sensitivity to a range of deep emotions — love, guilt, sorrow, joy.

Were it not for the existence of L, the critical fate of S might have been far different. The poem is usually referred to as "interpolated," a deprecatory term which minimizes its originality. Alexis S incorporates over 500 lines from the tradition known today from MSS L, A, P, and V, into a poem of 1331 lines, while altering the strophic form to laisses. This expansion is of the same order of magnitude as that found in the treatment of the first episode in the longer Moniage Guillaume II (2000 lines), compared to that in the shorter Moniage Guillaume I (850 lines). [49] In his amplification, the S-poet has added several new scenes or incidents: Alexis makes a pilgrimage to Jerusalem before going to Lalice (Laodicea); he overhears a conversation between his father's two servants and the innkeeper; he gives the cleric at Alsis a brief version of his life's story. There are two new characters, the innkeeper at Alsis and Danz Constentins who offers the unrecog-

---

[46] Crosland, 1956, p. 11. She appears, however, not to have read S very carefully. For example, she writes of Alexis' death that his wife "comforts him on his death-bed when he fears the devils will snatch away his soul, telling him that she can hear the angelic bells ringing to announce that all is well" (p. 10). At this juncture (997ff.) the text reads, "'Bele pucele,' çou dist sains A[lessins], / 'Oiés les sains, le Damedieu merci.'"

[47] In his introduction to S Gaston Paris had written (1872, p. 200) of its "popular," jongleuresque style: "...la rédaction du XIIe siècle a été certainement écrite en vue d'être remise à un chanteur populaire. Tout ce qu'elle a ajouté à l'ancien texte est composé dans cette vue."

[48] The version of M*, especially M¹ is far more didactic.

[49] Rychner, 1955, p. 32.

nized pilgrim hospitality at Rome. In addition the poet has expanded several scenes afforded only brief treatment in the earlier poem, notably the interview between the saint and his bride on their wedding night and the conversations between Alexis and his family on his return to Rome. In the Hildesheim manuscript, for example, the wedding-night scene occupies twenty lines — strophes 12-15 — and the girl remains silent. In *S*, the scene is 215 lines long, and the bride has 58 lines of dialogue. [50]

Many of the expansions or additions in *S* seem to have been created in response to questions an audience might be expected to ask:

1) "What was her (his) name?" *S* displays a veritable passion for proper names. In the Hildesheim manuscript most characters are unnamed. In *S* the mother is Bone Eurée (not Aglaes, her name in the Latin prose *vita* and in the vernacular poems directly dependent upon it), the daughter of Flourens. The emperor whom Alexis serves is Otevians (74), the bride is Lesigne, the daughter of Signourés (90).

2) "How did the bride react when Alexis told her he was leaving?" In *S* her feelings are explored in some detail, a point to which we shall return.

3) "Why, during the seventeen years he lived beneath his family's staircase, did no one ask Alexis who he was?" His father does ask, and the saint replies that he is named "Crestiens" (797).

The additions may remove some of the severe beauty and numerical symmetry for which *Alexis L* is highly admired. They serve, however, to create a more dramatic tale. The characters are better developed, easier to understand and, as a result, easier to identify with. In this sense, then, the poem has been "popularized."

The most telling area of difference between *L* and *S* is character development. In *S* the actors in the drama are portrayed fully and

---

[50] In its increased emphasis upon dialogue as a major narrative mode, *S* shares another feature of epic style. Nichols, 1970, pp. 376ff., discusses the ways the authors of epic and saga attempted to situate their works within the "life experience" of their intended audience; the use of direct discourse figured prominently among such techniques.

sympathetically. The poet explores their feelings. Indeed, he seems in some ways more concerned with the "human interest" side of his story than with the strictly religious message which the life of the saint exemplified, for he not only devotes more attention to the wife and mother that did *L*, he also softens the stern character of the ascetic saint.

In *S* the greatest change involves the bride. The treatment of her is perhaps the most significant contribution of *S* to the later tradition. The prologue indicates her increased importance, as she is mentioned in the third line:

> ...une feme que il prist a oissor,
> Qui il guerpi pour Diu son creatour,
> Caste pucele et gloriouse flour,

(3-5)

In *L* she remains a shadowy figure, a required element of the narrative but not a genuine participant in the action.[51] She is anonymous,[52] identified only as the daughter "d'un noble Franc" (40), a count of Rome (42). When Alexis tells her on their wedding night that he is leaving, she says not a word. In *L* she exists to be left; in *S* her role is more complex.

The poet's handling of this scene in *L* has been highly praised:[53]

> The silence of the bride — how effective is this background of utter stillness, against which the words of Alexis reverberate, unconfined, passing through her silence, down the ages to us. What could she find to say to words so final, to words conveying revelation, to the last words of a man saying farewell to this world? And if we

---

[51] In this respect the Hildesheim poem reflects more accurately the Latin biography. Johnson and Cazelles, 1979, p. 38, write of the bride, "Although the woman remains inactive and unnamed in the *Vita*, she serves as a literary device underlying Alexis' sudden vocation."

[52] For a cogent discussion of her anonymity, see Uitti, 1973, pp. 40-41. Of the names in the later tradition (omitting *S*), Uitti writes, "These names are typically literary: Adriatica, Sabina, even — in the late-medieval (post-Dante) Italian versions — the *donna angelica* incarnate, Beatrice" (p. 43).

[53] It has also come in for sharp criticism, primarily by Winkler, 1927: see also the defenses of Spitzer, 1932; de Gaiffier, 1947.

seek, out of curiosity, to probe into her feelings, we find
no point of access; similarly we are foiled if we attempt
to visualize this lonely, mute figure. She has no substance
in this scene. [54]

This is an aesthetic judgment. The girl's silence in *LAP* is moving,
perhaps evoking the restrained expressiveness of Romanesque
sculpture. But like Romanesque sculpture, it is not a very realistic
depiction, however beautiful it may be. Most women, medieval or
modern, could probably think of many things which they would
say under similar circumstances. [55]

But if the eleventh-century poet was not interested in the
bride's response, the twelfth-century one was. Her reactions are
given in detail, and she is painted with sensitivity and psychological
verisimilitude. We watch her pass from shocked disbelief ("Por
coi me lais? Ja m'as espousée," 167), to concern for herself. Having
been rejected (she feels) by her husband, Lesigne generalizes her
fears, anticipating that his parents will abandon her as well, as if
she had been his concubine (*asoignentée*, 171) instead of his lawful
wife. This anticipated fear of rejection is not rational, as the
ensuing action makes plain, but its intensity indicates the magnitude of the shock she has suffered.

> "Que porai dire ton pére ne ta mére?
> Sempres m'aront de leur terre jetée;
> Puis m'en irai com autre asoignentée;
> Tel honte arai, jamais n'iere hounerée."
>
> (169-172)

Alexis answers her anxiety concerning social status by explaining
his motivation, as he praises the life of the soul and laments the
sorry lot of the body, subject to corruption after death. Mortal
life is transitory: "Qui plus durra, vivera mout petit / Envers la
vie qui grans est a venir" (196-97). This exposition of Christian

---

[54] Hatcher, 1952, pp. 120-21.
[55] The biography of Christina of Markyate, for whom the St. Albans
Psalter may have been written, provides an interesting parallel for the
situation, with the sexes reversed. Christina's husband was far from
pleased with his wife's wedding-night rejection. See *The Life of Christina
of Markyate*, ed. Talbot, 1959.

doctrine, central to the meaning of the hagiographic poem, is thus presented as a spontaneous response to Lesigne's questions rather than as an unmotivated, unwished-for sermon, a far less sympathetic mode of discourse. Although not ceasing to weep, the girl gives Alexis her blessing:

"Sire," fet ele, "or te commant a Dé,
Quant autrement ne te puis retorner."

(207-208)

Delighted at her compliance, Alexis tells her as he prepares to leave that if she does not hear from him in a year, she will know that he is dead and that she can remarry (a detail of the plot which is never pursued). What follows is a careful piece of character drawing. At the mention of his possible death, the girl cries out:

Ot le la bele, si a jeté un cri;
Quide sa mére que il juast a li.

(221-22)

The bride, who loves her husband in spite of his behavior, has passed from worry about herself to concern for him. It is the thought of his death, not her own self-pity, which provokes the sharp cry of pain, a cry which the mother, her ear no doubt pressed to the bedroom door, interprets as that caused by initial penetration. The detail paints a vivid little picture of the intimacy of medieval life; its irony, however, is pointed, for Lesigne's cry signals the end, not the beginning, of the couple's physical union.

The bride next begins to question her husband, and in response Alexis spells out his plans, a dramatic device permitting the story to develop naturally. She first asks why he thinks so little of her; the question allows Alexis to protest his great love for her. Comforted, perhaps, by this knowledge, the girl continues to express her concern for *his* well-being. Her questions are natural ones: "What are you going to do?" (234); "When will you return?" (247ff.). Much of the didactic message of the poem is conveyed through Alexis' answers as he again tells her, to minimize her sense of loss, of the fragility of earthly pleasures and the durability of heavenly ones. He will pray that God receive them *both* into heaven. In spite of her sorrow, the girl concurs, and both weep at the impending separation:

> Dist li pucele, "Sire, voir avés dit;
> Les vos raisons doit on bien retenir."
> Estes les vous belement departis;
> Plorent des oels, ne se porent tenir.

(283-86)

Finally she asks why she cannot accompany her husband; she promises not to tempt him sexually (307ff.). [56] The rejection of her offer leaves her in tears as she begins to experience the grief that will be hers for the next thirty-four years ("Ele commence grant duel a demener," 318), and Alexis takes his leave.

Alexis S is unique in the emphasis it places upon the saint's winning the bride's consent and in the sympathetic picture painted of her (for *M* see below). The issues raised in this scene continue to dominate the poem — the concern with the explicit depiction of emotion and with Alexis' sense of guilt at leaving his family. Alexis' feelings are probed more deeply than in *L* or *M*. The Hildesheim *Alexis* maintains its customary reticence in describing the saint's midnight flight from Rome:

> Dunc en eissit de la cambre sum pedre;
> Ensur[e] nuit s'en fuit de la contrethe.
> Dunc vint errant dreitement a la mer.

(74-76)

"But how did he *feel?*" an audience might ask. *S* tells us. The departure is emotion-filled as Alexis is torn with conflicting sensations. For the third time the poet depicts the saint's joy at having won Lesigne's consent (323-25). As he makes his way from the city, Alexis climbs a hill and looks back at Rome; he first prays

---

[56] What she is proposing is "spiritual marriage," an institution in general rejected by the Church Fathers; see Labriolle, 1921. Hagiographic accounts, however, contain many examples of such unions; see below, and Gaiffier, 1946.

to Christ for the girl's salvation (330-33), then his thoughts turn to
his parents, and he weeps.

> Puis se li est de son pére membré
> Et de sa mére; si commence a plourer.
> Par lui meïsme s'en est reconfortés.
> Droit en la mer en aquels son esrer.
>
> (334-37)

Lines 334-36 are original to *S;* 337 picks up *L* 76.

Alexis successfully escapes the bonds of family life; he finds
them, however, hard to forget. Leaving Rome, he goes (in *S*
following a detour to Jerusalem) to Alsis, where he is eventually
found, though not recognized, by his father's servants. In *L* all
we are told is that he rejoices at escaping recognition ("Ne vus
sai dire cum il s'en firet liez" (125). [57] In *S* this scene is considerably
expanded as the saint follows the servants to an inn where he
overhears them tell the innkeeper about his family's sorrow.
Unfortunately the manuscript here contains a lacuna in which the
servants must have described the bride's fidelity and love. [58]
Hearing this news, Alexis is moved:

> "E cuers," dist il, "com estes adurés!
> Gente pucele, mout de mercis et grés;
> Jou t'ai fait mal et tu m'as houncré."
>
> (493-95)

There is nothing like this in *L,* where Alexis never mentions wife
or parents. Particularly innovative is his sense of having done harm
("Jou t'ai fait mal").

When the cleric at Alsis, instructed by the statue, discovers the
saint, the *S*-poet adds a conversation between the two. Here again
Alexis is haunted by his sense of sin and wrong-doing. He tells
the cleric about the bride he has abandoned and his doubts concerning his salvation on that score ("Qui çou a fait, comment porra

---

[57] Alexis' joy here contrasts with his family's grief described in the
next strophe (esp. line 128).

[58] Gaston Paris did not notice that *M** could be used to fill in the
gap here (see *M²* 326).

garir?" 565). Given the fuller, more sympathetic treatment of the bride in *S,* some sign of remorse on Alexis' part was probably necessary if the audience was not to reject the saint as cold and heartless. This is an important development to which we shall return.

The polarities which shape much of the action in *S* are joy and sorrow. Set off against the bride's grief is Alexis' happiness.

> De c'est mout liés, s'en loe Damedé
> Que la pucele l'en a congié donné.
>
> (323-24)

The extremes of joy and sorrow define the wedding-night scene, their evocation contrapuntally underlining the psychological factors involved and the enormity of the sacrifice on *both* sides. The magnitude of Alexis' choice seems clearer in this version of the story, which gives scope to the full range of feelings involved, than it does in the more sparely narrated accounts which omit all depiction of the emotional toll upon the actors. In *L* the saint seems motivated solely by negative emotions — unwillingness to anger his father (54), fear at losing God's love (60).[59] The twelfth-century saint's character is softened by love — his love for the girl and hers for him. This Alexis can weep, and his tears enable us to share the grief and to appreciate fully what he has abandoned.[60]

The midnight interview between Alexis and Lesigne is one of pathos, developed with concern for psychological realism and depth. It stands out as one of the great emotional scenes of medieval literature. The dialogue between husband and wife is expressive, colored by adverbs, as the girl speaks to her husband "gentement" (287), "doucement et souef" (303). Their tears mingle (286). The poet has highlighted the pathos of this story by the use of *laisses similaires* (15-16, 23-24), and by the lyrical refrain, repeated four times, "Jou te commant a Dé" (207, 297, 305, 315).

---

[59] Winkler criticizes the saint harshly, calling him a weakling who seeks to avoid conflict with his father (1927, p. 588).

[60] His is not the sterile *askēsis* of which Winkler, above note, complained.

The poet repeatedly depicts Alexis' joy at having obtained the girl's blessing and at her acquiescence in his plans (209, 245-46, 323-24). Her permission is important on two counts. First, it matters psychologically. Emil Winkler found the Hildesheim poem "poor in philosophical and moral values," [61] and he took particular exception to the saint's treatment of the girl:

> ... Alexius hardly takes the time in the bridal chamber to admonish her in a Christian way, and to share at least some of his own illumination with her. What a selfish asceticism! ... What a didactic, soulless asceticism! ... With unconcern Alexius beholds the suffering of the members of his family.... From the first moment on Alexius is excluded from our empathetic, *human* participation, like the relics at a Christian shrine, protected under glass and surrounded by billows of incense. [62]

Both the saint and the Hildesheim poem have been defended from this attack by Leo Spitzer, who maintained that Winkler's viewpoint was anachronistic in seeking from the saint's life an account with which we can empathize; instead the life transcends normal human experience and serves as an example. Spitzer then went on to quote André Jolles:

> ... Saints are ... individuals ... in whom the good ... is in a certain manner objectified. That is the reason why the community does not ask how the saint feels, when he is pious ... it does not consider him in this sense just another human being, it looks upon him as a means of seeing virtue objectified.... [63]

But these critics do not appear to have read *Alexis S*. Winkler might have found support for his position in this version. I suspect that twelfth-century audiences may have shared some of his discomfort at the severe, uncompromising asceticism of the Hildesheim saint. *S* shows Alexis to have feelings, to weep for his actions, although he does not swerve from his purpose. It is easier

---

[61] "Das Alexiuslied ist arm an philosophischen und sittlichen Werten" (Winkler, 1927, p. 588).
[62] Winkler, 1927, p. 598; translated by Odenkirchen, 1978, p. 69.
[63] Spitzer, 1933, quoted and translated by Odenkirchen, 1978, p. 71.

for audiences, medieval or modern, to sympathize with the saint's course of action, however virtuous it may be, if they believe that the girl concurs and has not simply been a passive victim. These modifications point as well to the secularity of the audience for whom *S* was intended, a mixed gathering of husbands and wives, mothers and fathers. [64] Hans Robert Jauss has written of the "admiring identification" with hero, saint, or sage, which affects the audience. Yet the evocation of such admiration rests on a delicate balance: if a section of the audience convicts the hero of unnecessary cruelty, admiration is dissipated. [65]

Lesigne's consent has significance in canon law as well. Marriage was no trivial sacrament, and Alexis did not renounce his wife until after the actual ceremony (which would, presumably, have been preceded by a betrothal). When Alexis tells his bride of his decision, her first question is (167), "Por coi me lais? *Ja* m'as tu espousée" — why are you leaving me now that you *just* married me? Baudouin de Gaiffier has pointed out that there are many hagiographic accounts in which a saint and his or her spouse determine on their wedding night to preserve their chastity. [66] In some cases they separated, in others agreed to live together without sexual relations. But by the twelfth century, the wedding was usually the second occasion on which a couple pledged faith to each other. [67] The betrothal constituted an equally solemn and

---

[64] *S* is intended for a mixed audience; cf. the address to the audience in the first line, "Signours et dames."

[65] Jauss, 1973-74. Particularly apposite is Jauss' discussion of the "hearts full of pity" with which the medieval audience viewed the Passion play (291).

[66] Gaiffier, 1946.

[67] The importance of the marriage to the *Vie de saint Alexis* is reflected by the manuscript illuminations. The one in the Hildesheim MS shows three scenes, as Alexis gives the girl the ring and belt, escapes from the house, and boards the boat (for a discussion of this miniature, see Pächt, 1960, 139-40). In *S* there is only one scene, the marriage. *M²* has no illumination, but *M¹* contains an illustration more in line with traditional hagiography as it depicts the saint's death; f. 393v has a tiny historiated capital C in which the dying saint is portrayed, surrounded by a man and a woman. The rubric also stresses the importance of his death: "Li vie saint Alesis. Et comment il morut." Similarly Latin authors seem more concerned with the second half of Alexis' story (the stay in Rome and his death) than the first; see Peter Damian's sermon on Alexis, *PL* 144, 652-660. Honorius Augustodunesis dismisses the wedding night

binding ceremony. The biography of a twelfth-century French saint shows what course a contemporary audience might have expected Alexis to follow. The *Life* of St. Ode (d. 1153), written before 1183, informs us that during the betrothal ceremony Ode's fiancé was asked three times by the officiating priest if he consented voluntarily to marry the girl. The man replied that he had come for that very purpose and promised to fulfil with all his energy the obligations of the marriage law. When Ode's turn came to reply to the same questions, the girl, wishing to devote herself to a life of chastity, refused to answer. [68] If the audience of *S* were expecting the saint to have participated in a preliminary ceremony at which he could have expressed his unwillingness to marry, his abrupt departure might have seemed even harsher and he still more in need, therefore, of the girl's consent.

Husbands and wives were to live together. [69] Voluntary separation after marriage was considered a sin and was expressly condemned, [70] although exceptions were made in unconsummated marriages for entry into a religious order by one (or both) of the partners. [71] Another contemporary biography, that of Christina of Markyate, shows that a vow of chastity taken prior to marriage, even if made in private, could be considered valid grounds for annulling a marriage, but Christina's *vita* makes plain the difficulty with which such an annulment was obtained in the face of the opposition of both her parents and husband. [72] With consent the problem was simpler. To a medieval audience, more attuned than a modern one to the niceties of the Church's attitude towards dissolution of marriage, such details might loom large.

---

with a single sentence: "Quam prima nocte in lecto reliquens peregre abiit..." (*PL* 172, 1045-46).

[68] Cited by Molin and Mutembe, 1973, pp. 65-66.

[69] Le Bras, 1968, p. 199.

[70] Le Bras, 1968, p. 201 (citing *Extra*, 4, 19, 3).

[71] The authority for this separation was Genesis (2:22) on the grounds that *unitas carnis* had not taken place (Le Bras, p. 195).

[72] The *Life of Christina* (ed. Talbot, 1959) attributes her difficulty to her father's bribing the Bishop to reverse himself and judge against Christina, but this is not the only possible explanation; the issue was complex, especially in the absence of consent. Considering the cruelty with which Cristina was treated by her father (who in his self-pity and concern for social status has much in common with the father of Alexis), one sympathizes rather more with Alexis' desire to slip away unnoticed.

The *S*-poet has also expanded the mother's role, seemingly in response to a desire for social and psychological verisimilitude. In *L* the mother is defined only by lack: she lacks a son and prays for his birth; that son leaves (first into exile, then in death), and she laments her loss. In *S* scenes are constructed with more concern for social realism, and so the mother is "on stage" more often. If grieving is her primary function, it is not her only one. She rejoices at her son's marriage (104; in *L* only the fathers are involved). Both parents conduct the couple to the bedroom, and the mother is the one to hear, and to misinterpret, the bride's cry. After Alexis' departure, her scene of grief in the abandoned bridal chamber is intensified by the creation of *laisses similaires* (32-33), although not otherwise altered. The depiction of her is romanticized, as she faints with grief (420-21).

The greatest expansion of the mother's role comes after Alexis returns to Rome (laisses 52ff.), and here we can observe the poet motivated not only by an interest in her for her own sake, but also concerned (as he was in his treatment of the wedding-night) to create a scene somewhat more in keeping with social norms. The Hildesheim poem depicts a world of deep emotion, but perhaps not one with which an audience could readily identify; it is abstract, bearing little resemblance to "everyday life." It is also a world dominated by men, while the society created by *S* gives to the two women roles more extensive than mere mourners. They have some part in the decision-making processes as well.

In *L* Alexis enters Rome and finds his father surrounded by a "grant masse de ses humes" (214; cf. *S* 658). Only the father hears and grants his son's request. In *S* the portrayal of an exclusively masculine society is replaced by a more intimate picture of family life. Alexis meets *both* his parents as they are returning hand-in-hand from church, talking about their son (660-664). Both mother and father participate in the decision to shelter the mendicant.

L asks us to believe that during the seventeen years Alexis lived beneath his parents' staircase they saw him often (236) but never recognized him or asked who he was or where he came from. Given normal human curiosity, this is not a very likely situation, but the *L*-poet is not interested in psychological realism. The *S*-poet is. First, the laisse telling us that Alexis' family saw him often (58) is doubled by a *laisse similaire* (59) recounting their feelings — they continue to grieve. While they do not immediately ask who the stranger is, they do so later. The father asks his name, [73] the mother wonders where he is from. Although she does not act upon her perception, she also notices the resemblance to her absent son:

> "Quant jel regart, menbre moi de mon fil;
> Pour un petit nel resamble del vis."
>
> (842-43)

Finally, the S-poet creates an interview between the saint and his mother three days before his death. Throughout the poem, Alexis has been painfully aware of the suffering for which he has been responsible. He is oppressed with a sense of sin and fears he will be called to account for it at the Last Judgment.

> "Quele amistié entre pére et enfant!
> Ces felonnies que jou lor fac si grans
> Me sont legiéres, ses trouverai pesans;
> Al grant juise me revenroit devant."
>
> (737-40)

When the saint knows that he is dying, he begs his mother's pardon for the pain he has caused her (867ff.), a scene without counterpart in L. With this episode the poet completes his depiction of Alexis' awareness that he has hurt the three people who love him most. The mother's pardon parallels the wife's consent on the wedding night; both actions serve to weaken audience hostility to the saint's conduct — if his family forgives him, so may we.

Alexis' seemingly heartless treatment of his family in the Hildesheim version of the story has bothered critics. [74] In S the question of the responsibility for their suffering is raised by Alexis himself on several occasions. Perhaps the more popular audience for whom S appears to have been intended, more sympathetic to the human than to the theological issues involved, brought it

---

[73] In M* the mother does so as well.
[74] Notably Winkler (1927); also perhaps Crosland (1956), although she is far less outspoken.

up. *S*, following a common hagiographic tradition, exonerates the saint from blame, as his ascent into heaven is depicted. But by having Alexis himself question his guilt, the poem is original. In his search for salvation and in dedicating himself to a life of ascetic renunciation, the twelfth-century saint has not wholly denied his humanity.

The hero of the Hildesheim *Vie* remains a remote figure, one to be admired, but not one with whom it is easy to identify. The twelfth-century saint and his family are more recognizable figures. The range of their emotional experiences has been explored sympathetically. Alexis' desire to devote himself solely to the love of God is not diminished by his acknowledging his love for his parents and wife. If anything, it makes his renunciation greater. This Alexis, we feel, is abandoning something he wants; with the Alexis of the Hildesheim poem, we are never quite sure.

A final example of the softening of the stern, uncompromising portrayal of the saint's life involves the treatment of the deathbed letter. In his attack on the seeming cruelty of the Hildesheim version, Winkler objected that the grieving father should have been the one to receive the letter, not the Pope.[75] Perhaps the creator of *S* (or the audience) felt something of the same impropriety, for the letter miraculously flies from the Pope's hand into the bosom of the abandoned wife (who, we discover, has been secretly wearing a hair shirt). The poet then explains the meaning of this miracle: if Alexis' stern asceticism is a way of life too severe for the average man to follow, his story can nevertheless be shown to contain a useful lesson. Alexis is held up not as an example of chastity and renunciation (as the Latin *vita* intended) but of correct behavior for all *married* men who are exhorted, following the Biblical injunction, to abandon father and mother and cleave to wife:

> Oiés, signour, con grande loiauté
> Tout home doivent a le moiller porter.
> Car tel moustrance fist le jour Damedés
> Que a sa mére ne vaut la cartre aler
> Ne a son pére ki l'avoit engenré,

---

[75] Winkler, 1927.

Mais a l'espouse ki bien avoit gardé
Le compaignie de son ami carnel,
La va la cartre par le plaisir de Dé.

(1093-1100)

In general, then, the effect of the material new to *S* is to soften the character of the saint, to explain more fully why an action occurred, to develop the characters of the two women — in short, to create a story with wide appeal, one which would attract and hold an audience.[76] The version of the *Vie de saint Alexis* contained in *S* reflects the twelfth century's growing concern with love and women, with problems of conscience, and with the individual.[77] If hagiographic accounts are largely exemplary in nature, *S* offers heroes with whom an audience can sympathize and forms of imitation more within the reach of the average man or woman.

2. *Alexis M*[2]

Alexis M converts much of *S* into rhymed laisses but leaves out many lines, paraphrases others and adds new details but no new scenes or characters. Omitting the jongleuresque prologue to the audience, the rhyming version opens with its rendition of the first line of *L* (= *S* 10), "Cha en ariere, au tans anchiseour." There is no announcement of the specific subject of the poem, and no mention of the bride.

Like *S*, *M** devotes considerable space to the wedding night scene (225 lines in *M*[1], 87 in *M*[2]). The bride's dramatic role is reduced, however, as she speaks only 24 lines (20 in *M*[1]), compared to the 58 given her in *S*. In *L* the girl is anonymous, and the poet indulges in no description of her. All later versions consider her worthy of more detailed treatment. *S*, as we have seen, abounds in proper names; the girl is Lesigne, the daughter of Signourés;

---

[76] That some form of the *Vie de saint Alexis* was part of a jongleur's repertoire we know from the account of the conversion of Valdesius (see below). For a discussion of the activity of pious jongleurs, see below; also Elliott, 1979.

[77] See M. D. Chenu, 1969, and Colin Morris, 1972; also Johnson and Cazelles, 1979, p. 23.

when Alexis gazes on her in the bedroom, she appears to him
"gente et couvoiteuse et bele" (*S* 125). In *M** she is again nameless,
but her beauty is described in greater detail.

> Qui tant par est courtoise et bien creüe,
> Et couvoitouse et blance la cha[r] nue ...
>
> (109-110)

Later in the poem she is characterized as "la pucele o le gente
colour" (442), "au gent cors precious" (1021). [78]

M^1 and M^2 treat the wedding-night interview in distinct ways
(it is in this scene that the two *M* manuscripts differ most radically).
Compared to *S*, the episode is bare, stripped of the psychological
development of the twelfth-century version; the girl's role is
restricted, and the lyricism is curtailed as the *laisses similaires* and
lyrical refrains are reduced to single statements. M^1 greatly expands
the didactic content of the scene by giving Alexis a long quotation
from a debate between Body and Soul. [79] M^2 omits this section.
Alexis speaks only nine lines in which he refers briefly to the
joys of heaven and then asks leave to depart. By contrast the girl
has a seventeen-line reply, largely reproducing her lament and
request to accompany her husband as given in *S*. Her grief-stricken
response to Alexis' rejection of this offer, however, has been
eliminated, and the treatment of this scene in M^2 lacks the emotional range and lyricism of *S*. But this poet has shunned as well
the sermons of M^1, thereby retaining some of the concern with
human values and feelings which typifies *S* (for the complicated
manuscript filiations, see the notes to the text).

In *M** the scene of Alexis' departure from Rome is also less
emotional. M^1 makes no mention of the *pucele;* in M^2 the saint's
first feeling is joy at having abandoned the enticements of worldly
esteem; then his thoughts turn to the girl, and he thanks God
for having obtained her blessing (184-190). The poet describes
Alexis' joy; he omits the vignette of the saint climbing a hill

---

[78] *Q* goes the furthest with such descriptions, as the girl lies on the
bed "tout nue; / Mout la vit blanche et tendre, bien faite et parcreüe)
(17a-b); "la pucele vermelle et coulourée" (18b).

[79] See below, n. 86.

and looking back at what he has left. As for Alexis' parents,
the M-poet tells us not a word of the saint's emotions, mentioning
instead the intense grief his mother and father will feel when
they learn what has occurred (191-96).

It is typical of the narrative technique of M^2 that the poet
prefers to describe rather than depict. In the scene of the parent's
grief, we are told that the mother cried out "come femme
foursenée" (M^2 255, M^1 400). The bride is characterized as "Irie"
(276). The episode, however, is considerably cut in comparison
with S (S 66 lines [394-459]; M^2 49 lines [253-301]). M eliminates
the *laisses similaires* of S (32-33), and omits the bride's speech
of grief for her husband, contenting itself with a summarizing
statement, "La demoisele regrete mout son dru" (269). It also
leaves out her request to stay with his parents, promising to live
"a loi de tourtereule / Qui pert son malle" (S 427-28).

If dialogue is cut in comparison with S, description is expanded.
Some passions are heightened. In S the mother fainted from grief
in the abandoned bridal chamber. In M, after Alexis' return to
Rome, she faints three times on hearing her son mentioned; in S
she only weeps (731). In the same scene, the father wrings his
hands with distress and drops his gloves. In S Alexis picks them
up, commenting on the power of love between father and son and
reflecting upon the "felonnies si grans" (738) which he has com-
mitted and for which he fears at the Last Judgment. In M^2 the
poet first characterizes Alexis' feelings ("Irés en est," 580), then
puts in his mouth a brief speech (4 lines compared to 8 in S):

> "Jhesus," dist il, "li Péres tous poissans,
> Quele amistés est de pére et d'enfant!
> Aide, Dieus, s'or me vont connissant,
> Tel joie aront c'onques n'orent plus grant."
>
> (583-86)

But although the saint perceives his family's pain, it does not touch
him personally (see also 462ff.). Gone is the brooding sense of sin
which oppresses the twelfth-century saint. The result, for all the
heightened emotional description, is a loss of intensity and complexity, particularly in the representation of Alexis' feelings.

The depiction of the saint in M* is more in line with the norms
of orthodox hagiography than is that in S. Alexis in the former

version is cognizant of sin but it is more sin in the abstract than
a specific feeling of remorse for the suffering he has provoked. He
is prey to generalized fears of persecution at the hands of devils
but does not dread punishment for any specific sin he has com-
mitted. He takes, moreover, an almost masochistic delight in the
refinement of his self-torture; Alexis selects a spot beneath his
father's stairs not because he is ill, as in *S*, but in order to torment
himself with temptation:

> La fera il, s'il peut, le sien lit estorer
> Si qu'il vera chascun jour au disner
> Les grans dentiés par devant lui passer,
> Non pas pour chou qu'il en veulle gouster,
> Ains le fera sa bouche desirer.
>
> (486-90)

In *M* Alexis specifically rejects any attempts by the servant to
make him more comfortable (602ff.). Only once in seventeen years
does he submit to a bath (601, 885). Such details suggest that, in
comparison with *S, M* was composed for a less popular, more
clerical audience for whom the specifics of Alexis' ascetic denial
had greater appeal.

Other indications of a clerical audience for *Alexis M* are
references to learning and to the liberal arts.[80] The Latin prose
vita describes Eufemien as "vir magnus et nobilis... dives valde
et primus in palatio Imperatoris."[81] This general characterization
is then amplified with details concerning his large retinue and his
acts of Christian charity. In the Hildesheim manuscript, Eufemien's
good qualities are referred to only briefly, and corroboration of his
virtue is found in the secular rather than in the religious sphere:

> Cons fut de Rome des melz ki dunc i ere[n]t,
> Sur tuz ses pers l'amat l'emperere.
>
> (*L* 17-18)

---

[80] Of *M*[1] Gaston Paris wrote: "La voilà, au treizième, par la main
de quelque *escrivain* habile, dans une *librairie* de cloître ou de manoir,
en attendant qu'une nouvelle métamorphose vienne attester la faveur dont
elle jouit toujours" (Paris, 1872, p. 265, his italics).

[81] Ed. Sprissler, 1966, p. 107.

The Latin poem, *Pater deus ingenite,* mentions Eufemien as one of the worthy princes of Rome but does not elaborate. *S* here agrees with *L:*

> Des belisors qui a cel jour i érent,
> Quens fu de Roume, de toute la contrée.
>
> (53-54a)

The poet of *M²* is the most specific, testifying to Eufemien's virtue by pointing to his scholarship as well as his piety:

> Quens fu de Romme et mout boins crestïens,
> Et sages hons des autours ancïens.
>
> (29-30)

In a similar fashion, *M* pays more attention to Alexis' schooling. *S* devotes only two lines to this subject (71-72), while *M* gives a detailed account of the saint's scholarly career — Alexis was a quick student. [82]

> laisses 6-7
> A donc le fisent a l'escole mener
> Et l'escriture ensignier et moustrer;
> En poi de tans sot bien lire et chanter
> Et en latin mout sagement parler. [83]
>
> Quant l'enfes fu des ars mout bien letré[s]
> Et des autours mout sagement fondés...
>
> (61-66)

The poet of *S,* on the other hand, chose to expand on the chivalric nature of the future saint's service to the emperor rather than on his education. [84]

---

[82] The *vita* (ed. Sprissler, p. 111), here reads: "Puer autem ut ad aetatem disciplinae congruam pervenit, tradiderunt eum ecclesiasticorum sacramentorum ac liberalium disciplinarum magistris, et ita Deo largiente edoctus est, ut in omnibus philosophiae et maxime spiritualibus floreret studiis."

[83] *M¹* adds another line: "Et une loi gentement visiter" (64).

[84] In *S* Alexis regrets his knightly career; in his conversation with the cleric at Alsis, he says, "Car jou fui clers, de letre bien apris, / Puis fui tant fols que chevaliers deving" (561-62).

> Li emper[er]es ot non Otevians;
> Illuec servi enfreci a .vii. ans,
> Et puis l'a fait son maistre cambrelenc.
> Se li carja tous ses commandemens,
> Et sa justice deseur toute sa gent,
> Cevaus et murs et palefrois amblans,
> Et plainnes males entre or fin et argent.
>
> (74-80)

The *vita* contains no mention of Alexis' serving the emperor. The author of M*, apparently finding such feudal details less interesting than he did the saint's schooling, refers to Alexis' service in general rather than in specific terms:

> Droit a le cour le roy s'en est alés;
> Tant le servi par se humilité
> Ki le a armes et garnemens dounés,
> Et les hounours dont ses péres est casés
> Li a rendues et des autres assés.
>
> (68-72)

The Alexis depicted in M* resembles closely the typical saint of the Latin hagiographic tradition, a wise and virtuous youth who spent his days in study rather than in sport (a *puer-senex*). Instead of enumerating details of Alexis' career as a public servant, the poet of M chose to focus attention on *how* he served — the saint's behavior was characterized by the display of a prime Christian virtue, "Tant le servi par se humilité." Seemingly motivated by a similar lack of concern with chivalry, at Alexis' death M* abbreviates the father's *planctus*, omitting Eufemien's regret (S laisse 102, L st. 83) that his son had not followed the family tradition of chivalric service.

Paralleling M's concern with scholarship is an interest in distinctions between the learned languages. The M-poet stresses the fact that Alexis learned Latin in school (*latin* in 64 appears to refer to the language of the schools, not to language in general). In M[1] when Alexis returns to Rome, not wishing his father to recognize him, he addresses Eufemien in Greek (479). Expressing his wish to write a deathbed letter, Alexis says, "Si escrirai un

petit de latin" (743, M^1 915). [85] Although the letter plays a large
role in S, the language in which it is written is not mentioned.

With the exception of the letter, there are no references to
reading in S, but several in $M*$. Once the poet refers to his written
source; of Alexis' arrival in Jerusalem, he says: "I va on bien, ce
trovons nos lisant" (M^2 209, M^1 351). In M^1 Alexis replies to Dans
Constentins' offer of hospitality by citing a written authority:
"Sire, dist il, nous le trouvons lisant" (677); in this same manuscript he caps his effort to persuade his bride that his course of
action is the correct one by citing a clerical literary genre, a
debate between Body and Soul, an authority which he introduces
with the phrase, "çou trovons nous lisant" (221). [86]

The final reference to writing in M is unparalleled in S (or
elsewhere), and it links the poem to the traditions of Latin hagiography. After giving the concluding lines of L (which are not
found in S), the poet, or the scribe, appends a final laisse in which
he voices a prayer in his own behalf:

laisses 100-101

> Aiiés, signour, cel saint homme en memore,
> Se li proiiés pour ki nous a assole [87]
> Et que·n cest sicle nous i otroit si grant joie
> Et ens en l'autre del regne Dieu le glore.

> Et de celui ki le romant escrit,
> A Dieu proions que il en ait merchi
> Et la soic ame en meche en paradis
> Avec le nostre et de tous nos amis,
> Pour la proiiere au boin saint Alesin. Amen.

---

[85] M^1 then goes on to provide details concerning the servant's prepara-
tions of the writing materials, details of interest, and perhaps only
known, to a clerical audience: "L'encre li a destempree et boulie" (923).

[86] For a discussion of this genre, with examples, see F. J. E. Raby
(1934, II, 299ff.). Additional examples are given in H. Walther (1920,
p. 215), "Altercatio Carnis et Spiritus" (for which Walther lists 62 MSS);
also a debate between *Corpus* and *Anima*, p. 218. See also T. Batiouchkof,
1891; Michel-André Bossy, 1976. In specific the reference in M^1 is to a
version in which the soul returns to the body on Saturday night, and in
which the soul is the only speaker. Gaston Paris conjectured that the
Visio Philiberti and the extract in M^1 go back to a common but unknown
source; see Batiouchkof.

[87] These two lines form the conclusion of S.

These lines are important not only for the mention of writing. They make a clear distinction between speaker and writer, between author and performer ("Que la soie ame en meche en paradis / Avec le *nostre*..."). M* is the only version of the *Vie de saint Alexis* to make this distinction; it is not found in the jongleur-esque S. In oral literature there is no such cleavage: the performing narrator is the poet. [88]

III

STYLE

S and *M* differ stylistically although they tell the same story, are genetically related in some fashion, and are both composed in epic decasyllables. In general, *S* shares many features of popular (epic) style — reliance on formulaic language, the use of linked laisses, *laisses similaires,* a jongleuresque prologue. [89] The work, moreover, is intended to be sung. [90] On the miraculous statue for whose sake Alexis goes to Alsis, the narrator comments at the beginning of laisse 28: "Iceste ymaige, signour, *dont je vous cant*" (368). In contrast, *M* seems intentionally to avoid features of epic style: there are fewer instances of linked laises; *laisses similaires* are usually reduced to a single statement. Furthermore, in describing the statue, the narrator remarks at the opening of laisse 33:

> Quant li sains [a] le bourc si enamé,
> N'en istra mais qu'il puist en son aé;

---

[88] In epic God is usually asked to protect the audience and the singer: cf. *Gui de Nanteuil,* M 2911-13:

> Sachiez que chi endroit est la canchon finee —
> Dex vous garisse tous qui l'avez escoutee
> Par si que moi n'oublit qui la vous ai chantee!

See also *Gui de Bourgogne,* 4302-04; *Floovent,* 2532-33.

[89] The length of *S* is also appropriate for recitation in a single session; Rychner, 1955, p. 49, suggests that in a two-hour session a jongleur might perform from 1000 to 2000 lines of verse. Cf. the story of the conversion of Valdesius in which the jongleur went to the merchant's house where he repeated his tale. *S* is 1331 lines; *La Charroi de Nimes,* 1486.

[90] For the importance of this mode of performance, see Rychner, 1955, p. 17; also Duggan, 1973, p. 29.

Le saint ymaige *dont je vous ai conté*
Le coutre del moustier en a araisonné:

(378-81)

The address to the audience is now the third line of the laisse, no longer, therefore, the solemn "vers d'intonation" as before. But far more important is the change in verb; the choice of *conter* in place of *canter* was not governed by the rhyme, so it may reflect a semantic distinction, as the narrator thought of himself as "telling" a story rather than singing one. In line 26 he also employed *conter* to describe his poetic activity — "Vous veul conter un essanple mout grant." This choice reflects a difference in performance conditions; I suggest that there is also a related difference in compositional technique perceptible in other aspects of style.

Perhaps the most marked difference between S and M is the degree to which they rely upon repeated hemistichs, upon formulaic language. The difference between the two is easiest to appreciate in tabular form; I include statistics from other works for comparison: [91]

	hemistichs	formulas	percent
Ste Marguerite	1704	191	11
12-syl. *Alexis*	2448	337	14
Buevon (D)	7762	1187	15
Alexandre (D)	1614	277	16
M^1	2551	408	16
M^2	2186	347	16
L	1250	262	21
Charroi (D)	2972	851	29
Gormont (D)	1318	380	29
S	2688	798	30
Guillaume (D)	7108	2172	31
Enf. Guillaume	6252	2961	47

---

[91] For fuller data, see Elliott, 1981. The figures given there for *S* and *M* are for Paris' edition of *S* and M^1. The methodology, as well as the definition of the formula, is adapted from the work of Joseph Duggan (1973). Those works concorded and analysed by Duggan are marked "(D)." For my concordances I used the following editions: Wace, *La Vie de sainte Marguerite*, ed. Francis (1932); the dodecasyllabic *Alexis*, a version independent of the Alsis-family of poems, ed. Stebbins; *L*, ed. Storey; *Les Enfances Guillaume*, ed. J.-L. Perrier (1933).

M* therefore has a formula density comparable to other works known to be composed in writing — e. g., other hagiographic texts, the decasyllabic portion of the *Roman d'Alexandre*, Adenet le Roi's *Buevon de Conmarchis*. In contrast, *S* has a density similar to the *chansons de geste* analysed by Joseph Duggan which average 29.8 % straight formula. [92]

Concerning the use of formulaic language, it is important to determine not only with what frequency a poet repeats himself but under what circumstances. I believe that for the orally composing poet (or for poems with a high formula density) the primary unit of composition is the hemistich, whereas for the poet who composes in writing (or for poems with comparatively low formula densities) the unit is primarily the line or some longer constituent. This distinction is responsible for some of the stylistic differences observable between *M* and *S*.

S relies much more heavily upon repeated hemistichs to frame its narrative than does *M** (30 % compared to 16 %, an increase of nearly 200 %). In poems with relatively high formula densities, there is a marked tendency to keep closely related grammatical constituents within the same hemistich. For example, a syntactic formula common to all versions of *Alexis* consists of a finite form of *venir* followed immediately by a gerund functioning as an adverb of manner. [93] In *L, A, P,* and *S*, this construction occurs a number of times, [94] and there are only two exceptions to the immediate juxtaposition of *venir* and the adverbial gerund: "Jusque an Alsis en vindrent dui errant" (*L* 113); "Dedens Ausis vinrent tout droit esrant" (*S* 463). In *M* the tendency to separate, and to separate more widely, these two constituents becomes pronounced. While the traditional grouping does occur ("cele part vient

---

[92] Duggan 1973, p. 26.

[93] Discussing this construction for twelfth-century poetry, C. W. Aspland (1970, pp. 72-73), writes: "A special group of gerunds expressing the relationship of manner with the main verb for the most part describe. rapidity of movement. They often have the force of adverbs too closely related to the verbs that they modify to convey a separate accompanying action. The most frequent of these adverbial gerunds are *corant* and *errant*, 'quickly, rapidly.' "

[94] For example, "la vint curant" (*L* 423), "puis vint currant" (*A* 75), "dunc vint errant" (*L* 76), "li serf Deu vint errant" (*A* 185), "ki vint plorant" (*L* 560), "se vont afoibliant" (*S* 29).

courant," 406; "vient fuiant," 430), on a number of occasions the M-poet elected to separate verb and gerund more widely:

Sains Alessins vint a le mer fuiant (M^2 197)
Si vinrent lues mil dÿable acourant (M^1 218)
Quant primes ving en ta grant court manant (M^2 714)
Quant jou premiers vinc en ta cort errant (M^1 884)

The first example constitutes a breakup of a potentially formulaic constituent since "vient fuiant" also occurs (430).

This separation of closely related constituents is indicative of a two-fold difference in compositional technique between M^* and the other versions of the Vie de saint Alexis. First, the poets of the rhyming versions seem consciously to avoid formulaic patterns of expression, and second, they tend to separate grammatically related constructions, sometimes going so far as to place one constituent in the first hemistich (or line) and the other in the second (cf. "Si vinrent lues mil dÿable acorant").

A far more significant instance of separation of grammatical constituents by the caesura involves an auxiliary verb and a past participle, a practice common in M^*. After Alexis' death, Eufemien is rebuked for having willfully concealed the saint's body. S reads, "Tant l'as celé, mout i a grant pecié" (953). In M the line is expanded to two, and the first-hemistich phrase, "Tant l'as celé," is divided between the first and the second hemistich:

"Certes," dist il, "fait as grant mesproison
Ke tant nous as celé cest saint baron."

(811-12)

Had the poet combined the auxiliary and participle in the same hemistich, he would have had a formulaic repetition of 409, "nous as celée tant."[95] Nor is this an isolated example. The M-poet in general appears to have felt little necessity to confine auxiliary and participle to a single hemistich. Compare the following lines taken from S with their rendition by M.

---

[95] It is also possible to view the line as a 6/4 decasyllable (instead of the normal 4/6), but for purposes of comparison, I have considered all lines 4/6.

Quant son avoir // lor a tout departi (*S* 389)
Quant li sires ot // departi son avoir (*M²* 241)

"Sire," dist il, // "Crestiens ai a non" (*S* 797)
"Chrestiiens sui // vraiement apelés (*M²* 668)

Va s'ent li pére // et li fils est remés (*S* 816)
Vait s'ent li peres // dolans et esfraés,
Et li fils est // remés [96] sor les degrés (*M¹* 842-43)

In a passage new to *M* there are three examples of separation of auxiliary and participle within three lines: [97]

Atant en est // li rices hons alés,
S'en a se femme // et ses enfans menés,
Et li sires est // en la place remés.

(595-97)

Such findings lead to the conclusion that for the *M*-poet the unit of composition was the line, while for the poet of *S* it was, to a far greater degree, the hemistich. In this respect the practices of the *S*-poet, composing in the verse form of the early *chansons de geste*, decasyllabic laisses in assonance, more closely resemble those of a formulaic epic singer than the stylistic tendencies of a writing poet. An examination of *L, S, M¹, M², Les Enfances Guillaume*, and one thousand lines each from *La Chanson de Roland* and *Les Enfances Ogier*, reveals the following statistics for auxiliary-participle separation.

	number of compound constructions	number of separations	percent
L	84	7	8
S	212	19	9
Roland (1-1000)	159	14	9
Enf. Guillaume	505	66	13
M²	235	68	29
M¹	195	73	37
Ogier (1-1000)	202	79	39

---

[96] *M²* reads *demeure par desous* (677).
[97] *M¹* contains an even more revealing example of such separation, as the auxiliary occurs in one line, the participle in the next; "Puis si

S, then, is comparable with two highly formulaic works, *La Chanson de Roland* (34 % semantic formula) and *Les Enfances Guillaume* (47 %), while the practice of the M-poet more closely resembles that of Adenet le Roi.[98]

Upon one occasion M* carries grammatical enjambment over three lines, a practice unparalleled in *L* or *S*. The grammatical pattern is as follows (I quote from M[1]):

Line 1: subject and transitive compound verb (doubled).
Line 2: object of the compound conjunction *(tant que)*,[99] a clause which itself consists of a subject and two compound transitive verbs.
Line 3: objects of the verbs in line 2.

Tant a li sires // et proié et ploré
K'eles li ont // guerpi et pardonné [100]
Ire et descorde et male volenté.

(894-96)

Such elaborate rhetoric and such complicated syntax do not occur in the earlier versions of *Alexis*. In both lines 894 and 895 the auxiliary verbs are in the first hemistich, the participles in the second; both participles are doubled, and the third line consists of three objects arranged as tricolon with crescendo. Line 894 makes use of alliteration. The effects are consonant with those praised by the rhetorical handbooks and similar to those found in the works of more rhetorically sophisticated poets who composed in writing such as Chrétien de Troyes and Adenet le Roi.[101]

---

m'*aroies* en es les quinse dis / Ensi *oublié* que ainc ne fusse vis" (199-200). There are no instances of this degree of necessary enjambment in any other version of *Alexis*.

[98] In general, these percentages increase inversely to the formula density. I do not have statistics for the formulas of *Les Enfances Ogier* but presume they are similar to *Buevon de Conmarchis*, calculated by Duggan to be 15 %. I analyzed *Les Enfances Ogier* instead of *Buevon* in order to reduce the variables; *Ogier*, like the works to which it is here being compared, is in decasyllables, *Buevon* in alexandrines.

[99] I quote from the manuscript (f. 398v); Gatto-Pyko reads "Quand." Gaston Paris' edition and the Carlisle manuscript both have *Tant* here.

[100] M² reads "K'eles li ont et bonement pardonné."

[101] Adenet is fond of enjambment; e. g. three instances from *Les Enfances Ogier* (ed. Henry): "Pour crestïens qui erent telement / Venu seur aus..." (637-38); "Rois Burnamons et Ogiers atendu / Ont trestout

Other differences in style appear to accompany the difference in treatment of the caesura noted above with regard to auxiliary-participle separation. Examining the Old French epic, Jean Rychner postulated that the individual decasyllable was the unit of composition rather than a series of lines. [102] In accord with this thesis, based on an analysis of 400 lines from the *Couronnement de Louis* (249-648), Rychner distinguished three principal types of decasyllables: [103]

> I. Aux deux hémistiches correspondent deux propositions, coordonnées, ou bien dont l'une est subordonnée à l'autre.
>
> II. Le décasyllabe est rempli par une proposition complète.
>
> III. Le décasyllabe est fait d'éléments syntaxiques qui se rapportent à un verbe figurant dans les vers précédents ou suivants. [104]

Of the first type, Rychner observes its metrical convenience to the performing jongleur and notes that he finds only one instance (line 494) where the caesura does not mark a grammatical division as well as a metrical break. Of the second type, he finds only four lines where the caesura does not indicate a minor grammatical break but falls instead between a noun or pronoun and its determiner. [105] My findings accord with Rychner's, especially concerning the importance of the caesura as a meaningful boundary. For the epic singer, I maintain, even more than the individual line the hemistich was the primary unit of composition. Lines of Rychner's type I, in which each hemistich is independent of the other, should therefore be more frequent in orally composed verse than in the works of writing poets.

---

quoi..." (3921-22); "Li rois Corsaubles en ot moult irascu / Le cuer,..." (5798-99).

[102] Rychner, 1964, p. 167.

[103] Rychner, 1964, p. 168.

[104] This category is not large and I have not considered it here, nor were there many examples found by Rychner. It is important to note, however, that the examples he cites from the *chansons de geste* do not involve as complex a degree of grammatical dependence as do those in *Alexis M*.

[105] One of these four (v. 285) involves that I would consider a break-up of a formula: "Celui a tot aveir commandé."

Type I lines offer the jongleur the greatest freedom. Consider the following first hemistichs (all taken from type I lines): "N'at mais (plus d') enfant"; "Vint en la cambre"; "Set ans tous pleins"; "Grant fut la noise." These formulas are followed by a wide variety of second-hemistich phrases:

> N'at mais enfant; lui volt mult honurer (*L* 43)
> bien le puet marier (*S* 91)
> Vint en la cambre, toute l'a desparée (*S* 412)
> plainne de mariment (*S* 406)
> o sa gente moillier (*S* 116)
> s'en a tret une broigne (*Prise* 967)
> .vii. ans tous plains, c'est li premier eés (*S* 637)
> ad estet en Espaigne (*Rol.* 2)
> avons ci conversé (*Girart* 6516)
> Grant fut la noise, si l'antendit la medre (*L* 422)
> si l'oirent Franceis (*Rol.* 1005)
> par tute la contree (*Rol.* 1455)
> de "Munjoie" escrier (*Rol.* 2151)
> et li cris et li tons (*Moniage* 75)

The syntactic flexibility offered by this type of line was not exploited by the M-poet to the extent that it was by the poet of *S*. On a number of occasions *M* has altered the syntax found in *I*. or *S*, preferring Rychner's type II line to type I. Grammatically this represents an entirely different solution although the thought expressed remains the same. Three examples of this alteration of surface structure involve expressions of naming (the first has already been discussed):

> "Sire," dist il, "Crestïens ai a non." (*S* 797)
> "Chrestiiens sui vraiement apelés." (*M* 668)
>
> Eufemien — si out a num li pedre (*L* 16)
> Eufemiens, ensi ot non li péres (*S* 52)
> Li Dius vassaus ot non Eufemïiens (*M* 28)
>
> Fud baptizet, si out num Alexis (*L* 31)
> Baptisiés fu, s'ot a non Alessis (*S* 69)
> Dant Alexins ont le fil apielé (*M*[1] 54)

To describe Alexis' flight from Rome (and his return) *L, A, P,* and
S all employ lines consisting of two independent constituents;
M prefers a type-II line of a single constituent: [106]

> Drecent lur sigle, laisent curre par mer (*L* 79; *S* 340, 583).
> Ourent lur vent, laisent curre par mer (*L* 192).
> Drechent lor voiles li maistre maritant (*M* 201).

M in fact demonstrates a markedly greater preference for lines
consisting of a single grammatical proposition than do other versions of *Alexis.* An analysis of one-hundred line segments for
type-II lines from four *Alexis* manuscripts and from the *Chanson
de Roland* shows the following distribution: [107]

	lines	percent type II
S	212-311	18
A	1-100	24
L	1-100	26
Roland	1-100	30
M^1	101-140, 236-296	48

Once again we find that *S* and *M* differ considerably in the way
they handle the hemistich, *S* treating it with more grammatical
autonomy than does *M.* In *S,* then, the tendency for the caesura
to mark a significant semantic and grammatical pause is greater
than in *M.* The practice of *S,* moreover, like that of *L,* tends to
resemble more closely that of the *chanson de geste.* [108]

With regard to formulas, the *M*-poet appears to seek to vary
the traditional patterns of repetition, avoiding semantic formulas
although using syntactic formulas with considerable frequency. The
quest for variety is the mark of the literate poet. In *The Nature
of Narrative,* Scholes and Kellogg remark, "Literary poets strive to
make the line unique, reserving repeated phrases for special

---

[106] Compare *Gui de Nanteuil: M* 1746, "Il drecierent lor sigle, s'ont
lor voile levee"; *V* 1909, "Il driçent lor velles, s'acoient lor estree."

[107] For *M* and *S* I chose lines original to that manuscript, not adapted
from other versions.

[108] In all the technical matters of style analysed here, *L* more closely
resembles *S* than it does *M*.*

effects." [109] The M-poet may be following the practice recommended by rhetorical teaching. Discussing *amplification* in the *Poetria Nova,* Geoffrey of Vinsauf, for example, recommended: [110]

> Si facis amplum,
> Hoc primo procede gradu: sententia cum sit
> Unica, non uno veniat contenta paratu,
> Sed *variat vestes* et mutatoria sumat:
> Sub verbis aliis praesumpta resume; repone
> Pluribus in clausis unum; *multiplice forma*
> *dissimuletur idem;* varius sis et tamen idem.

(219-25)

A very common phrase in the *LAPS* tradition is the second-hemistich formula, "e (a, de) le pedre e la medre," which occurs seven times in *L,* nine in *S.* There is only one instance of the combination of "father" and "mother" in a single hemistich in *M;* elsewhere the poet avoids the formula and turns to periphrasis and expansion. Concerning periphrasis, Geoffrey of Vinsauf advised: [111]

> ne ponas nomina rerum:
> Pone notas alias; nec plane detege, sed rem
> Innue per notulas...

(229-31)

So for instance the line "Or revendrai al pedra ed a la medra" (*L* 101, *S* 394) becomes "Or revenrai a chiaus de la contrée" (*M* 253). When Alexis' deathbed letter is read aloud, *L* and *S* utilize the formulaic hemistich, "Le non lor dist del pére et de la mére," *S* 1117; *L* 379). *M* expands the statement so that the mention of the saint's parents fills an entire line:

> Lors a le vie de chief en chief contée,
> Et son pére a et sa mére nommée [112]

(960-61)

---

[109] Scholes and Kellogg, 1975, p. 21.
[110] Faral, 1958, p. 204 (emphasis added).
[111] *Poetria Nova,* ed. Faral, 1958, p. 204.
[112] For the separation of auxiliary verb and past participle by the caesura, see above; see also the note to M^2 960.

In *L* and *S* the "father-mother" second-hemistich formula is often coupled with the formula "et la pucele" or "et la spuse" in the beginning of the next line (there are five examples in *S*, four in *L*):

> Tant i plourérent et li péres et li mére
> Et la pucele que trestout s'i lassérent.
>
> (*S* 1232-33)

M avoids this formulaic coupling, again preferring periphrasis and expansion: [113]

> Mout le regrete cieus ki lui engenra,
> Sa boine mére ausi ki le porta,
> Et la pucele ki tant forment l'ama.
>
> (1031-33)

Repetition, then, plays an important stylistic role in *S*, as it does in many *chansons de geste*. The *M*-poet, on the other hand, seems to have preferred variety of expression. Thus far we have been concerned with purely stichic repetition, but *S* demonstrates a similar fondness for repeating larger narrative units, although the two cannot wholly be separated. As Gaston Paris noted, *S* employs *laisses similaires* in a fashion highly reminiscent of the *chanson de geste*. The poem also contains linked laisses (i. e., "l'enchaînement des laisses"), and other types of narrative recapitulation. For example, Alexis twice travels by sea. The *S*-poet did not scruple to depict the saint's second voyage in the same terms used for the first (cf. 337-43 and 581a-89; also 627-28). The description of Alexis' two trips in *M*, however, do not repeat one another; there is only one hemistich common to both voyages ("done son pris," 200, 432).

Another form of repetition found in *S* also recalls the techniques of oral epic. This instance is of practical benefit to a performer. In *La Chanson de geste*, Rychner notes that the difficult conditions under which a jongleur performed necessitated the use of various techniques to link a story together and to remind the listeners of important sections of the tale which they might have forgotten

---

[113] Compare also *S* 755-56 with *M* 615-17.

or missed. [114] Rychner cites a number of scenes from the *chanson de geste*, as well as from Serbian oral poetry, in which a messenger delivers his message in exactly the same words with which he had been charged; in *S* the audience is given a detailed account of the contents of the Alexis' deathbed letter, an account repeated *verbatim* when the letter is read (911-16 and 1130-36). In *M* the contents of the letter are not described as Alexis writes it. When it is read, they are summarized:

> Lors a le vie de chief en chief contée,
> Et son pére a et sa mére nommée...
>
> (960-61)

No particulars, however, are given, presumably because the poet can assume that *his* attentive audience is sufficiently familiar with the story of Alexis' wanderings by now.

Multiple announcements of the subject of a poem are another practical form of narrative repetition. Rychner points to the reiterations of the subject at the beginning of *Moniage Guillaume II* [115] as indicating that the jongleur could not count on having his audience's rapt attention from the very first word; an audience might be slow to quiet down, late-comers might arrive, and so forth. Unlike other versions of the *Vie de Saint Alexis, S* opens with a 9-line prologue, of which Gaston Paris has written:

> Ces prologues sont tout à fait caractéristiques de la poésie des jongleurs.... Ils occupaient, par des vers de peu d'importance, les premiers moments où le chanteur-musicien prenait la parole, et pendant lesquels il n'avait pas encore obtenu de son auditoire un parfait silence. [116]

Only in *S*, moreover, is the hero's name stated at the outset (line 2); in all other versions the poet appears able to assume that his audience already knows it is to hear a poem about Saint Alexis

---

[114] Rychner, 1955, p. 54ff.

[115] Rychner, 1955, p. 55ff; Rychner notes that the *Chanson de Roland* is atypical of the *chanson de geste* as a whole because it contains very few comments by the jongleur. For a discussion of the prologues to the *chanson de geste*, see Gsteiger, 1959.

[116] Paris, 1872, p. 202.

and therefore he need not advertise. In laisse 2 the *S*-poet repeats
the announcement of the subject matter:

> Conterai vous del pére et de l'enfant,
> Qui de mençoigne n'i a ne tant ne quant.

(32-33)

Finally in laisse 3 he includes the line which in *L* serves to describe
the subject of the poem, "Pour çou vous di, d'un sien fil voel
parler" (*S* 51; cf. *L* 15).

The naming of the hero in the second line is similar to the
opening of, for example, the *Moniage Guillaume I*, composed,
according to Cloetta, about the same time as *Alexis S*, around
1160. [117] Epic prologues frequently summarize the contents of the
work and stress the veracity of the account to be heard. [118] The
prologue to *S* reviews the contents of the poem and asserts the truth
of the tale ("Que de mençoinge n'i a ne tant ne quant"). In contrast, *M* begins not with a jongleuresque prologue but with the
equivalent of the opening of the Hildesheim manuscript (the tenth
line of *S*). The poet waits until line 26 to announce his specific
subject:

> Vous veul conter un essanple mout grant
> D'un saintisme home et d'un sien chier enfant.

(26-27)

The poet thinks of himself as *telling* a story ("conter") which is
to provide his audience with an *example*, the traditional role of
hagiographic narrative. [119]

The *S*-poet's triple proclamation of his theme is typical of his
technique throughout the poem. Not only has he lengthened the

---

[117] Cloetta, 1911, p. 217, dates *Moniage I* between 1139 and 1170, and
closer to the latter date than the former. For the date of *S* see Paris,
1872, p. 199. In relation to Alexis' pilgrimage to Jerusalem and its
significance to dating the poem, see in this edition the textual note *ad loc.*

[118] Gsteiger, 1959, pp. 217-18; for classical epic, see Detienne, 1967.

[119] To give only one example, Sulpicius Severus, in his influential
biography of Saint Martin of Tours, wrote in the prologue to that work
that he was writing to provide "exemplo aliis" (*Vita Martini*, I, 6). See
also Jolles, quoted above, p. 37.

work by creating new characters and incidents, and by developing further sympathetic figures such as the wife and mother, he has also added to its bulk by extensive use of narrative repetition. The emotional wedding-night interview is lengthened by the addition of *laisses similaires* (15 is original to *S,* while 16 occurs in *L* although *S* has altered the last two lines). Of this scene Gaston Paris has stated:

> Nous nous trouvons ici en présence du fait bien connu de la répétition des tirades épiques, et nous pouvons constater à coup sûr au moins une des manières dont il se produisait: c'est uniquement pour s'arrêter plus longtemps sur un point de récit, sur une idée, sur une situation intéressante, que l'auteur... a ajouté cette strophe 15, d'ailleurs parfaitement inutile. [120]

S makes considerable use of several types of *laisse similaire* (we have already seen the reiteration of the poem's subject in laisses 1-3). Laisses 15-16, mentioned above, correspond to what Rychner has termed "l'horizontale lyrique." [121] The most poignant of the *laisses similaires* occurs during the bride's tearful farewell to her husband (laisses 23-24), a scene during which the reprise, "jou te commant a Dé," is heard three times in laisse 24, twice in the mouth of the girl and once from Alexis. The emotional intensity of the mother's grief at the departure of her son is also heightened by the use of *laisses similaires* (32-33); a fourth set of juxtaposed laisses treats the announcement of the saint's death (82-83). Each of these repetitions has occurred at a moment of high emotion (like the examples which Rychner cites from the *Roland*), and greatly enhances the lyrical nature of the poem.

A final type of *laisse similaire* involves the repetition of an idea at the beginning of two consecutive laisses which then give a separate development to the repeated idea. For example laisse 67 refers in a general way to the suffering Alexis endured for seventeen years at Rome, while 68, after reminding the audience of his seventeen-year stay at Alsis, gives more details of his deprivations. There are in all some eleven instances of *laisses similaires* in *S.* In

---

[120] Paris, 1872, p. 203.
[121] Rychner, 1955, p. 95; see also p. 125.

contrast there are only two brief examples of this form of narrative repetition in M^1 and one in M^2. [122] The other *laisses similaires* found in S have been reduced to a single statement without repetition.

An even more significant difference between these two versions of *Alexis* is the use of linked laisses. Performing was not easy. One technique, helpful to both performer and listener alike, was to link the laisses in such a way that the narrative syntax is clear and easy to remember. The laisses become not discrete entities but links in a chain; they follow each other in necessary order. In this technique, which Rychner christened "l'enchaînement des laisses," [123] the last line (or lines) of one laisse is repeated almost exactly as the opening line (or lines) of the next; Rychner gives a number of examples from the *chansons de geste;* I cite one (the repetition in boldface type):

> Par mi la herde l'en avint a fuir,
> **En sun estriu se fert un motun gris.**
>
> **En sun estriu se fert un gris motun.**
> Tant le turnad e les vals e les munz.

> *(Guillaume,* laisses 31-32)

In S both descriptions of the saint's sea voyages contain this type of link (24-25, 46-47), as do the transitions between laisses 4 and 5, 19 and 20.

> laisses 24-25
>
> En Jhersalem les conduist Damedés.
> **Sains Alessins est issus de la nef.**
>
> **Sains Alessins est de la nef issus;**
> Vint al sepulcre u nostre sire fu.

Like the example from the *Chanson de Guillaume,* these pairs of linked laisses contain a practical mnemonic device: the last line

---

[122] In M^1 laisses 29 and 30 begin similarly but develop different trains of thought; the last lines of laisse 76 are paraphrased in the first five of laisse 77. M^2 omits the equivalent of laisse 29 (30 = 16); laisses 76-77 = M^2 51-52.
[123] Rychner, 1955, pp. 74ff.

of one laisse contains the assonance word of the next — in *Guillaume,* for example, *motun gris* (assonance in *I*) and *gris motun* (assonance in *U*); in *Alexis S, issus de la nef* (assonance in *É*) and *de la nef issus* (assonance in *U*). In *S* at least twenty-two of the 135 laisses contain some sort of close verbal link, and four give the assonance word of the following laisse.

Some links extend over more than one line (Rychner points out that a "reprise" of two lines is especially characteristic of the *Chanson de Guillaume*). There are a number of two-line links in *S:*

laisses 35-36

Plourent emsamble del duel de lor ami,
L'une son fil et l'autre son mari.

Pleurent ensamble lor ami c'ont perdu:
Pleure la mére et la pucele plus.

This form of close verbal repetition is limited in *S* to links between laisses; it does not occur within a single laisse and therefore is not equivalent to *interpretatio* or some such figure praised by the Latin rhetorical teachers. [124] Of all types of narrative repetition, "l'enchaînement des laisses" is most indicative of epic style. [125] It is a practical, not an ornamental, device designed to aid the jongleur to remember what is to follow (and sometimes in what assonance), as well as to help the listener to grasp the thread of the tale. To my knowledge it does not occur to any appreciable degree in texts known to be created in writing. It is rare in *M.*

In addition to *laisses similaires* and linked laisses, *S* utilizes another form of narrative repetition which was of particular benefit to a jongleur performing before a somewhat noisy or inattentive crowd. An action is first described, then dramatized; the poet tells the audience what is to be said, and then says it. During the scene between Alexis and his bride, the poet first describes the division of the ring in laisse 17 but gives the dialogue which accompanies the act in laisse 20. If we follow the manuscript order for the laisses treating Alexis' return to Rome, we find the same phenomenon:

---

[124] Contrary to the opinion of E. R. Curtius (1937).
[125] Cf. Martín de Riquer, 1956, p. 318: "L'enchaînement des laisses est ce qui caractérise le mieux le style épique."

in laisses 47-48 the poet tells his audience of the saint's prayer to
escape recognition and God's granting his request; laisses 49-50
contain the words of the prayer quoted as direct discourse, and the
following laisses dramatize the interview between Alexis and his
parents in Rome. Similarly, the poet describes at the end of laisse
51 the saint's resolve to see his father; this laisse is linked to the
next (by *atapinés-s'atapine*) in which Alexis meets Eufemien. In 53
the encounter is described in greater detail, and the dramatization
continues through laisse 56. The same technique of indirect narration followed by direct is employed when Alexis becomes aware
that his death is imminent; the poet describes the saint's realiza-
tion and his desire to write a letter in laisse 64, while the writing
occurs in laisses 71-72.

Narrative repetitions, like stichic, are less common in M than
in S. M prefers amplification. Avoiding the multiple announcement
of the subject which occupies the first three laisses of S, the poet
instead chose to fill the second laisse with an expansion of the
religious and moral content of the work. M^2 has only two examples
of laisse-linking in 101 laisses, [126] and these differ somewhat from
those found in S:

> laisses 10-11 (M^2)
>> Tantost s'en issent, si l'ont faite widier.
>> Sains Alesins regarda son moullier.
>>
>> Quant li sains hons a le dame veüe,
>> Qui tant par est courtoise et bien creüe.

Here the second mention of the idea does not start from the same
point in time but somewhat later on: "Alexis looked at his wife";
"When Alexis had seen his wife" (there exist, however, parallels
for this shift in temporal perspective in epic; see the textual note to
S 863-64). More significant is the fact that the poet, in his quest for
variety (remember the injunction of Geoffrey of Vinsauf quoted
above), employs two different verbs, *regarder* and *veïr*, and two
different nouns for 'wife,' *moullier* and *dame*. The second instance
also demonstrates the poet's fondness for periphrasis instead of
strict verbal repetition:

---

[126] M^1 also links laisses 83-84.

laisses 70-71

> Et li serjans ki tant l'amoit forment
> S'en keurt au pére, se li dit coiement.
>
> Li boins serjans qui li pére ot tan chier
> Le court au pére, sovanet consellier.

What we have, then, is repetition of the same ideas, a form of *variatio,* not a verbal link which functions mnemonically.

Similarly, in reducing the *laisses similaires* to single statements, the M-poet does not avoid all forms of repetition but favors those recommended by teachers of rhetoric. For example, S devotes two laisses (32 and 33) to the mother's sorrowful stripping of the bridal chamber. M eliminates the narrative repetition, but expands the mother's first lamenting speech (I quote from M^1):

> "Fius Alesins, quel tristour m'as donnee! [127]
> Fils, tu t'en vas, s'as laissié t'espousee
> Que jou t'avoie si cortoise donnee:
> Tel duel me fais que ja serai dervee."
>
> (406-409)

There is indeed reiteration in this speech, but it is neither formulaic repetition nor the repetition of situation which typifies the *laisse similaire.* This repetition occurs within a single laisse; the phrase in 406, "kel tristour m'as donée" is paraphrased in 409, "Tel duel me fais," a form of *interpretatio* more in keeping with the tenets of the rhetorical schools than the jongleuresque repetitions of S. M*, then, reads like a clerical reworking of a more popular poem.

IV

CONCLUSION

The version of the *Vie de saint Alexis* contained in manuscript S forms an important chapter in the history of medieval hagi-

---

[127] M^2 here reads, "Fieus Alesin, douche rose honerée."

ography. The "popularity" of hagiographic texts has frequently
been noted, but by the observation most critics have meant little
more than that such works are many in number. Hagiographic
accounts have been considered the sole province of the Church,
their authors clerics, the occasion of their performance liturgical
feasts. [128] Cesare Segre, for instance, writes of the early vernacular
hagiographic poems, "nos textes sont nés dans ce milieu clerical
et y sont restés." [129] In a history of medieval French literature to
1300, Jean-Charles Payen notes the existence in works such as
the *Séquence de sainte Eulalie* and the Hildesheim *Alexis* of words
derived directly from Latin and writes of hagiography in general:
"Ce sont des poèmes de clers destinés à des clers." [130] For most
vernacular hagiographic texts, and all Latin ones, such views are
no doubt correct. But a poem such as *Alexis S* may be popular
in a different sense, and may owe its genesis to other sources.

As we have seen, *S* differs from earlier versions in a number
of ways, notable among which is an increased interest in the depiction of characters capable of arousing sympathy. The women, in
particular, are drawn in greater detail. Even the saint himself has
been humanized as he manifests concern for the pain he has caused.
He is a man with recognizable emotions, not an abstract embodi-
ment of *askēsis*. In this respect *Alexis S* may be called popular.
Similarly the style of the poem shares many features with that
popular genre par excellence, the epic — a high density of semantic
formulas, linked laisses, *laisses similaires*. *M**, by contrast, although
retaining in comparison with *L* many innovations of *S* such as
an increased interest in the *pucele,* has omitted details of a feudal
or chivalric nature and curtailed the portrayal of character, while
demonstrating a fondness for doctrine (particularly pronounced
in *M¹*) and for clerical lore. It avoids poetic techniques associated

---

[128] Mölk (1978), p. 339, argues for *L*, "il y a un rapport très précis
entre la genèse de la *Chanson* (= *L*) et le culte latin de saint Alexis."
He points to the words "oi cest jurn" in st. 109*L* as proof. This strophe,
however, is missing, as he notes, from *V*, but more significantly from *S*,
and from *M**. *S*, then, contains no reference to performance on the feast
of Saint Alexis. Pio Rajna (1929) and E. R. Curtius (1936) claimed that
strophes 109-10 were spurious.

[129] Segre, 1974, p. 309, emphasis added.

[130] Payen, 1970, p. 117.

with epic style. *M** suggests as its proper milieu the cloister, *S* the market place or seignorial hall.

In spite of its pious content, there is evidence that hagiography did not remain locked in the church, the exclusive possession of the clergy. A number of medieval texts testify to the activities of pious jongleurs. [131] In an often-cited passage Thomas of Chobham, for example, referred to the activities of those "joculatores qui cantant gesta principum et vitas sanctorum." [132] In the *Life of Saint Aybert* (d. 1140), Robert d'Ostrevand reports of the saint, "Cum esset juvenis et laicus in domo patris sui ... forte quadam die audivit mimum cantando referentem vitam et conversionem sancti Theobaldi et asperitatem vitae eius." [133] It is important to note that this quotation implies that the jongleur was performing in a private house, not in a church nor in conjunction with a liturgical ceremony.

Elioxe, the late-twelfth-century *chanson de geste* which opens the Crusade cycle, gives a more detailed picture of a jongleuresque *chanson de saint.* The subject is the life of a military martyr, St. Maurice (no *Vie saint Morise* has survived); the setting is the "mostier saint Wimer" (3177), to which a band of knights has returned after supper to keep vigil. [134]

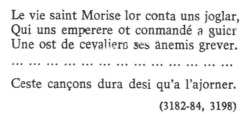

Le vie saint Morise lor conta uns joglar,
Qui uns emperere ot conmandé a guicr
Une ost de cevaliero ses anemis grever.
... ...
Ceste cançons dura desi qu'a l'ajorner.

(3182-84, 3198)

The jongleur's *Vie saint Morise* contains all the requisite narrative elements of the typical martyr's *passio* — a description of the saint's background, his accusation, punishment, and the aftermath of his death. In this case the saint was a soldier, so the details of his career are selected for their appeal to the chivalric audience

---

[131] For the eleventh-century *Triumphus sancti Remacli,* see Elliott, 1979.
[132] Thomas of Chobham, ed. Bloomfield (1968), p. 282.
[133] Cited by Faral (1910), p. 277.
[134] Ed. Mickel, 1977.

listening to the poem; Maurice was the commander of a large force, 6,666 men, "tous ber." The song, moreover, was no brief affair; the recital lasted from after supper "desi qu'a l'ajorner."

We know, moreover, that a *Vie de saint Alexis* formed part of a jongleur's repertory in the latter half of the twelfth century, the period to which is ascribed the composition of *Alexis S.* For the year 1173 an anonymous chronicler from Lyon recounts the conversion of Valdesius (better known as Peter Waldo) upon hearing a jongleur sing the life of Alexis. [135] The account is precious for the glimpse it gives us of the conditions of performance of a *Vie de saint Alexis:* the event took place on a Sunday. [136] The jongleur had gathered a crowd, so presumably he found hagiographic poetry popular and therefore profitable (the economic motives for singing such songs must have been important, at least from the performer's viewpoint). He was willing, furthermore, to go to the home of a wealthy merchant to repeat his tale. This account of Valdesius' conversion may well be legend, not history. If so, it is in many ways better evidence for the role played by jongleurs in hagiographic poetry. If the story is historical, it could have been a unique occurrence. But if it is a legend designed to lend romantic color to the conversion, it bears eloquent witness to the widespread activities of religious jongleurs, for no one would invent such a story unless it were well-known that jongleurs did perform poems about saints, and more specifically poems about St. Alexis.

S shows all the hallmarks of being such a jongleuresque creation, perhaps indeed, given its high density of semantic formulas, an orally composed poem. [137] There remains the question of the

---

[135] "Currente adhuc anno eodem, scilicet 1173, Dominice incarnationis, fuit apud Lugdunum Gallie civis quidam Valdesius nomine, qui per iniquitatem fenoris multas sibi pecunias coacervaverat. Is quadam die dominica cum declinasset ad turbam, quam ante ioculatorem viderat congregatam, ex verbis ipsius conpungtus fuit, et eum ad domum suam deducens, intente eum audire curavit. Fuit enim locus narracionis eius, qualiter beatus Alexis in domo patris sui beato fine quievit" (*M. G. H.* Script. XXVI, 447).

[136] Ulrich Mölk (1978, p. 340) points out that the performance occurred not on the feast day of the saint (17 July), but on a Sunday before Pentecost (Pentecost falls on the seventh Sunday after Easter).

[137] I do not claim that *S,* as we know it, is a verbatim transcription of an oral performance. Auerbach (1958, p. 284) issues a timely caveat

relationship between *L* and *S*. With the exception of the alteration of strophic form to laisses, *L* has more in common stylistically with *S* than it does with the more clerical *M²* (or than *S* has with *M²*). Yet the ecclesiastical connections of *L* seem clear. [138] The poem in the Hildesheim manuscript is preceded by a preface which may shed light on our problem. "Ici comuncet amiable cançun e spiritel raisun d'iceol noble barun, Eufemien par num, e de la vie de sum filz boneüret del quel *nus avum oït lire e canter* . . . ." This prologue has been interpreted to mean that the poem was intended for use in church. All it says, however, is that the life of the saint *has been* heard sung and read, presumably in church; it does not state that this precise version was so employed. But the words of the prologue do explain how a jongleur, even an illiterate one, might become familiar with the story of the ascetic saint — he had *heard* it in church.

As early as the Council of Tours in 813 it was ordained that sermons should be preached "in rusticam romanam linguam" for the benefit of those who did not understand Latin. [139] The badly mutilated "Jonas-fragment," remnants of a vernacular sermon, or notes for one, preserved by their inclusion in the binding of a tenth-century manuscript, testifies to such activity in the popular tongue by preachers prior to the composition of the Hildesheim *Vie de saint Alexis*. The details of Alexis' life might then have been acquired by some pious jongleur as he *listened* to a priest expound the story of the saint on his feast day. Just such an explanation has been offered to account for Old English religious poetry. John Miles Foley has denied the necessity of considering the cleric to be the only translator:

> What is to prevent an artist from hearing a translation of one of the Latin sources at, for instance, a religious service? Lord recounts numerous examples of a *guslar*

---

against such a conclusion in his discussion of the pervasive influence *not* of clerically trained poets but scribes. We cannot fully assess scribal influence.

[138] See the argument of Mölk, 1978, cited above n. 12.

[139] Concilium Turonense a. 813, c. XVII: "Et ut easdem omelias quisque aperte transferre studeat *in rusticam romanam linguam* aut thiotiscam, quo facilius cuncti possint intellegere quae dicuntur" (*M. G. H., Legum*, sectio III: *Concilia*, vol. I¹, ed. A. Werminghoff, 1906, p. 288).

learning an entire epic song at one hearing and reproducing it *in toto*, with personal modifications, the next
day. [140]

Bede's *Ecclesiastical History* provides us with the example of
Caedmon, an illiterate, formulaic poet who sang marvellous songs
based on what he had been told by *interpretes* of Biblical history. [141]
Such, then, may be the origin of *Alexis S*. The poet, rather than
having read the Hildesheim poem, may have heard it (or better,
a version resembling that poem) in church and have turned it to
his own purposes.

L has a formula density of 21 %, and many of these formulas
can be paralleled in the epic repertory. In my 1977 thesis I give
in Appendix III a list of 62 hemistichs contained in both *L* and
the *Chanson de Roland;* even a very cursory reading reveals at
least nineteen hemistichs common to *L* and the *Prise d'Orenge*,
twenty-one shared with the *Charroi de Nîmes*, and so forth. [142]
The presence of such familiar phrases would greatly facilitate the
task of a professional singer to assimilate the poem, and its comparative shortness (625 lines in the version we know) would make
its reproduction even easier, and perhaps explain as well the relative stability of the text. The Hildesheim *Alexis* is only 200 lines
shorter than the shortest complete *chanson de geste* extant, the
Pèlerinage de Charlemagne, and a reasonably faithful recreation
of its text should pose no problem for an experienced singer. [143]

---

[140] Foley, 1976, p. 220n. The reference to Lord is to *The Singer of
Tales*, p. 78.

[141] Edited by Colgrave and Mynors, 1969, p. 414. See also Donald
Fry, 1975.

[142] Similarly Duggan, 1966, p. 339, found 105 formulas in the *Couronnement de Louis* which occurred three or more times; of these 24 are
also found in the *Roland*, 21 in the *Charroi de Nîmes*, and 29 in the
Prise d'Orenge.

I find it easier to explain the presence of so many "external formulas"
by the existence of a common repertory of formulas than to assume that
the poets of these (and other) *chansons de geste* were consciously
imitating the *Vie de saint Alexis*. For a discussion of the utilization of
epic diction by an Anglo-Saxon religious poet in *The Dream of the Rood*,
see Wolf, 1970.

[143] The role of memory in oral performance is moot; see Lord, *The
Singer of Tales*, passim. See also Rychner, 1955, p. 33ff. Chaytor, 1945,
pp. 116ff. writes (p. 119) of the Yugoslavian singer: "He need hear a

Furthermore, the continued existence side by side with a popular version such as *S* (or even *L*) of the Latin *vita* would aid in reducing the number of new developments and characters introduced into the story. The result, I suggest, of such a symbiosis between ecclesiastical and popular culture would be a poem very like *Alexis S.*

Joseph Bédier attempted to account for the *chansons de geste* by considering them the fruit of a collaboration between cleric and jongleur, but he considered the cleric to be the creative member of this partnership, relegating the jongleur to the more passive role of propagator. Although recent scholarship has tended to reject Bédier's view of the genesis of the epic, the *Vie de saint Alexis,* particularly as contained in manuscript *S,* does, I believe, present us with a genuine example of religious and secular collaboration. The roles played by cleric and jongleur differ, however, from those assigned by Bédier, for the jongleur was the creative member of the team.

Nor is it likely that *S* is the only survivor from the works of pious jongleurs, though I suspect that we possess only a scattered handful of poems from a once numerous *corpus.* To give only one example,[144] E. C. Fawtier-Jones (1932) published a brief life of Saint Catherine of Alexandria (MS Tours 948, XIII-XIV c.; 164 decasyllables combined into 19 laisses in assonance) which she characterized as "une chanson de jongleur" (206).[145] The work is independent of Latin sources and does not follow the traditional order of events.[146] It opens with a jongleur's prologue, the call for

---

poem only two or three times to reproduce it; but the reproduction is by no means given in the same words.... Cases are known of minstrels who have doubled and even trebled the length of the poems which they had heard."

[144] Another work in decasyllabic laisses which employs epic phraseology is the fragment of a translation of Maccabees published in 1875 by Edmund Stengel. See also T. Hemming (1974) on the "Epître farcie de saint Etienne."

[145] For an assessment of the popular role of hagiography, and in particular of the share of oral tradition (though not necessarily of jongleur activity) in the formation of accounts of this saint, see Beattie, 1977.

[146] Mme Fawtier-Jones wrote of the poet, "Notre auteur a choisi dans la *Vie de Sainte Catherine* les épisodes qui lui ont paru pittoresques. Son public favori n'a que faire des discours théologiques d'une Clémence de Barking. Les épisodes choisis, notre poète les développe avec une liberté

the audience's attention and the praise of the poem to be heard
("n'oyrez onques plus bele!" 6). The work, although not formulaic,
contains many epic hemistichs and is intended to be sung, as the
narrator concludes:

> Mes prion Dieu que, por sa grant bonté
> Et por la voye de cuy *avons chanté,*
> Nos doynt sa payz et tignet en santé....

(160-62)

Maintaining too rigid a boundary between cloister and crossroads
is misleading. For all its originally Latin ancestry, hagiography
became a "popular" genre, created by and for the "people." Some
questions, however, about poems like *Alexis S* may ultimately
remain unanswered. Was the poem orally composed? I believe so,
though in the end proof is lacking, nor is this question the most
important one, in spite of the controversy surrounding the issue.
If it was the work of literate poet, that author was sufficiently
familiar with all the procedures of oral style that he could imitate
them with ease, and furthermore, wanted to do so.[147] If a cleric
composed it for dissemination by a jongleur (the Bédier position
for the epic), he understood fully the art of the jongleur, including
the advantages of linked laisses and formulaic language. Such may
be the genesis of poems like *S,* but I think that to accept this
explanation is more complicated than to accept the thesis that the
work is a genuine jongleur poem, composed by the performer
himself. If clerics were in the habit of writing pious works in

---

d'allure et une vivacité que nous ne retrouvons pas chez les auteurs qui
se sont efforcés de suivre un modèle quelconque. De toutes les vies de
sainte Catherine en ancien français que nous étudions c'est celle-ci qui
a le plus de vie" (1932, p. 208).

[147] For a discussion of such "transitional" figures, see the review
article of Curschmann, 1967, p. 45. A good example of a cleric who
did utilize techniques of popular narrative is Herman of Valenciennes,
whose translation of the Bible into rhymed laisses utilizes many hemistichs
drawn from the epic repertory. In his concluding laisse, Herman names
himself and states that "Prestre sui ordonez." He calls his work both a
"chançon" and a "live." See Meyer, 1891 (the quotations taken from
p. 208), and 1897; also Smeets, 1963. Bonnard, 1884, p. 14, characterized
Herman's *Bible* as a "chanson de geste ecclésiastique."

laisses [148] for lay singers to perform, it is suprising that so few
have survived since they would presumably have been written
down for the performer to memorize (the manuscript of the life
of Saint Catherine is small, characterized by Fawtier-Jones as
"peut-être un manuscrit de jongleur" [206]), and one would have
expected such texts to have had great interest for the clerical
scribes. If, however, these poems were usually created by secular
(and possibly illiterate) singers, they would have had less appeal.
Poems such as the Vie de sainte Catherine and Alexis S diverge
from the authoritative vitae to which clerics had easy access; they
would perhaps be judged faulty on that account and would be less
likely to be transcribed; it is suggestive that S survives in only
one manuscript, while all other versions have come down to us
in multiple copies.

Works like the two Alexis manuscripts edited here have
importance for the study of medieval literature. Ours is a fully
literate culture, our education the product of the printing press,
our training as scholars (and particularly as editors) often beginning
with the Greek and Roman classics. We respect the authority of
the written word, the fixity of the text. Medieval authors, however,
lacking our more developed sense of historical accuracy and of the
importance of verisimilitude, our awareness of the dangers of
anachronism, looked on the retelling of past events in a manner
different from ours. Their poems, once created (whether in writing
or orally), took on a life of their own. Discussing "The Interaction
of Life and Literature in the Peregrinationes and Loca Sancta and
the Chanson de Geste," Stephen G. Nichols maintains of the
Chansons de Roland:

> ... we should no longer continue to speak of Digby 23
> as the original poem, or the closest version to it, and
> of the later versions as reworkings. The distinction is
> invidious, and worse still has no support in mediaeval

---

[148] Florence McCulloch (1977) has calculated that "in a genre where
the octosyllabic rhymed couplet dominated from Wace's Vie de sainte
Marguerite in the second quarter of the twelfth century to the end of
the thirteenth, the six examples of monorhymed duodecasyllabic laisses
represent only seven percent of the total number of versions preserved
from this period" (p 174). Even fewer pious works are in decasyllabic
assonanced laisses.

literary practice. Poems on the same subject were not treated as so many imitations of an original version. It would be nearer the mark to think of them as a series of drafts in a continually evolving process of creation, a process which strove to present the truth of the past from the perspective of the present. [149]

Nichols' words are as true for the *Vie de saint Alexis* (and for many hagiographic accounts) as they are for the *Roland*. By concentrating almost exclusively on *L* (and on its sources), scholars have been guilty of distorting the medieval literary picture. Each of the versions, ultimately, has a source, but each leads nonetheless an independent life of its own. [150] The story of Alexis meant one thing to Peter Damian, another to the *S*-poet. The popularizations, if we may call them that, brought by the *S*-poet to his tale do not mark debasements of a pristine original, or fallings off from artistic perfection. They reflect the fact that this poem was composed for a different audience and was intended to be sung on a different occasion. The poet was a successful and artistic professional who correctly judged what his situation demanded. *S* reflects twelfth-century concerns: an increased interest in love and in women; a greater awareness of psychological nuance; a heightened sensitivity to the problems of conscience and individual responsibility. It is an important chapter in the evolving history of medieval ideas and ideals.

---

[149] Nichols, 1969, p. 77.

[150] The story of Alexis continued to thrive in popular culture, eventually making its way into Grimm's *Fairytales*, number 204, as one of the "Children's Tales." While details have been changed, the outline of the story remains the same. The hero, a king's son, spends seven years away from home disguised as a beggar. When he returns, he is so changed in appearance that no one will believe his true identity. His mother (not his father) takes pity on him, however, and assigns two servants to care for him; one is evil and gives the pauper only water, while the other brings him enough food to sustain life for a time. When the hero dies, the church bells ring of their own accord, and the priest who comes to shrive the corpse finds a letter relating the hero's adventures.

V

PRINCIPLES OF THIS EDITION

The conclusions reached concerning the popular, and possibly oral, nature of S, and concerning the independent existence of so-called "reworkings" of medieval literature have implications for the principles governing the edition of S and of M^2. First, in texts where oral composition and/or transmission are involved, contamination is the rule, not the exception. Therefore, we cannot postulate a *stemma codicum* drawn with the rigor of those for classical manuscripts, and no *stemma* accompanies the works edited here. Furthermore, for poems dependent in some way upon oral traditions and transmission, there are other consequences for the critic. First, scribal perfection becomes a less significant quality; a distinction exists between creator and codifier, between poet and writer. The *Chanson de Guillaume* is a case in point. This very beautiful and old epic survives in one manuscript, the work of a less than careful scribe. While the carelessness makes it more difficult for us to appreciate the epic, it tells us less about the poet than the scribe. The formal blemishes, although detracting from the artistic whole, may not be as important as they are when we deal with the works of an author known to compose in writing (and writing at leisure), a Vergil or a Chrétien de Troyes, where the task of the editor is to recover as nearly as possible the very words of the great poet. For orally created texts we cannot hope to do so.

Furthermore, if a poem indebted to the oral tradition is a living, changing creation in a way a work owing its genesis to a purely written tradition is not, "earliest" need not equal "best," nor is the search for the "original" version necessarily a fruitful one. Such a statement implies nothing about the originality of a particular singer, nor about the merits of a particular early version vis-à-vis later ones. It does mean that alterations, whether by an epic singer or later *remanieur,* merit our serious consideration.

Second, the premise underlying much editing based on classical or Lachmannian norms has been that scribes intended to reproduce their exemplars faithfully, and that all variants were therefore

"mistakes" to be "corrected" if at all possible. [151] Manuscripts of a
poem stemming from the oral tradition have a degree of autonomy
not possessed by those of works known to have a purely written
genesis. The divergent readings and innovations are valuable for
their own sake. Hence as an editor I may turn to other versions
of my poem to correct blatant errors or suggest ways to fill in
lacunae, but I do not assume that I am in the process necessarily
recovering an "original" (and therefore inherently more precious)
reading. A composite edition is, in many senses, a new poem; the
critic has assumed the role of *remanieur,* not the role he originally
set out to play.

The present edition strives to be conservative, preserving the
readings of the two unique manuscripts wherever possible. The first
edition of S and M^1, that of Gaston Paris in 1872, was in its own
way revolutionary, even if today we have for the most part abandoned the concepts on which it was based. Paris' edition was the
second to introduce the methods of scientific textual editing,
pioneered for New Testament and classical studies by Karl
Lachmann, to Romance scholarship (the first such enterprise was
Natalis de Wailly's 1868 edition of Joinville's *Histoire de saint
Louis*). This editorial principle, based on the "method of the common error," had caught the attention of medievalists through Karl
Bartsch's edition of the *Nibelungenlied* (Leipzig, 1866). Paris' edition of the *Vie de saint Alexis* was awarded the *prix Gobart,* and
was reprinted numerous times. [152]

In his edition, moved by a spirit of critical optimism, Gaston
Paris set out to recover the original poem as he felt confident
it must once have existed. Accusing Wailly of a "respect exagéré
pour le manuscrit," [153] Paris modified and emended his texts, often

---

[151] Protesting against the blanket condemnation of all scribes as
incompetents, with the concomitant exaltation of all authors as masters
of perfection, Urban Tigner Holmes questioned: "Why was every scribe
except the first a careless ignoramus, and every author a flawless wielder
of Old French metrics and case endings?" (1947, p. 469; cited in Foulet
and Speer, 1979, p. 34).

[152] Reprints: 1885, 1903, 1908, 1911, 1925. For an account of this
edition, see Foulet and Speer, 1979, pp. 12-14.

[153] In a review of Wailly in *Romania*, 3 (1874), 401-13, cited by Foulet
and Speer, 1979, p. 12. Paris was particularly critical of Wailly's preserva-
tion of manuscript orthography.

silently, to make them conform with his notion of the state of the French language at the time of composition. He regularized orthography and corrected grammar, notably the use of subject and object cases. In the later poems, particularly *S*, he frequently altered the text to underline its relationship to the Hildesheim manuscript (for discussion of some of his silent emendations, see the notes to the text).

In this edition, I have observed modern norms of word division, capitalization, and punctuation. I have regularized the use of *i* and *j*, *u* and *v*, and have silently expanded the following manuscript contractions: *m'lt* as *mout*, the commonest spelling of the word when it is written out; *p∞* as *pour*, *p̧* as *par*, *꜒* as *con* or *com*, the latter an abbreviation particularly common in *M²*. All other expansions are indicated in the text (e. g. *s* as s[aint] or s[ains] *ch* as ch[evalier], etc.). I have reproduced the manuscript's treatment of numerals. All other additions or changes are enclosed in brackets and the manuscript reading given in the *apparatus criticus* following the text. Words or phrases discussed in the textual notes are marked with an asterisk. In one respect I have deviated from contemporary editorial practice and followed Paris: the use of *é*. I have accented *pére* and *mére*, as well as words like *contrée*, because the poet of *S* usually took care not to combine *ó . . . e* and *e . . . e* in the same assonance (e. g. laisse 58).

VI

VERSIFICATION AND LANGUAGE

Gaston Paris' edition of the two manuscripts under consideration here gives an idealized, rather than an actual, picture of the poems. Both versions of *Alexis* contain unmetrical lines, faulty assonances and rhymes. In particular *M²* contains a number of irregularities; there are many alexandrines (listed below), and laisses 63 and 96-101 (the end of the poem) are in assonance, while other laisses frequently contain some words in assonance (indicated in the table of rhymes). In my edition I have left unemended most such "errors." Metrical irregularity was far from infrequent, [154] and hyper-correctness gives us a false sense of the state of medieval poetic practice.

Metrically irregular lines in *S:* 14, 24, 85, 146, 232, 290, 354, 372.

Alexandrine lines in *M²:* 27, 346-51, 353-58, 447, 486, 671, 690.

S: TABLE OF ASSONANCES

1. Masculine

-an (-en)	2, 5, 8, 10, 28, 32, 37, 56, 67, 121
-é	3, 6, 9, 14, 19, 24, 27, 40, 42, 46, 51, 55, 57, 59, 64, 66, 68, 70, 72, 76, 78, 84, 92, 95, 97, 99, 102, 104, 113, 119, 124, 126, 129, 135
-eu (ou)	123
-i	7, 18, 20, 23, 30, 35, 43, 45, 54, 65, 71, 80, 82, 85, 89, 106, 110, 117, 131
-ié	12, 22, 39, 44, 61, 69, 77, 83
-on (-our)	1, 53, 63, 75, 79, 86, 87
-ou	16, 88
-u	25, 36

2. Feminine

-a ... e	60, 90, 96, 107, 128, 134
-é ... e	4, 11, 17, 31, 33, 38, 48, 58, 94, 98, 103, 111, 115, 130, 132
-e ... e	13, 21, 26, 29, 34, 49, 62, 81, 91, 93, 101, 112, 114, 125, 127
-i ... e	41, 50, 105, 120, 133
-o(ou) ... e	47, 52, 73, 74, 109, 116, 118, 136
-u ... e	100, 108, 122

---

[154] Marjorie Windelberg, 1978, p. 6, points out that some 10 % of the lines in *Roland* "do not conform to the epic decasyllabic meter used in Old French."

M: TABLE OF RHYMES

-a	21, 89
-age (-aige)	81
-ant	2 (*Moÿset*, v. 10), 19, 27 (*courans*, v. 302; *douce-ment*, v. 308), 34, 43 (*noient*, v. 532), 47, 57 (*vraiement*, v. 721), 62
-é	5, 33 (*set*, v. 394), 51 (*set*, v. 646), 58, 61, 67, 72, 86, 88, 94
-ée	15, 23, 77, 85, 99 (asson.)
-ele	84
-ent (-ant)	8 (equally mixed)
-ent	4 (*tenemens*, v. 38), 13, 45 (*enten*, v. 551), 70, 78, 95
-er	6, 9, 12, 17, 29, 35 (*bers*, v. 429), 40, 46, 55 (*devier*, v. 700), 76, 98 (asson.)
-érent	90
-és	7, 48, 53, 64, 82
-eus	38 (four lines, -ous)
-i	16, 92, 101 (asson.)
-ie	18 (*merchi*, v. 187), 32, 37, 60, 75, 96 (asson.)
-ié	14, 25, 80
-iens	3
-ier	10, 50 (*garder*, v. 633; *principel*, v. 634; *disner*, v. 635; *resposer*, v. 636), 71
-iers	28
-iés	30 (*cergier*, v. 346; *pié*, v. 348)
-in	59 (*tapi*, v. 736)
-ir	44, 69
-is	42 (*Alesin*, v. 514; *pelerins*, v. 518; *vins*, v. 520), 56 (*Alesin*, v. 704; *pelerin*, v. 708), 68, 79 (*Alesin*, v. 980)
-i(s)se	39 (*service*, v. 473)
-ó ... e	63 (asson.), 100 (asson.)
-oir	22
-oit	26 (*foi*, v. 291)
-ommes	91

-on	41, 52 (*besoin*, v. 666), 65, 73
-on(d,p,t)re	93
-our (-or)	1 (*amor*, v. 2), 36 (*amor*, v. 443), 66 (*amor*, v. 821), 74 (*dochor*, v. 922; *honor*, v. 924; *doctor*, v. 927)
-ous (-ours)	87 (*jors*, v. 1023), 97 (asson.)
-u	20 (*rendus*, v. 215; *esmut*, v. 217; *connut*, v. 223), 24, 49
-ue	11, 54, 83 (*dure*, v. 1003)
-us	31

COMPARATIVE PHONOLOGY AND ORTHOGRAPHY

The language of *S* is less uniform than that of *M²*. Generally it resembles twelfth-century *francien* with, however, a strong admixture of Picard traits (e. g. *duërra, veïr*), etc. *M²* is a Picard text. [155] Note: Lines marked with an asterisk are discussed further in the textual notes. The examples given are not exhaustive.

1: Vowels

FREE *A*

1) -ALIS, TALIS, QUALIS > *els, eus* (graphy *-eus, ex*):

M²: teus (5*, 60*). Although not specifically Picard, vocalization of *l*, and subsequent loss of [w], > *ques* (< QUALIS, 619) [*Gossen*, 5].

S: > *tel, quel, ques* (482, 759; plural *tels* [635], *quels* [910], *ques* [418, 1119]).

2) *a* plus *yod:* -ATICU > *ai, a:*

M²: In Picard *a* and *ai* seem interchangeable: *-age*, as in *fran.*, as well as *-aige: ymage* (959), *ymaige* (380); *linaige* (993); see laisse 81 [*Gossen*, 6, 7].

S: > *ai:* usually *-aige; barnaige* (767, 781); *coraige* (515, 713); *imaige* (537), *ymaige* (525, 533, 540, 541, 544), but

---

[155] Segre (1974, p. 310) wrongly identifies the dialect of *M²* (= *Mb*) as *francien*.

ymage (517); *lignaige* (769, 1194); *saige* (526); but cf. *faice* (677) from FACIAT.

3) *yod* plus -ATA > Pic. *-ie*, fran. *-iée:*

> *M²:* irie (276,* see below) [*Gossen,* 8].
> *S:* estoie (1123*).

OPEN *E*

1) DĔUS:

> *M²* prefers *Dieu(s)* *(Diex)*, giving *Damedeus* only once (563), *Dé* (910) [*Gossen,* 9].
> *S*, as well as giving many examples of *Dieu(s)*, has *Deu* (1312), *Dé* (364; 9 ex.), *Dex* (692, 891), *Damedé(s)* (367; 13 ex.), *Damediu(s)* (113; 13 ex.).

2) ĕ[> Pic. *ie*, as in fran., sometimes monothongized to *i: M²:* entir (216) is the normal form of INTEGRU; *entier* (883) is preserved by the rhyme [*Gossen,* 10].

> *S:* see MELIUS.

3) ĕ] > Pic. *e, ie:*

> *M²:* M², in opposition to M¹, prefers *e*, e. g. *bele, certes, serjans.* (For the use of this phenomenon to localize literary texts, see *Gossen,* pp. 60-61; Hermann of Valenciennes and texts in Artois have *e*) [*Gossen,* 11].
> *S:* > *e.*

4) ĕ, ĭ checked by 1 > Pic. *eau, iau, au:*

> *M²:* BELLUS > *biaus* (99); ILLOS > *eaus* > *aus* (84, 465, 618; see *Gossen,* p. 62, n. 17); ECCE-ILLOS > *c(h)iaus* (253) [*Gossen,* 12].
> *S:* aus (963, 1242); *biaus* (112); *ciaus* (677); *cevaus* (79).

5) -ĬCULU: SOLĬCULU > *solel* plus *s* > *solaus:*

> *S:* solaus (325) [*Gossen,* 12].

6) MĔLIUS:

> *M²* > *miels* > Pic. *mieus* (292, 536) [*Gossen,* 14].
> *S:* miels (769, 1136), *mieus* (748, 916). MĔLIOR > *meldres* (40); MĔLIORE > *millour* (884), *millieur* (696); MĔLIO-RES > *millors* (460); see above, open *e*, 2) [*Gossen,* 12].

7) *an* for etymological *en:*

> *M².:* TEMPUS > *tans* (1, 10); *dame* > *demoisele* (269);
> SERVIENTE > *serjans* (353); INSIMUL > *ensanble* (35);
> *Constentin* (525). Learned words, EXEMPLU > *essanple*
> (26); SCIENTIA > *ensiant* (22) [*Gossen*, 15].
>
> *S:* *tans* (10, 19, 31, 853); *damoisele* (1022); *sergans* (121);
> *ensamble* (308); *tenremant* (744, < -MENTE); *Con-*
> *stentins* (681).

CLOSED *E*

1) ē, ĭ (e)[> ei > oi]:

> *M².:* The treatment of -ĬTIA shows a certain hesitation
> in Picard; *M²* has *rikeche* (427), probably the more recent
> formation, and the commoner form [*Gossen*, 16].
> *S: ricoise* (415, 576).

2) VIDĒRE, SEDĒRE:

> *M² > veïr* (464), perhaps by attraction to the 2nd conj.
> (but also *veoir*, 938, *seoir*, 242). Gossen notes that authors
> had both forms at their disposal (p. 68) [*Gossen*, 17].
> *S: veïr* (1191).

3) ē, ĭ, (e) plus nasal > Pic. *ain-e:*

> *M².: maine* (892); *paine* (376), [*Gossen*, 19].
> *S: mainne* (166); *plains* (< PLĒNU, 637).

-ILIUS, -ILIS > Pic. *-ius, -ieus:*

> *M².:* FILIUS > *fieus* (99); *gentieis* (57) [*Gossen*, 20].
> *S: fiels* (1139, 1147, 1197), *fiex* (455); *gentiels* (541), *gentieis*
> (1221).

OPEN *O*

ŏ (ǫ) plus l plus consonant > Pic. *au:*

> *M².: vaura* (479); *tauront* (456) [*Gossen*, 23].
> *S: vaura* (643), *volra* (700); *tolront* (612).

CLOSED *O*

1) ọ[> Pic. *ou* > *eu,* as in fran.:

> *M²: andeus* (271); *signour* (18), *signeur* (326); SUPER > *sour* (205, 240), *sor* (210), *desour* (144), *deseure* (687), [*Gossen,* 26].
>
> *S: deseur* (78).

2) -ŌRIA, -ŎRIA:

> *M²:* GLŌRIA > *glore* (44); MEMORIA > *memore* (1085) [*Gossen,* 27].
>
> *S: glore* (37, 61, 1322), *gloire* (929, 1317); *memoire* (1330); *victore* (1237).

3) o, ọ plus nasal > Pic. *o* (nasalized), often *ou:*

> *M²:* the hesitation between *Rom(m)e (saepe)* and *Roume* (238, 329) is common; forms in *ou* particularly frequent in Old Pic. (e. g. *noumer,* 81, 568, *douner,* 70, 98). In pretonic position followed by a nasal and cons. > *coun(n)oistre* (420, but *connoistre,* 690) [*Gossen,* 28].
>
> *S: ou* is the more common form: *houme* (109, 7 ex.); *hounerer* (573); *counut* (659) *Rome* (8 ex.), *Roume* (17 ex.).

UNSTRESSED VOWELS

1) Since the group *c* plus *a* is not palatalized in Pic., initial *a* can be conserved instead of becoming *e,* above all in hiatus: e. g. *caoir* (> *CADĒRE, 941) [*Gossen,* 29].

2) Reduction of romance pretonic *ei* before *s* to *i:*

> *M²:* ANTECESSORES > *anceisseus* > *anchis(e)our* (1, 5) [*Gossen,* 33].
>
> *S: ancissour* (48).

3) Initial and non-initial *e* plus *l, n* > Pic. *i, ie, e,* distinguishing Pic. from fran.:

> *M²:* SĒNIŌRE > *signour* (18) [*Gossen,* 34].
>
> *S: signour* (17).

4) Initial free *e* becomes *i* in some words:

M²: *iretier* (100) [*Gossen*, 35].
S: *iretés* (388, 1153).

5) Reduction of initial *o, i* to *e:*

M²: *kemant* (181).
S: *commant* (27).

6) Dissimilation of *o:*

M²: *honerer* (424, 944).
S: *hounerer* (573); *dolerous* (1139, 1223).

7) Dissimilation of *i:*

M²: *fenir* (544, 930) [*Gossen*, 37]. *fenies* (596*).

2: Consonants

GUTTURALS

1) *c* plus *e, i* > *ć* (graphy, *c, ch*):

M²: Many examples, e. g. *merchi* (158); *aproce* (207),
aproche (527, 843) [*Gossen*, 38].
S: *merci* (677); *aprocier* (266); *cerkié* (45); *cief* (253).
S: The only words beginning with *ch* in *S* are *chevaliers*
(483, 562) but *cevaus* (79); *chier* (109), but 5 ex. of *cier*
(e. g. 250); *cief* (488).

2) Vowel plus final *ce, t* plus *s* > *Pic.* -s, *fran.* -z (*ĉ*):

M²: CRUCE > *crois* (120) [*Gossen*, 40].
S: *crois* (317).

3) *c* plus *a* (and other vowels) at the beginning or interiorly
following a consonant > Pic. [k] (graphy, *c, k, qu*). For
all words *ch* variants exist as well, often in the same text:

M²: *cambre* (193, 264, 1013), *chambre* (105, 111, 260, 570);
cantant (772), *chantant* (63, 185); *cose* (41, 472, 787), *chose*
(886); *keü* (577, 1009); *kaitis* (121, 523); *blance* (110),
blanche (976) [*Gossen*, 41]. *K* is a common initial graphy
in *M²*: in addition to the words given above (plus *ke, ki*),
keulli (387); *keurt* (879); *kemant* (182).

S: cambre (116); *caitis* (1325), *cantant* (1049), *cangier* (111).
Initial *k: S* has only, in addition to *ke and ki, kenue* (1158).

DENTALS

-ATU (-ITU, -UTU, -ATE, -UTE) > Pic. -et, -it, -ut:

M²: p.p. ATU > *liet* (< LAETATU, 83), but *liés* (347, 354, 728); *couchiet* (136), but *couchiés* (445); *abaigniet* (218); *sakiet* (397); *herbegiet* (542); *proiiet* (724); *lassiet* (1045); *lendengiet* (396). Also *congiet* (344); *pechiet* (684, 758); *moitiet* (963), but *moitié* (143, 966) [*Gossen*, 46].
S: congié (242); *pechiés* (128).

SIBILANTS

1) Confusion of *-s-* and *-ss-:*
   M²: lassiet (1045) *lasié* (281); *-ss-* prevails, but only *Ausis* (304, 730) [*Gossen*, 49].
   S: only *-ss-*, but *Aussis* (362) and *Ausis* (878).

2) Interior *s > r* in some words:
   M²: Although normal in Picard, this phenomenon not found in *M².*
   S: desvée > dervée (1175) [*Gossen*, 50].

LABIALS

1) **-ABULU, -ABILE > Pic. *aule, avle:***
   M²: coupaubes (461) [*Gossen*, 52].
   S: hounerablement (98).

2) **POPULU:**
   M² > pule (786, 792, 804, 1057) [*Gossen*, 52].
   S: pules (519).

LIQUIDS

1) Passage of preconsonantal [ł] to [u]:
   M²: aumosne (< ALMOSINA(M), 243); *autre* (134); *Ausis* (304), also *Alsix* (233), *Assix* (227) [*Pope*, 383].
   S: aumosne (391); *autre* (171); *Ausis* (498); *aubes* (1295).

2) Metathesis of *er* > *re* and *vice versa*, typical of Picard [*Gossen,* 57].

   M²: No examples.

   S: couvretoir (155); *gouvreneour* (1063); *poverte* (781, 1163) but *povreté* (381, 766); *duërra* (see below, verbs).

3) Loss of intercalary *d* or *b* in the secondary groups *l'r, n'r, m'l:*

   M²: tenra (294, 295, 997); *tenrement* (131); *ensanla* (1020), but *ensanble* (35) [*Gossen,* 61].

   S: tenrai (432), *tenremant* (744).

4) *rr* > *sr:*

   S: esrant (462), *esrer* (331, 337, 581).

OTHER GRAPHIC VARIATIONS

1) Use of initial *w:*

   M²: weul (285); *widier* (106); *wy* (< HODIE, 981); *wys* (< OSTIU, 371, 405), *uis* (325).

   S: weut (1038); but *hui* (295, 302), *ui* (217); *uis* (319, 544).

2) *y* as a learned graphy for *i:*

   M²: foy (2, 6, 14, 56, 889); *yviers* (359); *ymage* (959); *wy* (981); *wys* (371); *Davy* (11); *Moÿset* (10, 511); *roy* (68).

   S: ymaige (363, 368); *martyre* (532), but *martir* (981, 1282).

3) Other peculiarities:

   M²: mongier (889), *maingier* (562).

   S:

   a) Confusion between [k] and [g]: *couvernent* (1277); *gouverne* (130).

   b) Confusion between [d] and [dz]: *dusqu'* (860, 918, 1312); *jusqu'* (1004).

   c) [ŋ] > gn, g: *signour, Signourés* (90), but *Sigoré* (818, 829).

MORPHOLOGY

1) Definite article:

M^2: For the feminine sing. subject case, primarily *li*, also *le* and *la; li barge* (213, 431), but *le barge* (435), *la barge* (449) [*Gossen*, 63].

S: li, la, and, less frequently than M^2, *le* (106,* 140,* 421, 450, 518, 829).

2) Demonstrative pronouns:

M^2: from ECCE-ILLE: masc. sing. nom. *c(h)il, chieus;* obj. *celui.* Fem. nom. subj. *cele;* Neut. sing. *cel.* Plu. masc. nom. *chil;* obj. *chiaus.* From ECCE-ISTE: masc. sing. subj. *cis;* fem. *ceste;* masc. obj. *cestui, cest.* Plu. obj. masc. and fem. *ces.* From ECCE-HOC: masc. *c(h)e, chu;* fem. *chou;* neut. *chu.* Of *icil* (the earlier form; see Foulet, 1920, p. 573), only *icel* (231, 6 ex.) and *icelui* (545) occur.

S: The regular *francien* forms are found, in addition to the Picard *ciaus* (677).

3) Possessive adjectives:

M^2: masc. sing. nom. *tes* (281); fem. *me* (507); masc. obj *sen* (218), fem. *se* (131, 683, 753, 934); plu. masc. nom. *mi* (463, 856) [*Gossen*, 66].

S: for the stressed forms, in addition to the usual examples, *vo* (obj. sing., 753); the unstressed forms are regular except *S* once uses *ten* (307), the Picard form, in place of *ton, se* for *sa* (481).

Nouns

In general the two-case system is maintained, although the ending *s* is treated with some irregularity.

M^2: the etymological nom. *hon (hom)* occurs three times (428, 805, 912); the usual form is *hons* (30), with the addition of an analogical *s*.

S: This MS has particular trouble with *pére*, on thirteen occasions giving the nom. as *péres* (23*).

Verbs

1) Infinitives:

   M²: veïr (464), characteristic of Picard [*Gossen*, 17].
   S: veïr (1191).

2) Strong perfects in -UI:

   M² typically employs the forms in *-o-* of *francien* alongside
   those in *-eu-* characteristic of the Northeast; *euc* (989),
   eus (988), *eut* (970), *ot* (241); *eurent* (1048), *orent* (36, 586),
   seuch < SAPUI (888); *sot* < SAPUIT (63); *seurent* <
   SAPUERUNT (53). PLACUIT > *pleut* (204), *plot* (211)
   [*Gossen*, 72].
   S: only *euc* (458), *eus* (1185).

3) 1st pers. sing. of pres. and perf. end in *c(h):*

   M²: och (568), *deuch* (859), *pauch* (885), *seuch* (888)
   [*Gossen*, 75].
   S: euc (458); *fac* (252); *quic* (865, 1014, 1112).

4) In sigmatic perf. and imperf. of subj., the loss of *-s-* occurs
   earlier in *francien* than in Picard; more sigmatic forms
   occur in *M²* than in *S:*

   M²: fesis (pf. 2, 984, 985), *fesist* (impf. subj. 3, 417) *gesist*
   (pf. 3, 193), also *gist* (770) [*Gossen*, 76].
   S: fesis (130), *fesist* (228); *presis* (1166).

5) Perf. indic. 6 in *-isent (francien, -irent):*

   M²: fisent (39, 61, 825); *misent* (920) [*Gossen*, 77].
   S: fisent (95); *misent* (68); but *virent* (497).

6) Pres. and fut. 4 (also pres. and imperf. subj.) in *-omes,* under
   the influence of *som(m)es:*

   M²: e. g. *sommes* (1040), *demenommes* (1041), *atendommes*
   (1042), *alommes* (1043), *devommes* (1044); also *cuidames*
   (339), *sachomes* (701) [*Gossen*, 78].
   S: With the exception of *som(m)es (soumes), S* has only
   one instance of *-omes, devoumes* (1329), but also *devons*
   (268).

7) Metathesis of *r:*

> Alongside of the very frequent future forms such as *durra* (*S*, 196), there exists a form with metathesis of *r:* *durera* > *duërra;* this form can be considered exclusively Picard [*Fouché*, 200].
>
> *S: duërra* (18*, 31, 198).

8) Pres. subj. in *c(h)e:*

> M^2: *face* (659), *bache* (< *battre*, *BASSIARE?, 460); *sache* (493), *sace* (872); *meche* (1091).
>
> *S: faice* (256, 677), *face* (193).

C'EST LI ROUMANS DE SAINT ALESSIN

[S]

1

Signour et dames,* entendés un sermon   [*51v*]
D'un saintisme home qui Allessis ot non
Et d'une feme que il prist a oissor,
Que il guerpi pour Diu son creatour,
5 Caste pucele et gloriouse flour,
Qui ains a li nen ot convercion.
Pour Diu le fist, s'en a bon guerredon;
Saulve en est l'ame el ciel nostre signour,
Li cors en gist a Rome a grant hounor.
10 Bons fu li siecles au tans ancineour*
Quar fols i ert et justice et amour;
Si iert creance dont or n'i a mais pro[u];
Si est mués, perdue a sa valour.*
Faut i li biens, n'i puet avoir vigour;
15 Ne porte fois* la moillier signour,
Ne li vasals n'est faals au signour.
A essient perdons nostre signour;
Fraisle est la vie, ne duërra* lons jours.

2

Al tans Noé et al tans Abraham*   [*52r*]
21 Et a Davi que Dieus par ama tant,*
20 Fu bons li siecles, jamais n'iert si vaillans.
S'est empierés et li biens va morant;
Ne porte foi li péres* son enfant

Ne li fius au parrin ne tant ne quant,*
25 Et li signour vont lor moillier boisant.
Li ordené vont le loi mal menant,
Trespassé ont le Damediu commant,
Et saintes glises, filles Jherusalem,
De tout en tout se vont afoibliant;
30 La fois del siecle se va toute falant.
Fraisle est la vie, ne duërra lonc tans.
Conterai vous del pére et de l'enfant
Qui de mençoigne n'i a ne tant ne quant.*
Sainte escriture em puis traire a garant.
35 Li fius servi bien Diu a son vivant;
Li cors en gist en or et en argent,
L'ame est en glore a Diu commandement.

3

Li péres fu preudom et hounerés;
Diu ama bien, si maintint carité,
40 Mais li fius fu meldres de lui assés;
A son vivant servi si Damedé
Qu'en blanc argent et en or esmeré
En gist li cors a Roume la cité.
Tout cil le sevent ki a Roume ont alé
45 Et cerkié ont par les maistres autés;
Li siens moustiers ne fu mie obliés.
Puis icel jour que Dius nos vint sauver
Nostre ancissour orent crestienté.
Fu nés uns sires a Roume la cité;   [52v]
50 Rices hom fu, de grant nobilité;*
Pour çou vous di, d'un sien fil voel parler.

4

Eufemiens, ensi ot non li péres,
Des belisors qui a cel jour i érent;
54a Quens fu de Roume, de toute la contrée.*
54b [Dunc prist moillier vaillant et hounorée,]
55 Fille Flourent, o non Boine Eurée.*

5

Bone Eurée, li pére ot non Flourens;
Il l'espousa au los de ses parens,
Puis conversérent ensanle longement.
Qu'enfant nen orent poise* lor en forment.
60 Diu en apelent andoi parfitement:
"E, Rois de glore, par ton commandement,
Soit ta mercis et tes otriemens
Qu'enfant nous donne[s]* qui soit a ton talent."

6

Tant li priérent par grant humilité
65 Que la moillier donna fecondité,
Un fil lor donne, si l'en seurent bon gré;
De saint bastesme l'on[t] fait rengenerer,
Bel non li misent selonc crestienté.

7

Baptisiés fu, s'ot a non Alessis;
70 Qui le porta volentiers le nourri,
Puis li bons péres a escole le mist;
Tant aprist letres ke bien en fu garnis,
Puis l'envoia l'empereour servir.

8

Li emper[er]es* ot non Otevians;
75 Illuec servi enfreci a .vii. ans,
Et puis l'a fait son maistre cambrelenc.
Se li carja tous ses commandemens,
Et sa justice deseur toute sa gent,
Cevaus et murs et palefrois amblans,   [53r]
80 Et plainnes males entre or fin et argent.
Son pére ama, si l'en a donné tant,
Et a sa mére, rice sont et manant.
Or voit li pére que mais n'ara enfant
Mais que ce seul que il par aimme tant,

85 Dont se pourpense del siecle en avant;*
    Sil velt qu'il prenge moillier a son vivant,
    Pour li a quise le fille un noble Franc.

9

    La pucele iert de mout grant parenté,
    Fille a un conte de Rome la cité
90 Lesigne ot non, ses péres Signourés;*
    N'a plus d'enfans, bien le puet marier.
    Emsamble en vont li doi pére parler;
    Les .ii. enfans veulent faire asambler.

10

    Noument le terme de leur assamblement;*
95 Quant vint au jour se fisent belement;*
    Ens el moustier saint Jehan de Latran*
    Sains A[lessis] al los de ses parens
    L'a espousée mout hounerablement.
    Mais de tout çou ne vausist il nient,
100 De tout en tout a a Diu son talent;
    Plus aimme Diu que nule riens vivant.

11

    Quant çou fu cose que il ot* espousée,
    De ses alues mout gentement douée,
    Mout en fu liés et li pére et li mére,
105 Et si ami et cil de la contrée.
    Puis l'emmena a le maison* son pére.

12

    Quant lor conroi orent aparellié,
    Et fait des noeces le premerain mangier,
    De cel saint houme que Diex par ot tant chier   [53v]
110 Et de la feme ke il prist a moillier,
    Dont va li jors, e vous la nuit cangier.
    Ce dist li péres, "Biaus fius, alés coucier
    Avoec t'espouse, a Damediu congié."

Ne vaut li enfes son pére corecier;
115 Sus se leva envis u volentiers;
Va en la cambre o sa gente moillier.
Li pére i fu et la mére au coucier.
Le cambre ont faite encenser et joncier;
Tendent i pailes* a or entrelaciés.
120 Quant il s'en issent si font l'uis verillier;
A .ii. sergans les font la nuit gaitier.
S[ains] Alessins a parlé tous premiers.

13

Sains A[lessins] esgarda la pucele;
Assés i ardent et candoiles et lanternes;
125 Mout la vit gente et couvoiteuse et bele.
Ses oels en torne vers le signour celestre
Qu'il amoit plus que nule riens terreste:
"Elas," dist il, "com fors pechiés m'apresse!
S'or nen m'en vois, jou crien que ne te perde
130 Qui me fesis, pére qui tout gouverne!*
Regarde moi de tes clers ex en terre,
Que ne perdés ne moi ne la pucele;
Donnés moi, sire, itel service faire
C'onques diables de nous .ii. n'ait poeste.
135 Mes péres m'aime; si cuide grant bien faire.
Qui me desfie de la vie terestre
Tollir me vieut nostre signour celestre."

14

Quant en la cambre furent andoi remés,*
Sains A[lessins] prist a li a parler;   [54r]
140 Le* mortel vie li prist mout a blasmer,
De la celestre li moustre verité.
Que lui ert tart ke il s'en fust tournés.

15

"Bele," dist il "celui trai a garant*
Qui nous raien[s]t de son precieus sanc,

145 Et de la viergene fu nés em Belliant,
Et baptistre presis* en e[l] flun de Jordant,
La soie vie n'ara ja finement.

16

"Bele," dist il, "celui trai a espous
Qui nous raienst de son sanc precious,
150 Car en cest siecle nen a parfite amour.
A mout grant joie s'asamblent peceour,
Mais il desoivrent a doel et a tristour."

17

Quant ses paroles li ot issi contées,
E la pucele les ot issi [es]co[u]tées,
155 Del couvretoir l'a puis acouvetée.
Prist un anel dont il [l']ot espousée,
.ii. pars en fist al trencant de l'espée;*
L'une partie l'en a recoumandée,
Se li pria qu'ele soit bien gardée,
160 S'on li demande, k'[ele] soit aprestée;
Emsamble lui en a l'autre portée,
Que se jamais revient a sa contré[e]
Et il li moustre les ensegnes prouvées,
Que l' recounoisse entre li et sa mére.
165 Dist la pucele, "Or sui mout esgarée!
Mainne me la dont tu m'as amenée.
Por coi me lais? Ja m'as tu espousé[e].
Que querras ore en estrange contrée?
Que porai dire ton pére ne ta mére?   [54v]
170 Sempres m'aront de leur terre jetée;
Puis m'en irai com autre asoignentée;
Tel honte arai, jamais n'iere hounerée."
"Bele," dist il, "n'estes mie senée.
A Diu te tien, si devien s'espousée;
175 T'ame iert el ciel roine corounée.
Em Paradis iert mise et alevée.

18

"Bele," dist il, "ja sés tu bien de fi
Que l'ame estuet de nos cors departir;
Que caut del cors quant en tere porrist?
180 L'ame iert mout lié qui Diu ara servi;
Droit en ira es ciels dont elle vint
Al Saint Espirt dont Damedius le fist.
Li cors est tere*, dont il fu establis

[LACUNA]

Li cars deduist, li os ne puet porrir,
185 Doucement flair comme flors en avril,
Et del mort home refera Dius le vif.
Las, li meffait que porront devenir?
Qui estora del cors au departir
Dont li cors put et li os est pouris;
190 Ens en abisme trebuce al maleis,
Sous limo tere* dont ja n'iert revertis;
Ne sains ne sainte nen iert ja si hardis
Que ja li proit qu'il li face merci.
Pour Diu, pucele, enten çou que jou di,
195 Car tu ne sés que t'est a avenir.
Qui plus durra, vivera mout petit
Envers la vie qui grans est a venir
Del nouvel siecle qui duërra toudis.

19

"Qui fait le bien se reçoit Damedés,   [55r]
200 Et qui le mal, cil est mal eurés;
Ens en infer le trebuce maufés
So limo terre dont ja n'iert racatés.
S[ainte] escriture ne set avant aler.
Dolant celui ki ne puet amender."
205 S'ele ert dolente,* ne l'estuet demander;
Ot le la bele, ne cesse de plorer:
"Sire," fet ele, "or te commant a Dé,*
Quant autrement ne te puis retorner."

Cil fu mout liés, si volt del lit lever,
210 Et en apres le prist a rapeler:
"Bele pucele," dist A[lessins] li ber.*

20

"Bele pucele," ce dist sains Alessins,
"Or m'en irai en estrange païs,
Mais jou ne sai com iert del revenir.
215 De cest anel que jou ai departi,
Ceste moitié qu'en m'aumoniére ai ci,
D'ui en un an le renvoierai ci*
Par .i. mesaige u moi se jou sui vis.
Se ne revieng, puis pues prendre mari;
220 Savoir porras que alés sui a fin."
Ot le la bele, si a jeté un cri;
Quide sa mére que il juast a li.*
"Bele," dist il, "vous me volés hounir."
"Par Diu," dist ele, "aiés de moi merci.
225 "Sire," dist ele, "mout ai mon cuer mari;
Se moi em poise pour coi me as plus vi[l]?"*
"Certes, nen ai," çou dist s[ains] A[lessins],
"Ains vous aim plus que riens que Dius fesist,
Sans cel signour qui nous forma et fist;   [55v]
230 Ja le querrai u il fu mors et vis,
Et au sepulcre u il rexurexi,
Qu'il nous reçoive el saint paradis."*
"Sire," dist ele, "Dius vous i laist venir.

21

"Frans hom," dist ele, "quel le vauras tu faire?
235 Gehis le moi pour Diu et en confesse;
Se je [d]i home, Diu em puisse jou perdre."
Quant il oï que pour Diu l'en apele,
Dont ne laissat pour nus avoir de tere,
"Certes," dist il, "Damediu irai querre,
240 Qu'il nous reçoive a son regne celestre.
Il ne faut mie a houme qui le serve."
"Au congié Diu, sire," dist la pucele;

"Grant duel arai et nuit et jors a certes;
Jou remanrai caitive en ceste terre."

22

245 Quant il oï qu'elle l'ot otroié,
Sou ciel* n'a home qui [l'] peust courecier.
"Sire," dist ele, "com ert del repairier?
Di me le terme, sel ferai metre em brief.
Mout as dur cuer qui or me veus laiscier,
250 Et pére et mére qui par t'ont si tres cier.
Jou sui mout fole, si ne fas mie bien,
Quant ne te fac et piés et mains loiier."
Dont ploura il des biaus oels de son cief:
"Certes, pucele, del terme ne sai nient;
255 L'en set quant va, mais l'e[n] ne set quant vient.
Que que jou faice, a Damediu te tien."
"Que Dius vous doinst a joie repairier;
Se ne te voi, mais n'arai mon cuer lié."
"Bele," dist il, "pour Diu ne te targier.   [56r]
260 De Diu servir plus ne te voel proiier,
Car peciéres n'en iert si eslongiés
Par saint glise ne puisse repairier:
C'est li services ke Dius par a mout cier."
Dist la pucele, "Sire, vous dites bien,
265 Car se Diu plaist, or le ferai mout bien,
Se Dius tant m'aime que m'i laist aprocier."

23

"Bele pucele," çou dist s[ains] Alessins,
"Ne devons mie nos cors si raemplir
De grans ventrées que veulent recuellir;
270 Car endementre que li peciére vit
Et tient le bien dont li cors doit garir,
Il en doit bien pour s'ame departir;
A la grand joie qui est em paradis,
La est la vie qui ja ne prendra fin.
275 Dolant le cors qui tout veut engloutir,
C'ara dont l'ame quant li cors a trop pris?

Quant ja li hom n'ara si cier ami
Puis qu'il est mors et alés a sa fin,
Que ja le veulle plus oïr ne veir
280   Ains li est tart que il soit enfouis.
A male eure* cil est engenuis
Qui se travaille pour infer deservir!*
Dist li pucele, "Sire, voir avés dit;
Les vos raisons doit on bien retenir."
285   Estes les vous belement departis;
Plorent des oels, ne se porent tenir,
Et la pucele gentement li a dit,
"Or t'en va, sire, Dieus te laist revenir
Quant autrement ne te puis retenir.   [56v]
290   Dolante e[r]t* cele qui te nori,
Si ert li péres qui toi engenui,
Et jou meïsme qui t'avoie a mari.
Jou remanrai en estrange païs*
Et esgarée entre tous mes amis.
295   Hui verrai noeces a grant duel departir;
S'encor ne [t'] voi, de duel m'estuet morir.

24

"Or t'en va, sire, jou te commant a Dé
Quant autrement ne te puis retorner.
Cil ert dolans qui t'avoit engenré,
300   Si iert ta mére qui te porta en lés,
Et jou meïsme qui sui en vevés,
Hui v[errai] noeces a grant duel desevrer."
Il le signa, si le commande a Dé.
Elle l'apele doucement et souef:
305   "Sire," dist ele, "jou te commant a Dé.
Con faitement m'en porrai consirer?
S'a ten consel le peusse trouver
Qu'ensamble toi me laississes aler,
Ja me veroies gentement conreer,
310   Tondre mes crins, .i. capel afubler,
Et prendre escerpe et .i. bourdon ferré;
Servirai toi de tes dras relaver,

Ne ja luxure ne [m'] verras demener,
Ne adultére ne autre put[eé]."
315 "Non ferai, bele, ains te commant a Dé,
Li glorious qui pour nous fu penés
En sainte crois pour son pule sauver."
Ele commence grant duel a demener.
Il vint a l'uis, sel deffrema souef;   [57r]
320 A mienuit s'en fuit de la cité
Si que ses pére et sa mére nel set,
Ne li serjant qui l'orent a garder.
De c'est mout liés, s'en loe Damedé
Que la pucele l'en a congié donné.
325 Quant il fu jors et solaus fu levés,
Descent .i. val, s'a un tertre monté
A .iiii. liues de Roume la cité;
Regarde Rome et en lonc et en lé.
Envers le ciel en a son vis torné;
330 Estroitement a Jhesu reclamé
Que la pucele dont issi a esré
Doinst en cest siecle tel vie demener
Que l'ame en soit el saint regne de Dé.
Puis se li est de son pére membré
335 Et de sa mére; si commence a plourer.
Par lui meïsme s'en est reconfortés.
Droit en la mer en aquels son esrer;*
Preste est la nes u il porra entrer.
Donne son pris, si est tous [seus] entrés.
340 Drecent lor sigle, laissent courre par mer;
En Jhersalem les conduist Damedés.*
Sains Alessins est issus de la nef.

25

Sains A[lessins] est de la nef issus;
Vint al sepulcre u nostre sire fu.
345 Fist ses priieres, si s'est confés rendus.
.ii. jors sejourne et .ii. nuis i estut
Qu'il ne manja ne sa bouce ne but.
Apres en est al flun Jourdan venus

U li baptesmes de nostre signour fu.   [*57v*]
350 Et li apostle s'i baptisiérent tuit.
     Il se despoille, si se baigna tous nus,
     Puis prist des palmes, si s'en est revenus.
     Pour les Juis n'i osa estre plus,
     Car a cel jour que li sains i fu
355 N'i avoit il des Crestïens nesun.
     Droit a le Lice a son cemin tenu.

26

     Droit a le Lice, une cité mout bele,
     Illuec s'en va sains A[lessins] par terre.*
     Mais jou ne sai com longes i converse:
360 U que il soit, de Diu servir ne cesse;
     De sa maisnie veut il a tous jors estre.

27

     Apres en va en Aussis le cité
     Pour une ymaige dont il oï parler
     Que angle fisent par le commant de Dé,
365 El non celi qui porta sauveté.
     Onques faiture ne fu de sa biauté
     Sans nostre dame, la mére Damedé.*

28

     [I]ceste ymaige, signour, dont je vous cant,*
     Çou n'est de fust ne n'est d'or ne d'argent,
370 Mais li sains angles ki fist l'anoncement
     De nostre dame u Dius prist car et sanc
     Esgarda bien son vis et son samblant,
     Si fist l'ymaige par Diu commandement,
     Pour soie amour le mist non Marien.

(29)

375 Marie ot non, comme la mére Dé;*
     Si vint des ciels de sainte maïsté
     Par un devenres de la crois aourer,

Que nostre sire transi pour nous sauver;
. Par icel jour de la passion Dé   [58r]
380 Le mist li angles issi en la cité;
Ainc en la tere nen ot plus povreté.
La le requist sains Alessis li ber;
Tout son avoir que il en ot porté
A departi, ains riens ne le'n remest.
385 Larges aumosnes par Ausi la cité
Douna as povres u qu'il le[s] pot trouver.
Pour nul avoir ne vaut estre emcombrés,*
Ne ne volt perdre del ciel les iretés.

30

Quant son avoir lor a tout departi,
390 Entre les autres s'asist sains Alessins,
Reçust l'aumosne la u Dius li tramist.
Tant en retint que son cors en soustint;
Le remanant en rent as poverins.

31

Or revenrons au pére et a la mére,*
395 Et a l'espouse ki seule est reméoc;
Quant il çou sorent ke il fuis s'en ére,
Çou fu grans deus que il en [d]emenérent,
Et grans complaintes par toute la contrée.*
"Fius A[lessins], de ta dolante mére,*
400 Tu [m']es fuis, dolante en sui remése.
Le liu ne sai ne ne sai la contrée
U jou te quiére; toute en sui esgarée.
Ja n'ierc lié, biaus fius, si n'iert tes pére
Se ne reviens en iceste contrée."
405 Çou fu grans deus que il en demenérent.

32

Vint en la cambre plainne de mariment;
Si le despoille que n'i laissa nient.
N'i laisse paile ne nul cier garniment;

Tost a tourné a grant duel son talent.   [*58v*]
410 Par grant dolour se dejete souvent.
Ains puis cel jour n'en fu lié granment.

33

Vint en la cambre, toute l'a desparée:
Si l'a destruite comme ele ert la vesprée,
Ostent les pailes et les courtines lées,
415 Sa grant ricoise a a grant duel tornée.
Ains puis cel jour ne fu lié li mére:*
"Cambre," dist ele, "mal fuissiés atornée,
Contre ques nueces vous avoie parée!
Jamais en vous n'iert leëce trouvée."
420 Tel duel en ot, a poi ne ciet pasmée,
Quant par le main* le relieve li pére.

34

De la dolour s'asist li mére a tere
Ne s'assist mie ne sour banc ne sour sele.
Si fist l'espouse saint A[lessin], la bele:
425 "Dame," dist ele, "jou ai fait moult grant perte;
Jou ai perdu mes nueces les nouveles.
Or mais vivrai a loi de tourtereule
Qui p[e]rt son malle, puis ne veut autre querre.
Quant n'ai ton fil, emsamble toi voel estre;
430 Servirai Dieu, car miex ne puis jou faire.
S'il ne revient, ne a toi ne repaire,
Jou me tenrai devers le roi celestre,
Car a nul houme n'aurai jamais a faire;
Ne me faura s'il voit que jou le serve."   [*59r*]

35

435 Respont li pére,* "Que bone feme a dit,
S'ensamble o moi te voloies tenir."
"Servirai toi pour amour a ton* fil."
"Ja n'aras mal dont te puisse garir;
Faille me Diex, se te fail a nul di."

440 Dist la pucele, "Sire, vostre merci.
    Il m'espousa al los de mes amis.
    Or sui malvaise, si me doit Diex hair,
    Se moi ne membre de çou que il me [d]ist
    A icel eure que de moi departi.
445 Quant [tu] pour lui me vauras retenir,
    Trés or tenrai Damediu a mari;
    Ne me faura se jou le voel servir."
    Quant [ot la mére que la pucele] dit,
    Que Damediu servira pour son fil,
450 Tout em plourant le baise enmi le vis.
    Plourent emsamble del duel de lor ami,
    L'une son fil et l'autre son [mari].

36

    Pleurent ensamble lor ami c'ont perdu:
    Pleure la mére et la pucele plus.*
455 "Dius," dist la mére, "qu'est mes fiex devenus?"*
    Çou dist li péres, "Peciés le m'a tolu."*
    "Dius," dist l'espouse, "com petit l'ai eü.
    Hier euc signour, mais n'en ai ore nul
    Sans Damediu, le glorious la sus."

37

460 Dont prist li pére de ses millors serjans,
    Par mout de terres fait querre son enfant.
    Dedens Ausis vinrent tout droit esrant;
    Illuec trouvérent dant A[lessin] seant;
    Entre les autres va l'aumosne querant;   [59v]
465 Ne recounurent son vis ne son samblant.

38

    Dont ot li enfes sa tenre car muée,
    Sa vesteure desroute et despanée
    Qu'il ot porteé par estranges contrées.
    Ne[l] recounurent li doi sergant son pére;
470 A lui meïsme ont l'aumosne donnée.

39

Nel recounurent, ne ne l'ont entercié.
Sains A[lessins] en loe Diu del ciel;
Des sers son pére qui il ert aumoniers —
Ains fu lor sire, ore est lor [provendiers]: *
475 Ne vous sai dire comme il par s'en fist liés.

40

Li doi serjant s'en vont a lor ostel; *
Il les poursuit tant que les vit entrer;
Pour l'ocoison de l'aumosne donner
S'en va a l'uis lor raison escouter.
480 Li serjant fisent lor oste o les disner;
Se feme et il prisent a demander:
"Signour," dist il, "ques hom est que querés?"
".I. ch[evalier], un jovene baceler,
.I. gentil houme, * si iert de Roume nés;
485 Onques ses péres, qui l'avoit engenré,
N'ot plus d'enfans, sel pooït mout amer

[LACUNA]

Sous ciel n'a houme, s'il l'ooït regreter,
Ne li estuece des iex del cief plourer.
Avoirs nous faut, n'avons mais que donner;
490 Veulli[ons] u non, nous en estuet aler."
"Dius," dist li ostes, "qu'en feriés vous el?"
Sains A[lessins] a bien tout escouté:
"E, cuers," dist il, "com estes adurés!
Gente pucele, mout de mercis et grés;   [60r]
495 Jou t'ai fait mal et tu m'as houneré."
Pitié en ot, si commence a plourer.
Li serjant virent qu'il ne porent trouver;
.iii. fois l'ont quis par Ausis la cité;
Par mout de teres l'ont quis et demandé.
500 Il [nel] counurent, si ont a lui parlé;
Puis s'en repairent en Rome la cité.
Noncent au pére qu'il ne porent trouver;

S'il fu dolans, ne l'estuet demander;
Veullent u non, metent el consirer
505 Mais lor grant duel ne puent oublier.
A[lessins] est en Ausis la cité;
Son signour sert par grant humilité
Que anemis ne l'em puet encombrer.

41

Dis et .vii. ans ainc rien n'en fu a dire;
510 Pena son cors en Damedieu service.
Ce ne fist il pour ami ne amie,
Ne pour hounor qui li en fust a dire,
Mais pour celi* qui fu nés de la virge;
Pour nul avoir ne s'en tornera mie.

42

515 Quant son coraige ot a çou atourné
Que ja son vel n'istra de la cité,
Dius fist l'ymage pour A[lessin] parler.
Par un miedi de le Nativité
Que tous li pules fu par matin levés*
520 Pour le service qu'il durent escouter.
Il i vint ains que sains i fust sonnés
Si com li hom qui·n iert acoustumés.
En es le jour que Damedieus fu nés
Fist Dieus l'ymaige iii* fois pour lui parler.   [60v]
525 L'ymaige en a Ermener* apelé,
.I. saige clerc qui servoit a l'autel.
Çou dist l'ymaige, "Apele l'oume Dé
Car il est dignes d'en Paradis entrer,
Et pére et mére guerpi pour l'amour Dé
530 Et son avoir et tout son parenté.
Bon guerredon l'en rendra Damedés;
A grant martyre a son cors atourné."

43

Çou dist l'ymaige, "Fai l'ome Diu venir
En cest moustier, car bien l'a deservi,
535 Car il est dignes d'entrer em Paradis."
Cil va, sel quiert, mais il ne set coisir
Icel saint home de cui l'imaige* dist.
Devant l'imaige revint tous esbahis.

44

Li clers revint esmaris al moustier;
540 Devant l'ymaige commença a prier:
"Gentiels ymaige, ne sai qui entercier;
Angle te fisent par commant Diu del ciel;
Tel paour ai, tous sui desconsilliés."
Çou dist l'ymaige, "Celui qui les l'ui[s] siet,
545 Pres est de Diu et del regne del ciel.
Par nule guise ne s'en veut eslongier."
Ot le li clers, s'est issus del moustier.

45

Ot le li clers, fors del moustier issi.
Par les ensegnes que l'ymaige li dist
550 Le recounut, onques riens n'i fa[i]lli;
Cele part vint, a apeler le pris:
"Com as tu non? car me di, biaus amis." *
"Sire," dist il, "j'ai a non A[lessins],   [61r]
Uns peciére hom, se voel espeneir.
555 A ceste feste c'on dist Arcedeclin,
Que nostre sire forma d l'aige vin,
Adonques iérent .xvii. ans acompli
Que jou issi tous seus de mon païs;
Ainc puis ne vi nul home de mon lin.
560 Ne sai se Dius m'i feroit revenir,
Car jou fui clers, de letre bien apris,
Puis fui tant fols que ch[evaliers] deving,
Feme espousai et mes nueces en fis,
Ains le guerpi que li plais departist.

565 Qui çou a fait, comment porra garir?
    N'en orés plus," Alessins li a dit.
    Ot le li clers, si l'en a fait enclin;
    As piés li ciet, et cil le recuelli.
    E vous la noise par trestout le païs
570 Que cele ymaige parla pour A[lessin];
    Tout l'en hounorent, li grant et li petit.
    Si fust evesques se le vausist souffrir.

46

    Quant il voit çou que [l'] veulent hounerer
    E[t] vesque faire en Ausi la cité,
575 "E Dieus," dist il, "ci ne voel mais ester.
    De grant ricoise et d'orguel demener
    Ne puet on mie Damedieu acater."
    A mienuit s'en fuit de la cité.
    Ne quist congié ne n'osa demander;
580 Contre son gré ne l'i facent ester.
581a Droit a la mer en aquelt son esrer; *
581b [Pres est li barge qui outre doit aler.]
    Donna son pris, si est devens* entrés.
    Drecent lor sigle, laissent courre par mer.   [61v]
    La prendront terre u Dius l'a destiné:
585 Droit a Troholt* quidiérent ariver,
    Mais ne puet estre, c'autre part sont tourné;
    Tout droit a Roume les conduit li orés,
    A .i. des pors qui plus pres de Roume est.*

47

    A un des pors qui ert plus pres de Roume,
590 Illuec arive li nés a cel saint home.
    Quant voit son regne, mout forment s'en redoute.
    Fait ses priiéres, a orisons se coce,
    Diu en apele et saint Piére de Roume,
    De ses amis qui nel counoissent onques
595 Ne de l'onor del siecle ne l'encombrent.

48 [50]

Quant issi ot ses priéres fenies,*
Se li a Dieus de trestout raemplies,
Qu'envers lui orent lor veues tourblées;
Nel recounurent li pére ne li mére,
600 Ne si ami ne cil de la contrée,
Ne la pucele qu'il ot espousée,

(49) [48]

"E Dius," dist il, "glorious rois celestres,*
Se toi pleust, ci ne vausise estre.
Se me counoissent la gens de ceste tere,
605 Il me prendront par force et par poeste;
Se j[o]u's en croi, il me trairont a perte.

50 [49]

"Ajue, Diex, qui nous as em baillie;
Se vel avoir le vraie compaignie,
Et deservir. vostre durable vie.
610 Se me counoist ma mére l'esmarie,
Et mi parent, et m'espouse, et me sire,*
Il me tolront le vostre compaignie.
Sil me rembatent en ceste compaignie,   [62r]
Deffent me Diex, de toutes males visces
615 Et del diable que il ne m'escarnisse;
Ne puis mue[r] le cuer ne m'asouplice.
Et ne pourquant mes péres me desire,
Si fait ma mére plus ke feme ki vive,
Si fait l'espouse que je lor ai guerpie.
620 A tous les jors que jou avoie a vivre
N'estoit mais eure, plus lié ne m'en fesise;

[LACUNA]

Com Diex me doinst, sire,* par itel guise
Que bien les voie et sace lor couvine;
Ne me counoissent, ne nus hom ne lor die!

625 Puis m'en iroie faire vostre service,
    Si esteroit l'ame moie garie."
    Ist de la nef quant s'orison ot dite.*

51

    Sains A[lessins] est issus de la nef;
    Tout un cemin s'en commence a aler.
630 Sous une espine s'asist pour reposer;
    Il est malades, si est mout enfremés.
    Si crient morir par estranges ostés.
    Son sautier a parfondement prée;
    Il [l'] a ouvert, si a devens gardé.
635 Si a tels letres el parcemin trouvé
    Que la mére a son enfant a garder
    .vii. ans tous plains, c'est li premiers eés,
    Et puis li pére*, s'il ciet en effretés,
    Toute sa vie que il a a durer.
640 Or vauroit sur son pére araisonner;
    Par itel guise peust a lui parler,
    Nel couneust a son roumanc parler,
    Et sa prouvende li vaura demander,   [62v]
    S'a Dieu pleust qu[e] li vausist douner.
645 Si vauroit miés ses aumosnes user
    Que les autrui dont il fust emcombrés,
    S'en esteroit plus sauls a Damedé;
    N'en son herbec ne vauroit ja ester,
    Mais ça defors gesir sour* son degré,
650 Puis atendroit le merci Damedé
    Et le juise qu[e] li a destiné.
    De sa despoille est tous atapinés;
    Va s'ent en Roume a son pére parler.

52

    Si s'atapine que on ne le counoisse;
655 Toute la rue s'en est alé[s] en Toivre,
    Parmi les rues u il fu ja bien cointes;
    Autre puis autre, et son pére i encontre;

Ensamble lui grant masses de ses homes.
Bien le counut, par son droit non le noume.

53

660   [S]on pére encontre ki revient d'orison;
      Si iert sa mére qui le tient par le poing.
      Del moustier vienent saint Piére le baron;
      A messe furent et a pourcession.
      Del fil parloient, mais il n'iert gaires lonc;
665a Il l'apela, si l'a mis a raison:
665b ["Eufemiien, escoute ma raison;]*
      Car me herbeges, pour Diu, en ta maison,*
669   Biaus sires, puis que j'ai tel dolour.*
667   Enfers hom sui; pais moi, pour Diu amour.
670   Et pour ton fil qui Allessis ot non;
668   Que Dieus del ciel itel talent li doinst
      Que il reviegne a tou[s]* en ta maison."

54

      Quant ot li pére ramentevoir son fil,
      Pleure des oels, ne s'en pot astenir: [*63r*]
      "Pour Diu," dist il, "et pour mon cier ami,*
675   Tot te ferai, bons hom, çou que tu dis,
      Lit et ostel et pain et car et vin;
      Que Damedius faice tous ciaus merci
      Qui le herbegent par estrange païs.
      xvii. ans a que de mes oels nel vi;
680   Elas, peciére, ne sai s'est mors u vis."
      Uns rices hom iert la, [dans] Constentins,*
      Et voit le pére ki herbege le fil.
      Le pére apele, gentement li a dit,
      "Laissiés le moi, sire, vostre merci.
685   O moi venés, biaus sire pelerins;
      Herbegiés estes, s'o moi volés venir.
      Emsamble moi [se] vous volés [t]enir,
      Ne vous faura ne pains ne cars ne vins.
      S'ains muir de vous, Diex ait de moi merci,
690   Et vous ament par coi puissiés garir."

"Sire," dist il, "de Diu .v.c. mercis;
Dex herbege toi en son saint Paradis.
Hom sui estranges, si vieng d'autre pais
Et ostel quier et pour Diu i sui mis*

[LACUNA]

695 Et celui laisse que il a recuelli,
Et milleur quiert pour son cors miex servir,
S'en celui muert, pris est a male fin;
Diu a perdu et son saint Paradis.
La me tenrai u primiers me sui pris,
700 Quant on pour Diu m'i volra recuellir."
Ot le la mére, si l'a al pére dit:
"Sire," dist ele, "ja t'a il ostel quis.
Car le herbeges, pour Diu et pour ton fil."   [*63v*]
"Dame, dist il, "pres en sui et garnis."
705 Ot le la mére, si rapela son fil:
"Herbegiés estes, biaus sires pelerins.
Ensamble moi vous em poés venir,
Et pour l'enfant pour cui l'avés requis
Ja n'arés mal dont vous puissiés garir."
710 "Dame," dist il, "de Diu mout de mercis,
Et le signour ki vous doit maintenir;
Et a l'enfant c'aviés engenui
Doinst tel coralge que il puist revenir.
Il revenra, pour voir le vous plevis."
715 Ot le la mére,* si l'en a fait enclin.
Pleure des oels et li mére autresi.

55

"Eufemien, biaus sires, rices ber,
Herbegié sui, la merci Damedé.
Enfers hom sui, soufraitous de parler;
720 Un grabeton me fai sour ton degré
Pour cel enfant ke tu pues tant amer.
Que Dius te doinst itel home trouver
Que* si te saint qu'a li puistes parler."
"Bons hom," dist il, "pour amor Damedé

725 Et mon enfant pour coi l'as demandé,
      Herberc aras et pain et car assés,
      Et puis del vin quant vous boire en vaurés.
      Que Dius assoille toute crestienté
      Que [l'] me herbet par estranges ostés!
730 Mout a dur cuer que si m'a oublié."

56

Pleure la mére le duel de son enfant;
Tot ramentoivre le duel dont ot le cuer dolant.*
Li pére en va ses mains si detorjant   [*64r*]
Que a la tere en cairent si gant.
735 S[ains] A[lessins] s'abaisse, se li rent.
      "E Dius," dist il, "vrais pére tous poissans,
      Quele amistié entre pére et enfant!
      Ces felonnies que jou lor fac si grans
      M[e sont]* legiéres, ses trouverai pesans;
740 Al grant juise me revenroit devant,
      Pour pére et mére qui me pourmetent tant,
      Que si par fac coreciés et dolans.
      Ajue, Diex, s'en sont si desirant!"
      Com il les voit plourer si tenremant,
745 Iriés en est mais il n'en fait samblant;
      Crient et redoute nel voisent ravissant.
      De tout a mis en Jhesu son talent;
      Mieus aimme Diu ke nul home vivant.
      "Dius," dist li pére, "cor eusse un sergant
750 Qui le gardast trestout a son talant!
      S'il estoit sers, jou le feroie franc."
      I. en i ot qui s'en presente avant.
      "Vés me ci, sire, sel garc par vo commant."*

57

Par nule guise ne l'em puet on blasmer.*

[LACUNA]

(58)

755 Souvent le virent et li pére et li mére,
Et la pucele que il ot espousée;
Par nule guise onques nel ravisérent.
Il ne lor dit, n'il ne [li] demandérent,*
Ques hom estoit et de quele contrée.

59

760 Souvente fois lor vit grant duel mener,
Et tout pour lui et nient tout pour el,
Et de lor eus souventes fois plourer.
Il les esgarde; sel met el consirer,   [64v]
N'a soig que [l'] voie si est a Diu tornés.

60

765 Sour le degré u gist sour une nate,
La le paist on del relief de la table;
Sa povreté deduist a grant barnaige.
Il ne veult mie que sa mére nel cace;
Miels aime Diu que trestout son lignaige.

61

770 De le viande qui del ostel li vient
Tant en retient que son cors en soustient,
Le remanant en rent as prouvendiers.
N'en fait mugot pour son cors encraissier;
As povres gens le redonne a mangier.
775 En sainte eglise converse volentiers;*
A Diu servir se commence efforcier;
S[ains] A[lessins] ne s'en voelt eslongier.

62

Sous le degré ou il gist et converse,
La li apporte a mangier la pucele

780 Qu'il espousa et sa feme doit estre.
    A grant barnaige deduit sa grant poverte;
    Li serf son pére, qui le maisnie servent,
    Lévent lor mains, hanas et escueles,
    Les laveures li getent sour la teste.
785 Ne s'en courouce ne i[l] nes en apele.

63

    Mout* l'escarnissent et tienent a bricon;
    L'aige li getent et moillent son liton.
    Ne s'en courece icil saintismes hom,
    Ains prie Diu que trestout lor pardoinst
790 Par sa merci, mais ne sevent qu'il font.
    Par une feste de sainte Rouvison
    Monta li pére les degrés contremont,
    Et voit* gesir son fil el grabaton.   [65r]
    Il l'apela, si l'a mis a raison:
795 "Biaus crestïens, ne savons vostre non.
    Faut vous conrois? De coi aiés besoing?"
    "Sire," dist il, "Crestïens ai a non,
    Et trestout cil qui levé sont des fons.
    Qui cest non garde s'en a bon guerredon,
800 Et qui nel fait, mor[t] morians* a non.
    Li cors p[o]rist, l'ame toute em pert on
    Fors de la garde des mains nostre signour.

64

    "Par mon droit non, sire, m'avés noumé
    Se tant sui bons que m'en puisse garder.
805 En s[aint] baptesme, en fons, me sui donnés,
    Mais jou criem* perdre par mal siecle mener.
    Conroi ai tant que ne le puis user.
    Celui em puisse grassier et loer
    Pour cui amour le me faites donner;
810 Il vous remaint l'enfant* ke tant amés."
    "Bons hom," dist il, "ke me ramentevés?
    N'est mie vis qui tant a demouré.
    Salve en est l'ame se Dieus l'a commandé,

Et Dius em penst par sa grant pieté.
815 Mout a dur cuer qui si m'a oublié."
Va s'ent li pére et li fils est remés.
E vous le mére qui descent al degré,
E la pucele, la fille Sigoré;*
Çou fu l'espouse, un mantel affublé*
820 D'un paile brun, d'un hermin engoulé.
Quant il les voit, s'est mout espoentés
Que par pecié ne lor soit endité.
Quant il les voit et venir et aler,   [65v]
Et vair et gris et blïaus trainer,
825 Par desor lui et descendre et monter,
N'est tant hardis qu'es ost abandonner
Que nel counoissent a son roumanc parler,
Que nel rembatent ens el pecié mortel.
Li mére apele le fille Signoré:
830 "Savés, pucele, dont m'ara mout pesé?
Moi est avis cis pelerins me het;
Mout longement a o nous conversé,
C'onques nul eure ne me vaut aparler.
Il est malades, si est mout enfremés;
835 Ne vivra gaires car mout est descarnés.
Car li faisons ses drapiaus relaver;
Çou iert aumosne, si nous en sara gré.
Savoir vauroie de quel païs est nés;
Nel sarons mais puis k'il iert deviés."
840 Dist li pucele, "Alons li demander."

65

Çou dist li mére, "Jou i vois mout envis.
Quant jel regart, membre moi de mon fil;
Pour un petit nel resamble del vis.
Lors plour des oels, ne m'en puis astenir;
845 Çou est li dels dont m'estora morir."
Cele part vint, a apeler le prist:
"Dont estes vous, biaus sire pelerins?"
"Dame," dist il, "pour amour Dieu, merci.
Jou sui* malades, si sui pres de ma fin.

850 Je ne devroie vous ne autrui mentir,
    Car par mençoignes pert on saint Paradis;
    D'ui a tierc jour le sarés bien de fi."*
    Car on aproce al tans et a sa* fin,   [66r]
    Et au juise ke il devoit morir,
855 Mais ains qu'il muire vaura faire un escrit;*
    Si metra tout par letre el parcemin
    Si com li sire qui bien en est garnis,
    Et tres bien set et letres et escrit.
    "Aprociés moi," dist il, "dame, un petit."
860 Ele s'aproce dusc'au lit u il gist.
    Il s'abaissa, as piés se li caï;
    Puis le baisa, se li cria merci.
    "Sire," dist ele, "quel pardon m'avés quis?*

66

    "Sire," dist ele, "quel pardon me querés?"
865 "Pour mon malaige quic jou estre emcombrés."*
    "Sire," dist ele, "tout vous soit pardonné."
    "Vostre grant painne que eü en avés,
    Pour amour Diu, si le me pardonnés."
    Et la pucele les a bien esgardés;
870 Se li pardonne, ele fait autretel.
    Ele s'en tourne, cil est mout liés remés.

67

    Iluec converse issi .xvii. ans.
    Nel recounurent ne li serf ne li franc,
    N'onques nus hom ne sot de ses haans.
875 Fors sol li lis u il a geü tant;
    Ne pot muer, cil fu aparissans.

68

    Dis et .vii. ans a prouvendiers esté,
    Et autretant en Ausis la cité.
    Ne but de vin ne de car n'a gousté,
880 Mais del relief qui li vint de l'ostel

Poi en manja a l'eure del souper,
A tout le mains qu'il s'en pot consirer.

69

Quant li sergant li dounent del relief,
Tout le millour en rent as prouvendiers,
885 Et le plus pesme retien[t a son mangier].
ii. jors jeune, puis si manjue au tierc;
Ore est fourment ses cors afoibliés.
Se li a Dius pardonné ses peciés.
Sa fins aproce, s'en loe Diu del ciel.

70

890 Trente .iiii. ans a si son cors pené;
Dex son service li velt guerredonner.
Sa fins aproce ke il doit devier;
Se li a Diex ses peciés pardonnés.
Ses cors est nes comme argent esmerés.
895 Mout li agrieve li soie enfremetés,
Et il set bien que il s'en doit aler;
S'en est mout liés, s'en loe Damedé.
Cel sien serjant a a lui apelé.

71

"[O]s tu, serjans, qui tant jour m'as servi,
900 Dius et sa mére le te puisse merir,
Povres hom sui, ne t'ai que departir.
Quier moi, biaus frere, et enche et parcemin
Et une penne; si ferai une escrist.
N'escris pieça; or m'en est talens pris.
905 Esbatrai moi, pesans sui de morir."
"Au congié Diu," li serjans respondi.

72

Cil li va querre, si li a aporté.
Quant il le tint, s'en loa Damedé.
Tout i escrit quanqu'il a manouvré,

910 Et çou i mist de quels parens il ert,
Com s'en ala en Ausi la cité,
Et com l'imaige fist Diu pour lui parler,
Et pour l'ounour dont le vaut emcombrer   [*67r*]
S'en rafui en Roume la cité;
915 Sen boin serjant n'i vaut mie oublier,
Que mieus l'en sot quant tant jour l'a gardé.
Les lui le tint, ne vaut pas demoustrer,
C'om nel counoisse dusqu'il s'en soit alés,
Car ainc n'ama loenge seculer.
920 Sa fins aproce, li cors est agrevés;
Droit entour none s'acoise de parler.
En es le jour que il dut devier;
"Diu consumate" em prist a apeler;
Onques nus hom ne l'oï d'el parler.
925 En la semainne que il s'en dut aler
Vint une vois .iii. fois en la cité
Fors del sacraire, par commandement Dé,
Por son ami qu'il en voloit mener.
Preste est la gloire u il porra entrer;
930 Cel jour a dit, "Car querés l'oume Dé."

73

A haute vois lors vint autre semonse
Que l'oume Diu quiérent qui gist en Roume.
Quant il l'oïrent, durement le redoutent.*

74

Sains Innocens iert adonc apostoiles;*
935 A lui en vinrent et li rice et li povre,
Requisent li consel de cele cose
Qu'il ont oïe, qui si les desconforte.
Ne gardent l'eure que terre les engloute.*

75

Li apostoile et li empereour —
940 Li uns A[caire],* l'autre Onorés ot non —

Et tous li pules par commune raison,
Deprient Diu que consel lor en doinst
De cel saint home par qui il gariront.   [67v]

76

Trestout deprient la soie pieté
945 Qui lor ensaint u le puissent trover.
Vint une vois qui lor a endité:
"A le maison Eufemien querés
Car illuec est, iluec le trouverés."

77

Tost s'en tournérent sour dant Eufemien;
950 Alquant le prendent forment a blastengier:
"[I]ceste cose deussiés anoncier
A tout le pule qui ert desconsilliés.
Tant l'a[s] celé, mout i a grant pecié."

78

Il s'escondist que li hom qui ne set;
955 Il ne l'en croien[t], a her[b]ec sont alé.
Il va devant sa maison [aprester],
Si la fait bien torcier et atorner
A l'apostoile ki ens devoit entrer.
Forment l'enquiert a tous ses menestrés,
960 Mais il respont* que nus d'els riens ne'n set.

79

Li apostoile et li empereour
Sient en banc pensif et ploureos,*
Et entour aus li prince et li baron.
Deprient Diu que consel lor en doinst
965 De [cel] saint home par cui il gariront.

(80)

Endementiers que il ont iluec sis,*
Deso[iv]re l'ame del cors saint A[lessins];

D'iluec en va tout droit em Paradis.
Ja iert en tra[n]se quant la pucele vint;
970 Adont l'esgarde, si le vit empalir.
"Sire," dist ele, "mout [vous] torble li vis."
"Bele," dist il, "car pres sui de ma fin;
Grant paour ai car pres sui de morir.   [68r]
Car or voi çou que onques mais ne vi;
975 Voi quantes mains me voelent recuellir.
Hui perirai se Dius ne me garist.
Pense del cors qu'il soit ensevelis;
L'ame ara çou que ele a deservi."

81

Il li a dit, "Pour amour Diu, pucele,
980 Ma fins aproce, ne viverai mais gaires.
981a Sains Bonifaces, que on martir apele,*
981b [Avoit en Roume une eglise mout bele;]*
Porter m'i fai, se m'i fai metre en tere;
Quant tu morras tu i vauroies estre."
"Au congié Diu, sire," dist la pucele.

82

985 "Bele pucele," çou dist sains A[lessins],
"Se or eüsse tant Damediu servi
Que jou peüsse les sains souner oïr,
Dont fuisse liés, si [s]eüsse de fi
Que m'ame eüst son liu em Paradis,
990 Si recouvrast vers Damediu merci."
A icele eure que li sains hom le dist,
Li saint commencent tout ensanle a ferir.
Sounent a force, la cités retentist;
N'i avoit saint, tant soit grans ne petis,
995 Ne sont plus cler que onques mais ne fist.
Ains que il muire les a bien cler oïs.
"Bele pucele," çou dist sains A[lessins],
Oiés les sains, le Damediu merci.
Ma fins aproce, dont je ne puis garir,
1000 Qui a tous homes fait tous avoir guerpir,

Sans les aumosnes com nen ses puet tollir.
Vois ci mes palmes que j'ai a tout l'espi;
De Jhersalem l'aportai quant jou ving;   [68v]
Bien sont gardées jusqu'au jour de ma fin.
1005 A mon cavet, quant jou iére enfouis,
M'en faites crois et as piés autresi;
Dius pensera del croistre et del tehir;
L'anoncemens d'un angle le m'a dit.
Jou ne sui mie de mo[ut] lontaing païs
1010 Quant mi parent seront al sevelir,
Si ert mes pére et ma mére autresi,
Et une espouse que jou ai deguerpi."
Ot le la bele, si jeta un souspir.
"E Dius," dist ele, "jou quic c'est mes amis!
1015 Sire," dist ele, "sont il bien lonc de ci?
Mandas lors tu par més qui lor desist?"
Ne pot parler, s'est transis l'esperis.
Donc fu dolante que plus ne l'ot enquis.
Li bons serjans qui tant jour l'ot servi,
1020 Il va au pére, si li a tantost dit:
"Sire," dist il, "mors est li pelerins.
Ma damoisele l'a fait ensevelir."

83

Li bons serjans qui servi volentiers,
Il le nonça son pére Eufemien.
1025 Souef l'apele, se li a consillié:
"Sire," dist il, "mors est tes prouvendiers.
Çou m'est avis qu'il ert bons crestïens.

84

"Mout longement a[i] o lui conversé;
De nule cose, certes, nen sai blasmer.
1030 Çou m'est avis que çou est li hom Dé."
Tous seus en est Eufemiens tornés;
Va a son fil u gist sour son degré.
Le drap souslieve dont il iert acouvetés;*   [69r]
Vit del saint home le vis et bel et cler,

1035   Et en sa main sa cartre et son seel.
       Ens a escrit trestout le sien convers.
       Eufemiens veut savoir k'ele espialt.

(85) [86]

       Il le weut prendre mais ne li pot tolir;*
       A l'apostoile revin[t] tous esbahis:
1040   "Sire, pour Diu, aiés de moi merci!
       Or ai trouvé çou que tant avons quis.
       Sous mon degré gist mors uns pelerins;
       Tient une cartre mais ne li puis tolir."

86 [87]

       Sains Innocens entendi la raison
1045   Qui apostoiles estoit a icel jour,
       Et ot les sains ki sonnent* a un son
       Dusqu'a la nuit de lor gré toute jour,
       Et des sains angles vit la pourcession,*
       Qui portent l'ame cantant nostre signour.
1050   De cele cartre li prist mout grans paours,*
       Et tous li pules esmaris environ.
       Sous le degré vinrent al grabaton;
       N'en apelérent car ne sorent son non.

87 [88]

       Li apostoiles et li empereour*
1055   Devant lui vienent, getent s'a orison;
       Misent lors cors [en grans afflictions,]*
       Se li deprient par mout bele raison:
       "Merci, merci, merci, saintisme on,*
       Ne te connumes, ne ne te connisson.

(88) [89]

1060   Ci devant toi soumes doi peceour,
       Par la Diu grasse clamé empereour;
       C'est sa mercis qu'il nous consent l'ounour.

De cest empire soumes gouvreneour;
De ton consel soumes mout soufraitous.

89 [90]

1065 "Cis apostoiles doit les ames garir;
C'est ses mestiers dont il a a servir.
Rent li la cartre par la toie merci;
Si nous dira qu'il treuve en escrit.
Si nous doinst Dius qu'encor puissons garir."

90 [91]

1070 Li apostoles mist sa main a la cartre;
S[ains] A[lessins] la soie li alasque.
Cil le reçut ki ert de Rome pape;
Quant il le tint, si le moustra as autres.
Illuec fist Dieus un glorious miracle,*
1075 Que de sa main s'en ala droit la cartre;
A la pucele s'en ala a la place,
Ens en son sain, en son blïaut de paile.
Empres sa car ot vestue la haire;
Ele ne veüt c'omme ne feme nel sace.*
1080 Doucement sert le glorious mirable.
S[ains] Innocens esperdi son coraige;
Si ot vergoigne des houmes de la place
Et paour a ke Damedius nel hace.

91 [92]

Sains Innocens quant ot la cartre ouverte*
1085 Et vi les letres ke li sains hom ot fetes,
Ains li escape que le peust espialre
Tout droit en va el sain de la pucele,
Sous son blïaut, entre ses deus mameles,
U ele pleure les mals et les soufraites
1090 Que li sains hom sour le degré a traites;
Ne si ne set c'a lui eüst a faire,
Mais perdre en crient le glorious celeste.

92 [93]

[O]iés, signour, con grande loiauté
Tout home doivent a le moiller porter.   [*70r*]
1095 Car tel moustrance fist le jour Damedés
Que a sa mére ne vaut la cartre aler
Ne a son pére qui l'avoit engenré,
Mais a l'espouse ki bien avoit gardé
Le compaignie de son ami carnel,
1100 La va la cartre par le plaisir de Dé.
Cil qui le virent furent espoenté.

93 [94]

Or est remése la cartre a la pucele
Par le plaisir le glorious celestre.
Plus tost que pot le prent a la main destre;
1105 Saint Innocent l'apostre en apele:
"Sire," dist ele, "que porra de moi estre?
Car me consille, que par sui mesfete."

94 [95]

"Bele," dist il, "buer fuisses tu ains née.
Toi[e] est la cartre que Dius le t'a donnée;
1110 Qui que toit plaist doit estre delivrée."
"Sire," dist ele, "jou sui mout esgarée;
Faire quic cose dont li cors sains me hée."
Il esgardérent* les clers de la contrée;
A saint Ambrose ont la cartre livrée.
1115 Cil ert evesques et cancelers s[aint] Piére*
Il list la letre; li autre l'escoutérent.
Le non lor dist del pére et de la mére,
Et de celi que il ot espousée,*
Et si lor dist de ques parens il ére,
1120 Et la moitié de l'anel ont trouvée
Dedens la cartre tres bien envolepée,
Dont la moitié li ot recommandée.
Ele l'ot bien estoié* e[t] gardée.   [*70v*]
Il li demande; ele l'a aprestée;

1125 Il les assamble, si se sont acordées.
Dist l'apostre, "Ceste ensegne est prouvée."
"Sire," dist ele, "quel m'aviés tant celée?
Si les eüsse rendues et moustrées."
Grans fu li diex, a terre ciet pasmée.

95 [97]

1130 Et si lor dist com s'enfui par mer,
Con s'en ala en Ausis la cité,
Et com l'ymaige fist Dius pour lui parler,
Et pour l'ounor dont le vaut emcombrer
S'en rafui a Roume la cité.
1135 Sen bon serjant n'i vaut mie oublier,
Que miels l'en soit* qui tant jour l'a gardé.

96 [98]

Quant ot li pére ke on troeve en la cartre,
A ses .ii. mains desront sa blance barbe:
"E fiels," dist [il], "con dolerous mesaige!
1140 Jou aesmoie ke tu vis repairasses,
Pour Diu merci, si me reconfortasses."

(97) [99]

[A] haute vois prist li pére a crier:*
"E fius," dist il, "que dels m'est demorés!
Com male garde ai fait sous mon degré!
1145 Et jou peciére, com par sui avulés!
Tant l'ai veü c'ains ne sot aviser.

98 [100]

"Fiels A[lessins], de ta dolante mére,
Tante dolour a pour toi endurée
Et tant gran fain et tant soif trespassée,
1150 Et tantes larmes pour le tien cors plourées!
Cis dels l'ara sempres par acorée
Qui est mout grans; anqui sera tuée.*

99 [101]

"Fils, qui* seront mes grandes iretés,   [*71r*]
Mes larges teres dont jou avoie assés,
1155 Mi grant palais en Rome la cité?
Par toie amour m'en iére mout penés;
Se tu vesquisses, t'en fusses hounerés.

100 [102]

"Blanc ai le cief et le barbe kenue;
Mes grans onors avoie retenues;
1160 Je vous servoie, mais vous n'en aviés cure.
Si grans dolors m'est hui cest jour [v]enue!
Fils, la toie ame soit el ciel absolue!

101 [103]

"A tel dolour et a si grant poverte,
Fils, es deduis par alienes teres;
1165 Et de cest bien qui tous deust tiens estre*
Poi em presis en la toie herbege;
Se Diu pleüst, sire en deussiés estre.

102 [104]

"Toi couvenist lance et escu porter,
Espée çaindre comme tes autres pers,
1170 Et grant maisnie ricement conreer,
Le gonfanon l'empereour porter;
Si fist tes pére et tous tes parentés."

103 [105]

De la dolour que demenoit li pére
Grans fu la noise; si l'entroi sa mére.
1175 La vint corant comme feme dervée,
Batant ses palmes, corant, escavelée.
Voit mort son fil; a terre ciet pasmée.

104 [106]

Qui dont le vit son grant duel demener,
Son pis debatre et son cors degeter,
1180 Ses crins derompre, son vis desmaiseler,
Et son mort fil detraire et acoler,
N'ot si dur cuer nel estuece plourer.

105 [107]

Desront ses crins, si debat sa poitrine.   [*71v*]
A grant duel met la soie car meïsme:
1185 "E fiex," dist ele, "com me eus enhaïe!
Et jou caitive, com par sui avulïe;
Nel recounnui onques tant le veïsse."

106 [108]

Pleure des oels, si escrie a haus cris,
Puis se regrete, "Ma[r te] portai, biaus fils!
1190 Et de ta mére, c[o]m nen eüs mercis?
Pour toi veïr desiroie a [morir];
Çou fu mervelle que p[i]tiés ne [t'] em prist.

107 [109-10]

"Fils A[lessins], de la toi[e] car tenre*
Si adoisaisses tout ton gentil lignaige.
1195 Se une fois a moi seule parlasses,
Ta lasse mére si le reconfortasse[s],
Qui·st si dolan[te], biaus fiels, buer i alasses.

108 [111]

"E lasse mére, comme fort aventure,
Que ci voi morte toute ma noureture!
1200 Ma longe atente a quel duel m'est venue!
Que porrai faire, dolante creature?

(109) [112]

"Ains que t'eüsse en sui si dolerouse; *
Quant tu fu nés, sen fui issi joiose.
Çou poise moi ke ma fins tant demore.

110 [113]

1205 "Signor de Rome, pour l'amor Diu merci;
Aidiés me a plaindre le duel de mon ami.
Grans est li dels qui sor moi est vertis.
Ne puis tant faire que mon cuer est saisi.
Il n'est mervelle, n'a[i] mais fille ne fil."

111 [114]

1210 Entre le duel del pére et de le mére,
Vint la pucele qui il ot espousée,
Que il laissa en la maison son pére:
"Sire," dist ele, "com longe demourée!   [*72r*]
Atendu t'ai en la maison ton pére;
1215 Tu m'i laissas dolante et esgarée.
Sire A[lessins], tant jour t'ai desirée,*
Et tantes larmes pour le tien cors plourée"
(Et tot pour bien et nient tout pour el[e]).

112 [116]

"Sire A[lessins], de ta jouvente bele,*
1220 Com sui dolante quant toi porrira terre!
E gentiex hom, si dolante puis estre!
Com atendoie de toi bones nouveles!
Et or les voi dolerouses et pemes.

(113) [117]

"Se te seüsse ça defors le degré*
1225 U as geü de longe enfremeté,
Nus hom qui vive ne [m']en peust tourner
Qu'ensamble toi ne m'este[üs]t poser.

114 [118]

"Or par sui veve, sire," dist la pucele;
"Jamais leëce n'arai car ne puet estre.
1230a N'a carnel houme n'arai jamais a faire;
1230b [Diu servirai, le roi qui tout governe;]*
Ne me faura s'il voit ke jou le serve."

115 [119]

Tant i plourérent et li péres et li mére
Et la pucele que trestout s'i lassérent
Endementiers le saint cors conreérent.*

116 [120]

1235 "Signour, que faites?" çou dist li apostoles.
"Que vous ajue cil deus ne ciste cose?*
Car par celui arons boine victore."

(117) [121]

Trestout le prendent qui porrent avenir;*
Cantant emportent le cors s[aint] A[lessin]
1240 N'estuet semonre cels qui l'orent oï.
Tout i acorent, et li enfant petit,*
Et tout li prient que d'aus tous ait merci.

118 [122]

Si s'en esmurent toute la gens de Roume;   [72v]
Plus tost i vient qui plus tost i puet courre.
1245 Parmi ces rues en vinrent si grans routes;
Ne quens ne rois n'i puet faire entreotes,
Ne cel s[aint] cors ne puent porter outre.

119 [123]

Entr'els em prisent li signor a parler:
"Grans est la presse, nous n'i porrons passer;
1250 Pour cel saint cors que Diex nous a presté

Liés est li pules qui tant l'a desiré.
Tant en i vienent, c'om nes em puet torner."

120 [124]

Respondent cil qui le regne baillissent,
"Estes, signor, nous en querons mecine;
1255   De nos avoirs faisons grans departies;
La gens* menue qui l'aumosne desirent
S'or nous font presse, si en iermes delivre."

121 [125]

[D]e lor avoir prisent l'or et l'argent;
Si l'ont geté devant le povre gent,
1260   Pour çou quidiérent avoir descombrement.
Que lor ajue? Il nen veulent nient;
A cel saint cors ont torné lor talent.

122 [126]

A une vois crient la gens menue,
"De cest avoir, certes, n'avons nous cure,
1265   Mais del saint cors que il nous face ajue,
Car par celui nous iert vie rendue."*

123 [127]

Sours, n'avulés, ne contrais, ne lepreus,
Ne crestiens qui tant soit languereus,
Ensorquetout nus hom palasinex,
1270   Icil n'i vint qui·n n'alast refuses,*
Ne nus n'i vient qui report sa dolour.

(124) [128]

N'i vient enfers de cele enfremeté*
A cel saint cors, lués ne soit rasenés;   [*73r*]
Auquant i vienent, auquant s'i font porter.
1275   Si vraie espesse lor a Dius demoustré,
Qui vient plorant, cantant l'en fait aler.

125 [129]

Li doi signour qui le regne couvernent,
Quant il en virent les vertus si apertes,
Alquant le prendent et li auquant le servent.
1280　Auques par p[r]oi et auques par poeste
Passent avant, si desrompent la presse.
S[ains] Bonifaces que on martire apele
Avoit en Roume une eglise mout bele;
Illuec portérent s[aint] A[lessin] acertes.

126 [130]

1285　La gent de Roume qui tant l'ont desiré
vii. jours le tinrent sor terre a poesté.
Grans fu la feste, ne l'estuet demander.
De toutes pars l'ont si avirouné,
Sous ciel n'a home qui i puist habiter.

127 [131]

1290　El mesme* jour fu faite sa herbege
A cel s[aint] cors, a la gemme celestre.
Traient s'en sus, si alasquent la presse.
Vellent u non, le laissent metre en terre.

128 [132]

A encensiers, a [a]ures camdelabres,
1295　Clerc se revestent en capes et en aubes.
Cel saint cors metent en un sarcu de marbre.

(129) [133]

D'or et d'argent fu li sarcus parés*
U cel s[aint] cors veulent metre et poser;
Si l'enfouirent a vive poesté.
1300　Pleure li pules de Rome la cité,
So siés n'a home qui[·s] puist reconforter.

130 [134]

Ore avons dire du pére et de la mére
Et de l'espouse comme il le regretérent.   *[73v]*
Le jour i ot .D. larmes plourées.

131 [135]

1305 Quant sour la tere n'en porent mais tenir,
Vellent u non, le laissent enfouir.
Prendent congié al cors s[aint] A[lessin],
"Biaus sire pére, aiés de nous merci,
A ton signour nous soiés boins plaidis."

132 [136]

1310 Va s'ent li pules, et li péres et li mére
Et la pucele onques ne desevrérent.
Ensamble [furent] dusqu'a Deu en alérent.
Lor compaignie est boine et hounerée;
Pour cel saint home ont lor ames sauvées.

133 [137]

1315 [C]om bones oevres, Diex, et com bon service
Fist cil sains hom en ceste mortel vie!
Ore en est s'ame de gloire raemplie;
Quant que vaura, n'en est un point a dire;
Ensorquetout et si voit Diu meïsme.

134 [138]

1320 Bele pucele, dont il se fist estrange,*
Or sont privé, emsamble sont lor ames.
Or sont en glore sans nule repetance;
Illuec conversent et si lisent lor salmes.
Ne vous sai dire comme lor joie est grande.

135 [139]

1325 Elas, caitis, com somes emcombré
Que porrons dire? Trop sommes apressé;

Pour nos peciés sommes tout avulé.
La droite voie nous ont entroublier;
Par cel saint home devoumes ralumer.

136 [140]

1330 Tenons, signour, cel saint home en memoire;
Çou li prions de tous mals nous asoille.

12. pror, *G. P. corr.*
13. mues *followed by a dot.*
16. Que li v.
54. *54b is from P.*
59. poisent *G. P. corr.*
63. donne.
65. sa.
67. lon.
74. emperes.
119. i. pailes.
122. S. Alessins ąpaȓręllię a.
144. raient.
146. presist en efflun.
154. issi contees, *G. P. corr.*
156. il ot esponsee, *G. P. corr.*
160. li, *G. P. corr.*
162. contre, *G. P. corr.*
167. espouse, *G. P. corr.*
191. limontere, *G. P. corr.*
194. entenį.
202. Solimonterre.
219. prendre amari, *G. P. corr.*
226. vis *G. P. corr.*
236. Se je vi, *G. P. corr.* se je l' di.
246. qui peust, *G. P. corr.*
255. mais le ne set, *G. P. corr.* l'en ne sait.
264. Sireș.
281. A male eure, *corr. in Ms.* A con male eure.
290. Dolante est, *G. P. corr.* Dolante en ert.
296. ne voi, *G. P. corr.*
302. venra, *G. P. corr.*
303. se *corrected with a heavier stroke to* le.
313. ne verras, *G. P. corr.*

314. puterie, *G. P. corr.*
339. tous tens, *G. P. corr.*
352. des bąp palmes.
368. ceste; *the scribe did not leave enough room for the initial* I.
371. Dius fist, *G. P. corr.*
386. le pot, *G. P. corr.*
393. poureins, *G. P. corr.*
400. Tu nes, *G. P. corr.*
405. ce menerent, *G. P. corr.*
416. *After 416 the scribe repeated lines 412-416 as a new laisse.*
428. part, *G. P. corr.*
443. fist, *G. P. corr.*
445. Quant ni pour, *G. P. corr.*
448. la pucele ot que la mere dit, *G. P. corr.*
452. son ami, *G. P. corr.*
468. portees, *G. P. corr.*
469. Ne recounurent, *G. P. corr.*
474. aumouniers, *G. P. corr.*
490. Veullies, *G. P. corr.*
497. vinrent, *G. P. corr.*
500. Il le counurent, *G. P. corr.*
544. celui qui lui siet, *G. P.,* Celuy qui les l'uis.
545. *After this line the scribe has repeated 543.*
550. fallli.
573. que veulent, *G. P. corr.*
574. En vesque, *G. P. corr.*
581b. *is from* M[1]
606. iaus, *G. P. corr.*
609. dę.
616. muel, *G. P. corr.*
634. Il a ouvert, *G. P. corr.*
638. et puis li prie.

644. qui li., *G. P. corr.*
649. sour son, *G. P. corr.*
651. qui il. *G. P. corr.*
655. alee, *G. P. corr.*
660. Ton.
669. jen ai.
671. a tout, *G. P.* a toi.
681. la u constentins, *G. P.* dant Coustentins.
687. moi vous en voles venir, *G. P. corr.*
692. herbegent.
729. Que me, *G. P.* Qui l' me.
739. Mest legieres, *G. P. corr.*
758. lor demanderent, *G. P. corr.*
764. que voie, *G. P. corr.*
785. neis nes en, *G. P. corr.*
800. mors morians, *G. P. corr.*
801. prist, *G. P. corr.*
880. relief qui si, *corrected by scribe to* li.
885. retiens as prouvendiers, *G. P. emend.*
899. Es tu, *G. P. corr.*
940. Li uns ara del autre oneres ot hounour non.
953. Tant la cele, *G. P. corr.*
955. croien al herenc. *G. P. corr.*
956. atorner, *G. P. corr.*
965. De saint, *G. P. corr.*
967. Desoure, *G. P. corr.*
969. trase, *G. P. corr.*
971. most, *G. P. corr.*
988. eusse de fi, *G. P. corr.*
995. clerc.
1009. mon lontaing, *G. P. corr.*
1028. aolui, *G. P. corr.*
1032. sour son se.
1036. Ens en a, *G. P. corr.*
1039. reving, *G. P. corr.*
1056. cors getent sa orison, *G. P. corr.*

1078. nel feme, *G. P. corr.*
1086. espialre.
1093. *The rubricator omitted the capital.*
1107. que se par sui mesfete.
1109. Toi est, *G. P. corr.*
1111. Il lesgarderent, *G. P. corr.*
1123. estoie esgardee.
1139. dist ele, *G. P. corr.*
1142. Haute, *G. P. corr.*
1148. dolour ai, *G. P. corr.*
1161. tenue, *G. P. corr.*
1164. est deduis, *G. P.* t'es deduis.
1170. "ricement maisnie".
1189. mais tel, *G. P. corr.*
1190. cam, *G. P. corr.*
1191. a veir, *G. P. corr.*
1192. ne lemprist, *G. P. corr.*
1195. mois seule.
1196. reconfortasse, *G. P. corr.*
1197. dolans, *G. P. corr.*
1208. na mais fill ne fil, *G. P. corr.*
1218. pour el.
1226. ten peust, *G. P. corr.*
1227. mestent, *G. P. corr.*
1230. *A line missing; 1230b, supplied by G. P.,* = LAP 494.
1244. i vienent, *G. P. corr.*
1258. Se lor, *G. P. corr.*
1270. refuses, *G. P.,* malendos.
1278. vinrent, *G. P. corr.*
1280. poi, *G. P. corr.*
1294. oures, *G. P. emend.* oires.
1301. qui puist, *G. P. corr*
1312. Ensamble dusqua, *G. P. corr.*
1315. Hom, *G. P. corr.*
1325. sil lisent, *G. P. corr.*

ALEXIS S

NOTES

1. The address to a mixed audience is unusual but not unparalleled. At least two *chansons de geste* contain similar openings. MS *C* of *Gaydon* (ed. Guessard and Luce; fonds fr. 1475 [olim 7551], XV c.) begins: "Seigneurs et dames, vous plaise à escouter / Bonne chançon qui moult fait à louer" (p. xxvi). So too in laisse 11 of *Jourdain de Blaye* (ed. Dembowski) the narrator addresses the audience: "Oiéz, seignor, damme de bonne foi!" (281, see also 575).

sermon: here not necessarily a 'sermon' but an 'account'; cf. *Les Enfances Ogier* (ed. Henry), 261.

10. *ancineour:* G. P. read this as *aucineour; u* and *n* are often difficult to distinguish. Furthermore, medieval scribes often used *n* and *u* without distinction; see McCormack, *Gui de Nanteuil*, p. 59. This line = the first line of *L*.

13. After this line G. P. inserts, "Jamais n'iert tels com fut as ancesours," = *LAP* 4.

15. *fois:* obj. for nom (cf. line 23), a common error (*Foulet*, 45). *moillier:* with the exception of epic, this word is very rare in Old French literature (see Grisay *et al.*, 1969, p. 88). There are four occurrences of it in *L*, 7 in *S*. G. P. changes *signour* to *baron* to avoid the repetition of the same word in three consecutive lines.

18. *duërra:* the poet uses this 3-syllable variant here (also in 31, 198) for the meter; he also employs the more usual *durra* (196). For the Picard form, see the introductory section (VI), verbs, 7.

21ff. Such moralizing prologues are not the exclusive property of clerical literature. Compare, for example, *Fierabras* 17-22 (ed. Guessard, 1860):

> Moult par est puis li siecles empiriés et mués :
> Se li peres est maus, li fix vaut pis assés,
> Et du tout en tout est li siecles redoutés,
> Ke il n'i a un seul, tant soit espoentés,
> Ki tiegne vraiement ne foi ne loiautés.
> N'en dirai plus, s'arai avant alé.

23. *péres:* the inflection of this word caused difficulty; there are 13 examples of *péres* being used for the sing. nom. rather than the plu. obj. case (use of analogical *-s* is not uncommon).

24. The MS reading is hypermetric; G. P. emends silently to "au parrin tant ne quant."

33. Assertion of the truth of his poem is an important part of a jongleur's claim to authority; poems are better not because more beautiful but because more *true*. Cf. *Fierabras*, 3, "Ce n'est menchoigne, mais fine verités"; *La Prise d'Orenge* (ed. Katz), 4-5; "Ceste n'est mie d'orgueill ne de folie, / Ne de mençonge estrete ne emprise." For a discussion of the importance of truth-telling in Greek oral poetry, see Marcel Detienne, 1967; for Yugoslavian poetry, see Lord, p. 18.

50. An epic line; cf. *La Siège de Barbastre*, 589, "Que riches hom estoit et de molt grant fierté."

54. *S* is missing a line referring to Eufemien's marriage.

55. *S* is the only member of the Alsis-family of manuscripts in which Eufemien's wife or his father-in-law is named. In the Latin *vita*, Alexis' mother is named Aglaes. A good example of the possibly allegorical nature of the names in *S; Bone Eurée* = 'Blessed' (cf. the preface to *L*, "... la vie de sum filz boneürét."

59. *poise*, MS *poisent*: here, as elsewhere, *S* has trouble with agreement, following a rough agreement of logic rather than of strict grammar. Perhaps the MS reading should be retained; Ruelle (*Huon*, p. 51, 36) notes 3rd sing. forms ending in -nt (*amoinent*, 6422; *dient*, 10079).

63. *donne[s]*: omission of a silent (?) *s* (see 130).

74. *emperes*: the Oxford *Roland* has the same mistake in lines 1 and 16. Only in *S* is the emperor named. Octavian (= Augustus) is unhistorical; were the tale history, the emperor would presumably have been Theodosius.

85. *siecle en avant*: G. P. emends to "a en avant" to create a metrically regular line.

90. The proper names are, again, unique to *S*. They are all capable of allegorical interpretation.

94. *assamblomont*, cf. *AΓ*, *usemblement*, *L* 46, *adaisement*. APS create a closer laisse link.

95. *se fisent belement*: G. P., *se. l' f*. The scribe frequently omits the d. o. pronoun; see 102.

96. *saint Jehan de Latran*: another instance of *S*'s fondness for proper names, and for names unique to it; in the Latin tradition the couple is married at St. Boniface's (cf. the dodecasyllabic *Alexis*, 153; *vita*, ed. Rohlfs, pp. 15-16: "et impositae sunt eis singulae coronae in templo sancti Bonifaci").

102. *que il ot*: G. P. emends to *que il l'ot*. The omission of the d. o. pronoun is particularly common when two of the same letters are involved (an aural mistake? cf. 95, 156, 246, 469, etc.); the mistake is so characteristic of the MS that I do not always correct it.

106. *le maison*: *S* occasionally uses *le* for *la* (as does *M²*; the form is normal in Picard); see also 140, 450, 518, 829, etc.

119. *Tendent i pailes*: the MS reads *Tendent i. pailes*, as if the scribe thought that *i* was the number *une* rather than the adverb.

130. *gouverne*: G. P. emends, probably correctly, to *gouvernes*, but for the identical confusion between second and third person forms in prayers, see 63.

138. *furent andoi remés*: here *AS* align against *LP (tut sul remes)*; see Contini, 1970, p. 363.

140. *le:* the fem. def. art.

143-52. Laisse 15 is original to *S;* laisse 16 similar to *L* (see introduction). The result is the creation of classic *laisses similaires.*

146. *presis:* a 2nd sing. form; the expected 3rd sing. is *presist* but the *t* has been expunged in the MS. G. P. emends to regularize the meter, "el flum de Jordant" (the *m* of *flum* is a mistake); *S* contains a number of alexandrines.

157. *espée:* this line is new to *S,* and the detail is found elsewhere only in the seemingly independent dodecasyllabic *Alexis. S* utilizes, however, the assonance word of *LAP.*

183. *Li cors est tere:* G. P. emends to "Li cors en tere." Emendation in passages involving *lacunae* is risky, and in this case unnecessary since the notion of the body's being clay is common.

191. This unfamiliar Biblical expression caused trouble for the scribe (cf. 202). Compare Genesis 2:7, "Formavit igitur Dominus Deus hominem de limo terrae . . . ."

205. *S'ele ert dolente:* G. P., considering this line part of Alexis' speech, emends to "S'il ert dolenz." If, however, the line is taken as a comment by the narrator describing the bride's concern at the strange way her husband is behaving on their wedding night, no emendation is necessary. The line is a whole-line formula, repeated at 503 where it describes the father's response to bad news. For another probable intervention by the narrator, see 1218.

207-208. For the lyricism of this scene, and the stress upon the bride's consent, see the introduction.

211. G. P. omitted this line without comment. It creates an additional instance of "laisses enchaînées."

217ff. Alexis' promise to send word of his condition in a year, not followed up on, is unique to *S.*

222-23. This detail, found only in *S,* paints a lively picture of medieval family life, as we must imagine Alexis' mother standing with her ear pressed to the door of the nuptial chamber.

226. The scribe has confused the subject case *(vis)* with the object *(vil).*

232. *el saint paradis:* a five-syllable hemistich. Seeking metrical regularity, G. P. emends to *en el.*

246. *Sou ciel:* an aural mistake? G. P. emends silently to "sous ciel."

281. *A mal eure:* In the space between the capital and *mal, com* has been written in, G. P. claims by a "later hand," but I detect no differences. The ink is the same color.

290. *ert:* G. P.'s correction of *est* to *ert* is no doubt correct, but in the MS the long *s* is clear (see 588).

293. *en estrange païs:* this statement is not strictly logical since the bride is a native of Rome (89); it reveals her sense of alienation, underscored in the next line: "Et esgarée entre tous mes amis."

337ff. *S* now picks up the story as told in *LAP,* st. 16.

341. The journey to Jerusalem is new to *S* (in *M** it is due to a storm which blows the saint off course). G. P. uses this detail to date *S* prior to the fall of Jerusalem in 1187.

358. A good example of the misleading nature of G. P.'s use of roman and italic type to distinguish lines derived from *L* and those original to *S.* He prints this line in roman letters, when in fact it is a conflation

of two lines and resembles more closely *AP* than *L*. MS *P* reads (st. 17): "iloc ariue sainement la nacele / dunc en issi forz danz alexis a terre" (*L*, a certes).

367. Again G. P. prints this line in roman type, but all it has in common with *L* is the assonance word, *Damedé*. *LAP* read, "sainta marie ki portat damne deu" (90).

368. *dont je vous cant:* the hemistich occurs in epic; cf. *Le Charroi de Nîmes*, 1092. 368-382 are new to *S*.

375. There is no indication of a new laisse here. The capitals normally alternate red and blue; the *D* of laisse 26 is red, the *A* of 27 blue, the capital of 28 was omitted (the scribe did not leave enough room), and the *Q* of 30 is blue. Therefore the rubricator, at least, thought the manuscript should have one more laisse break than did the scribe, and continued the alternation of colors on that assumption. For a discussion of the difficulties of ascertaining the number of laisses in the Oxford *Roland*, see Hunt, 1973, p. 310.

387. *emcombrés:* G. P. rather consistently, although without MS authority, spells this verb *encombrer*.

394. G. P. mistakenly numbers this laisse "XXX."

398. I suspect a line is missing here identifying the mother as the speaker. *L* reads: "la bone medre s'em prist a dementer / e sun ker filz suuent a regreter" (129-30). *M** gives "Li dame crie com femme foursenée" (*M²* 255). On the other hand, if *S* is a text intended for performance, the absence of such lines, while awkward, is less surprising since a good jongleur could by changing his voice indicate who was speaking (for the pride of a medieval performer in this mimetic ability, see the epitaph of the mime Vitalis, quoted by Richard Axton, 1974, p. 17).

399. Without manuscript authority, G. P. signals the beginning of a new laisse here on the basis of a change in strophes (from 21 to 27) in *L*. At this point *S* significantly alters the order of strophes found in *L*; 394-98 correspond approximately to st. 21; 399-452 (with much amplification) to st. 27-31; 453-475 to st. 22-25. *M** abbreviates this scene, and follows the order 21, 28, 22, 30, 23. MS *Q* reverts to the order of *L*.

416. The scribe here repeated lines 412-416 *verbatim* as a new laisse; this is evidence, then, that he was working from a written exemplar. The aural mistakes (if such they are) will therefore have occurred during a prior copying.

421. *le main:* G. P. emends to *la* although *le* for the feminine definite article is common (also 140, 450, 518, 829, where G. P. also changes the spelling). *Le* for *la* occurs in *L* (see *L* 236 and Storey's note *ad loc.*).

435. In *LAP* it is the mother who responds. *M** follows *S*. The second hemistich is original to *S*. *a dit:* G. P. emends to *as;* another example of confusion between second and third person.

437. *ton:* G. P. emends silently, but perhaps correctly, to *mon*. The MS reading, however, is defensible if we image the line to be the girl's reply.

454. This line, attributing the greatest grief to the bride, is new to *S*, and reflects her increased importance in this version.

455-59. Approximates st. 22, but shows the textual freedom of *S*, suggesting a memorial, rather than a reading, knowledge of *L* (ed. Foerster):

> Co dist li pedres cher filz cum tai perdut
> respont la medre lasse qued est devenut.

co dist la spose pechet le mat tolut
e chers amis si pou vus ai out
or sui si graime que ne puis estre plus.

456. *peciés le m'a tolu:* the switch of this line fom the bride to the father is important. When spoken by the girl (as in *L*), the line has served as one of the focal points in the controversy concerning Alexis' abandonment of his bride (see introduction, and Winkler, 1927; Richter 1932, 1933; de Gaiffier, 1947); to avoid having the bride appear to criticize Alexis, scholars have been forced to translate *pechet* (*L* 108) as "His feelings of sin" (Odenkirchen), instead of the more natural "Sin has taken him from me" — i.e. it is a sin that he has gone away. Leo Spitzer, 1932, 487, interprets: "Nicht *seine,* sondern *meine Sünde,* indem ein Unglück als schuldverusacht aufgefasset wird." By transferring the line to the father, who never does understand his son's motives, *S* avoids the problem. In *M** the line is spoken by the mother (for a discussion of the line in *L,* see Hatcher, 1952, p. 125).

474-75. Cf. *M*[1] 457-58: "De ces siens siers cui il est aumosnans. / Il fu lor sires, or est leur aumosniers" (the second line begins a new laisse). *M*[2], 312-13, supports G. P.'s emendation.

476ff. This scene is an invention of *S*. It provides an additional occasion for Alexis to express his feelings for his bride (esp. 493-95; for further discussion, see the introduction).

484. *houme:* G. P. gives *homme* but there are only five minims.

513. *celi* (fem.) for *celui* (masc.).

519-20. Agreement again by logic rather than by strict grammar, as the sing. antecedent of 519 ("li pules *fu*") leads to a plural relative clause, ("qu'il *durent* escouter"). See the notes to 960 and 1256.

524. *iii:* the scribe omitted the dots usual with numerals.

525. *Ermener:* again *S* reveals its fondness for proper names; in *LAP* this "saige clerc" is an anonymous "servitor."

537-38. *imaige:* without manuscript authority G. P. silently regularizes the spelling of this word.

552ff. This conversation between Ermener and Alexis is an invention of *S*. It allows Alexis to dwell upon his sense of sin, a detail which is important in light of the debate between Winkler and B. de Gaiffier, among others.

581ff. Alexis' second sea voyage is described in almost the identical terms used for his first (336-339).

581b. A line appears to be missing. G. P. supplies *L* 191, "Dans Alexis entra en une nef." I have preferred *M*[2], on a parallel with 338.

582. *devens:* G. P. emends to *dedens* but see 634.

585. *Troholt:* MS consensus lacks here. According to the *vita,* and *LA,* Tarsus was Alexis' destination; *P* names Rome (a mistake), *M*Q* Corsant (see note to *M*[2] 433). What is interesting about the proper names given in *S* is that they are 1) unique, and 2) wrong.

588. A close link with the following laisse. G. P. emends, perhaps correctly, *est* to *ert*. Tense irregularities, however, are well-documented in the Old French epic, and should not always be emended (see 290).

596. The order of laisses here is troubling. I follow the MS order, considering laisses 47 and 48 *laisses similaires;* laisse 47 tells us that Alexis has prayed, and 48-49 contain the contents of that prayer (see introduction and the note to 628). G. P., in contrast, follows the order

of *L*, but *S* has deviated from *L*'s order of strophes before. Laisse numbers enclosed in square brackets are those of G. P.'s edition.

G. P. emends *fenies* (which he reads as *finies*) to *finées; fenies* is a Picard graphy (for dissimilation of *i*, see Gossen, 1970, 37). In the next line, G. P. changes *raemplies* to *escoutées* for the sake of more perfect assonance. The assonances of *S* are, however, not always perfect.

602. The MS does not indicate a new laisse here, making in this instance no apparent distinction between *-ée* and *-ee*.

611. *me sire:* the scribe seems not to have heard the *s* of *mes* (nom.) because of the following sibilant.

622. *Com Diex me doinst, sire:* G. P. emends (perhaps rightly) to "Conduit me doinst." I keep the MS reading, awkward though it be, with the precedent of the other, similarly awkward switches between second and third person (e.g. 63, 130).

627-28. A classic laisse-link, containing in 627 the assonance word *(nef)* of laisse 50. In order to preserve this link, I have followed the MS order of laisses. Even if the MS order is an error, the assonance-link was, I suggest, strong enough in the scribe's mind to be responsible for that mistake in the first place. The similarity of this laisse-link to that between 24 and 25 (concluding the saint's first voyage) argues for retention of the MS order.

638. A corrupt line. G. P. emends "Et puis li prie" to "Et puis apres."

649. *sour:* G. P. emends *sour* to *sous* but cf. 720, 765 for the preposition. For confusion between *sus* and *sur* ($<$ SU(R)SUM), see Roncaglia, 1971, p. 169.

665b. A line is missing (cf. 659, "par son droit non le nomme"). G. P. supplies "Eufemiens, biaus sires, riches hom" (*LAP* 216, *S* 717); I have used the equivalent line (507) from *M²*.

666. After this line, G. P. adds, "Sous ton degré me fai un grabaton" (*LAP* 219); *S*, however, does not follow *L* slavishly, and the line is not necessary for the sense.

669. Quoting this line, G. P. writes, "ce qui ne donne pas de sens"; he emends to "Qui te guerpist, dont tu as tel dolour." With only minor modification, however, and with reordering of the lines, the MS reading can be preserved: "Shelter me, for God's sake, in your house (666), good sir, since I am in such pain (669); nourish me, for the love of God (667). And for your son who is named Alexis (668), may God in heaven grant him the inclination (670) to return to all in your house" (671). The only problem with this reconstruction is *en* in 669.

671. *a tou[s]:* G. P. emends the MS *tout* to *toi*. This reading limits Alexis' meaning to his father; the emphasis placed in *S* upon the saint's concern for his wife suggests that his concern is for *all* residents of his father's house.

674ff. In *L* this scene is restricted to the father's three-line speech. *S* expands it to 75 lines (674-749). The added lines serve largely to show in detail that the grief of Alexis' parents at the loss of their son has not paled during his seventeen-year absence.

681. *Constentins:* G. P. reads *Coustentins* but the *n* is clear; the character is new to *S*.

694. Lines are missing in which Alexis spells out his reasons for not changing lodging; see *M²* 534-36.

715. *mére:* G. P. emends to *pére. M¹* 698, reads, "O le la mere, si

gieta .I. souspir"; M^2 548, "Od le li péres, si geta un soupir." The MS reading is defensible if we understand Alexis to be the subject of *pleure;* that he too should be in tears is natural enough, and he is frequently depicted weeping in this version. A better solution, however, might be to emend *mére* in 716 to *pére.*

723. *Que:* G. P. emends to *qui,* but confusion between the subject and object forms of the pronoun is common in medieval romance languages, and should not be altered (cf. 729); see Foulet, 1930, 247.

732. An alexandrine; M^2 also contains a number of alexandrine lines.

739. *Mest:* G. P.'s correction to *me sont* is probably right, but there are other instances of mistaken agreement between subject and verb (e.g. 59, 519-20, 960 and the note there).

753. After this line G. P. adds, "Par toie amour en soufrirai l'ahan" (= *LP* 230). *A* lacks the line as well.

754. Following this line, without any indication in his *apparatus criticus,* G. P. adds four lines (= *L* st. 47). There is clearly a lacuna but its precise contents are less apparent. In the MS 754 is the first line of a laisse which concludes at 759. M^2 expands on the nature of the serjant's service to Alexis for 19 lines (596-614), M^1 for 20.

758-59. In fact Alexis' father does ask who he is.

775. After this line, G. P. adds, "Chascune feste se fait acomungier" (cf. *LP* 257; the strophe is missing in *A*). M^* contain G. P.'s added line but lack 775. Both lines are not necessary to the sense.

786. *Mout:* G. P. changes to *Tout,* commenting that here, as elsewhere, the rubricator "a mal rempli l'espace qui lui avait été laissé." At laisse 28, the rubricator had omitted the *I* but the scribe had not left him enough room; the page has been trimmed and it is impossible to tell whether the scribe had indicated the capital correctly in the margin. Elsewhere it is still possible to detect these letters (e.g. fol. 69v, line 1093). For the laisse in question, other MSS read "Tout," although *M* and *T* are not easily confused in this MS.

793. *voit:* G. P. emends silently and unnecessarily to *vist.*

800. *mor[t] moriens:* G. P., emending the MS, explains the phrase as "morte moriens."

806. *jou criem:* G. P. adds the missing d. o. pronoun, "jou l' criem." Omission of such pronouns is very typical of this MS. G. P. inserts them systematically; I have not done so.

810. *l'enfant:* G. P. emends silently to *celui.*

818. *Sigoré:* here and at 829, the MS represents [ᚷ] by *g.*

819-20. These details of dress occur elsewhere only in M^1 (847-49), but in the negative.

> C'ainc puis cele eure ne fu giu veüe
> Ne de chier paile ne d'ermine vestue,
> Qu'ele en la cambre fu seule remansue.

The version of M^1, in which the bride underlines her devotion to her husband by her renunciation of courtly dress, makes better sense.

849. *jou sui:* G. P. corrects unnecessarily (and silently) to *suis* (Pope, 1934, 951).

852. The ability to predict precisely the day of one's death is a stock attribute of a saint.

853. *sa fin: la fin?* Elsewhere (304) the scribe has confused *s* and *l,* where it is corrected in the MS.

855-57. These lines about writing the letter seem out of place here. In *M** all mention of the letter comes after Alexis begs his mother's forgiveness.

863-64.   Linked laisses; in *Les Enfances Guillaume* there is a similar example of two laisses linked by a change in verb tense:

L'enfes Guillames le sien peire en apelle.
L'enfes Guillames ait son peire apelley:
(laisses 71-72, 2812-13).

865.   G. P. suggests, on the basis of M^1, that several lines are missing from the beginning of Alexis' speech (cf. M^2 712-723). *M**, however, expands freely some portions of *S* while curtailing others, so that its testimony is not wholly reliable. On the other hand, the scene in *S* is rather abrupt as it stands. Both versions *(SM*)*, in comparison with *LAP*, heighten the pathos, exploring the human emotions involved.

933.   After this line G. P. adds, "Si li depreient que la cités ne fonde" (cf. *L* 298). The line, however, is not necessary. *M** does not contain it, although this portion of the narrative is considerably amplified there; instead line 933 (which approximates *L* 301) is expanded to four lines (M^2 778-81).

934.   *Sains Innocens:* Innocent I, Pope from 401-417 A. D.

938.   *engloute:* a good example of G. P.'s method of emendation: He alters *engloute* to *encloe;* cf. *L* 305, "nes anglutet": *A* "les encloe"; *P* "les asorbe." See Storey's note *ad loc. M** lack lines 937-38. *S* freely combines words in *o-e* and *ou-e* in a single assonance (see 931-33 for another example).

940.   *Li uns A[caire], l'autre:* ms. *Li uns ara del autre.* The unfamiliar name caused trouble for the scribe. Arcadius and Honorius, sons of Theodosius, were respectively emperor of the East (395-408) and of the West (395-423). For *M**'s troubles with this line, see the note to M^2 783.

960.   *respont:* another instance of *S*'s difficulty with verb agreement; the singular verb with a plural subject *(menestrés)* takes its agreement logically from *nus.* For a similar switch in person, see *Huon* 1655-56, *Dient François:* "Cil doit estre esbaudis; / Par lui ert certes, *je cuit,* li ans conquis." In M^1 602-603 there is a plural subject governing a singular verb. Of these lines Gatto-Pyko writes (p. 100): "Sujet au pluriel ... et verbe au singulier est trop fréquent au moyen-âge pour être corrigé. Cf. Williams, *Floriant et Florete,* p. 248, note 1873." So, for example, *L* 17, "des melz qui dunc i eret." See also Rutebeuf, "La Vie de Sainte Marie l'Egyptienne," 718.

962.   *pensif et ploreos:* G. P. emends to "et pensif et plouros" (cf. *L* 327).

966.   The scribe does not begin a new laisse here. The final deathbed interview between Alexis and his wife is new to *S*, as is the miracle of the church bells which ring in reply to the saint's dying wish. Both details are in keeping with the more romantic cast given to the story in this manuscript.

981.   For Alexis' connection with the cult of St. Boniface, see Mölk (1978), p. 343.

981b.   A line is missing; I have supplied 1283. G. P. writes, "Cil a en Rome une eglise mout bele."

1033. G. P., following *L* (st. 70), begins a new laisse here although to do so involves considerable emendation. G. P.'s version brings *S* much closer to *L*, although 1035 shows the difference between the two (cf. *L* 348, "En sum puing tint le cartre le deu serf"). For the inclusion of *espialt* in an assonance in *é*, see 1086 (assonance in *e-e*).

1038. The scribe did not indicate a new laisse here.

1046. *sonnent:* G. P. reads *sounent;* the MS gives *soñent.*

1048. Direct entry into heaven prior to the Last Judgment is the reward for sainthood, and the sight of this splendid angelic procession is a common detail in hagiographic narrative (for example, St. Anthony's vision of the soul of Paul of Thebes in St. Jerome's account, or in epic, the death of Roland in the *Chanson de Roland*).

1050. After this line G. P. adds "Vers le degré s'en courut a bandon," taken from M^1 (M^2 "de randon"). M^*, however, have no line equivalent to 1052, and two lines describing the movement to the stairs are unnecessary. *L* says merely "venent devant" (357, = *S* 1055).

1054. Laisse 87 is in the same assonance as is 86 (see also 73-74).

1056. *en grans afflictions:* the scribe's eye apparently slipped up one line. The correction (= *LP* 358), is Paris'.

1058. *saintisme on:* G. P. changes to *saintismes hom,* and in his apparatus indicates that the MS reading was one word, *saintismeon.* In fact the MS plainly has two words here. The scribe consistently has trouble with the nom. ending, *-s.*

1074. The miracle of the letter's flight is an apparent invention of *S,* perhaps to explain why the Pope himself did not read the letter but gave it to "un boen clerc et savie" (*L* 375).

1079-80. G. P. inverts these two lines, but the MS order appears to make better sense. The bride does not, in her humility, want anyone to know that under her fine clothes she is wearing a hair shirt (a detail found only in *S*).

1084. Laisse 90 is a *laisse similaire* with laisse 91.

1113. *Il esgardérent:* G. P. emends to *Ele esgarda.* The MS reading has both St. Innocent and the wife look around together, an interpretation supported by *ont* (1114), which G. P. must emend to *a.*

1114. *saint Ambrose:* *S*'s fondness for proper names gives rise here to a certain anachronistic piety. Saint Ambrose (Bishop of Milan, not "cancelers saint Piere") died in 397 A. D., four years before Innocent became Pope. In the Latin *vita* the letter is read by a cleric named Ethio, in *L* by "Li cancelers cui li mestres en eret" (376), in M^* by an unnamed cardinal. The name "Ambrose" shows *S*'s independence of the Latin tradition; the poet chose a familiar name from the approximate period.

1115. Without MS authority or change of assonance, G. P. begins a new laisse here on the basis of *L*. M^* continues the same laisse.

1118. The inclusion of the wife and the finding of the ring (1120ff.) are new to *S*, and are in keeping with greater interest in the girl in this version.

1123. *estoie:* it is possible that the MS reading preserves the Picard feminine participle here; for *yod* plus -ATA giving *ie*, see Gossen, 1970, 8.

1136. *soit:* = *sot;* for the graphy, see Gossen, 1970, p. 67 n. 23.

1142. There is no indication of a new laisse here.

1152. The last hemistich of this line, for which there is no equivalent in *LA*, approximates the last line of st. 80 in *P:* "cest dels lara enqui tuee."

1153.   *qui = cui* (Foulet, 1930, 254).

1165ff. Laisse 101 approximates *LAP* st. 84, while laisse 102 approximates st. 83. *M** omits them, as well as st. 82.

1193ff. *S* diverges here from the strophic order of *LAPV*, and the assonances of laisse 106 reveal some confusion. 1193 = the first line of strophe 91; 1194 = the second line of strophe 90. G. P. adds the rest of strophe 91 following 1193, and, as his laisse 110 (107 in this edition), the first line of strophe 90 before 1194. Laisse 108 = strophe 89. M^2 has a lacuna here (1002), and as a result gives only four lines to the mother; M^1 does not have a lacuna but develops the mother's speech quite differently from *LAPV*.

1202. *dolerouse:* G. P. emends to *desirouse* on the basis of *L* 456, *desirruse*. It looks as if the scribe or poet has conflated two lines at this point, for *V* reads:

> Anz ketousse sin fui mult desirouse
> anz kele ueisse mult enfui dolorouse.

1216. G. P., following *L*, st. 95, begins a laisse here, altering *desirée* to *desiré*, and *plourée* to *plouré*. If, on the other hand, the MS readings are retained, as I have done, the feminine past participles are admittedly grammatical errors. Another solution, which preserves the MS reading more closely (and which makes good sense) is to emend *el* (1218) to *ele:* she wept only for the good and nothing for *herself*. For the pronoun, see Foulet, 1930, 154-55. G. P. prints 1218 in roman type although it corresponds to no line in *L;* the closest approximation is *L* 475, "Pur felunie nient ne pur lastet" (a controversial line; see Richter, 1932). *AP* lack the line.

1219. Laisse 112 corresponds to strophe 96, laisse 113 to st. 98. Strophe 97 is missing in both *S* and *A; V* rearranges the order of strophes here.

1224. There is no laisse break here.

1230h A line seems to be missing which supplies the antecedent for *il* in 1231. See the critical note.

1234. After this line G. P. adds on the basis of *L* 499-500:

> Tot cil seinor et bel l'acoustumérent.
> Felix tot cil qui par foi l'honerérent.

M^1 reads (1223-35):

> Molt bielement le Diu serf atornerent
> Devant tout chiaus ki[l] aluec honerent
> Et ki le jor de bon cuer l'ounererent.

M^2 1038-39 reads (utilizing in 1038 the verb of *AP*):

> Mout belement le serf Dieu aprestérent.
> Boineuré tout cil qui l'ounererent.

In point of fact, *S*'s text makes the best sense of *any* version at this point. The next laisse or strophe opens with St. Innocent's violent denunciation of the excessive grief for Alexis' death. The lines omitted from *S* describe those mourning the saint as happy *(felix, LP)* or blessed *(boineuré, AM²)*. Therefore these lines contradict and weaken the effect of the Pope's outburst. In *S* his protest follows directly upon the description of the grief of the saint's family.

1236. *cose:* G. P. emends, perhaps rightly, on the basis of *LAP* to *noise. M** is lacking. After this line he adds. "Qui que soit doels a nostre oes est-il joie," a reworking of *L* 503.

1238. There is no capital indicating a new laisse here.

1241. This line begins with a blue capital *T*, indicating a new laisse.

1256. *gens:* an agreement problem again, a singular collective noun here taking a plural verb, *desirent.* G. P. emends to *gent.* But see Ruelle, *Huon,* p. 51, 36, for *-nt* as a singular ending.

1266. *S* here omits strophes 108, 109, 110. For a discussion of the ending of the poem, see Elliott, 1980.

1270. *refuses:* G. P. emends to *malendos,* commenting: "la vraie correction n'est sans doute pas *malendos,* mais je ne la trouve pas." See the note on *M²* 1071.

1272. There is no indication of a new laisse.

1290. *mesme:* G. P. conjectured, probably correctly, *setme* (cf. *L* 576, "Al sedme jurn fut faite la herberge").

1297. There is no laisse break, the scribe perhaps not noticing the change in assonance from *á-e* to *é (parés).*

1320. Before this line, G. P., following *L* st. 122, adds:

> Sains Alexis est el ciel sans doutance
> Ensemble o Dieu en la compaigne as angres.

The equivalent lines are lacking in *M**. This laisse, which approximates st. 122, follows the equivalent of st. 123 (laisse 133). For *bele pucele* G. P. emends to *et la pucele.*

VERS D'ALEXIS [M²]

1

Cha en ariere, au tans anchiseour,   [*112r*]
Foys fu en tere et justice et amor
Et verités et creance et douchour,
Mais ore est frailes et plains de grant dolour.
5 Ja mais n'ert teus* con fu as anchisours.
Ne portent foy li mari lor oisiors,
Ne li vasal feute leur signours.
Tous li mons est tornés en grans esrours;
Chu mauvais siecles ne doit durer lons jours.*

2

10 Al tans Noé et au tans Moÿset,
Et a Davy cui [Dieus] par ama tant,
Boins fu li siecles, n'arons mais si vaillant.
Vieus est et frailes, tous se va declinant.
Ne portent foy as péres li enfant,
15 Et li filleul vont les parins boisant.
Li justichier le lour Dieu malmenant,
Pour lui ne laissent le mal ne tant ne quant;*
Li signour vont leur moullier ahontant.
Joie et leëche va toute remanant;
20 Sous ciel n'a home qui de l'avoir ait tant
Qu'il ne si crieme del tans en avant.
Pres est li fins par le mien ensiant,
Car tous li biens del siecle va morant.*
En l'onor Dieu, le glorieus poissant,   [*112v*]

25 Ki nous cria trestous a son sanblant,
    Vous veul conter un essanple mout grant
    D'un saintisme home et d'un sien chier enfant.*

3

    Li D[i]us vassaus ot non Eufemïiens;
    Quens fu de Romme et mout boins crestïens,*
30 Et sages hons des autours ancïens;
    Tous jours mena grant tenchon sur paiens
    Et sainte eglise ama sur toute riens;
    De felonnie n'ot onques en lui riens,
    Et prist moullier puis k'il fu [anchïens].*

(4)

35 Puis conversérent ensanble longuement;*
    S'orent assés et or fin et argent
    Et vair et gris et vies vin et fourment
    Et bo[i]s et viles et rices tenemens,
    Et grant bien fisent a leur menue gent,
40 Et sainte eglise visitérent souvent.
    Mais d'une cose mout leur poise forment,
    K'il n'ont enfans, caït lor tenement.
    Dieu en apelent andoi parfitement:
    "Oiés, roys de glore, pur ton commandement,
45 Un fil me* done qui soit a ton talant."

5

    Tant li prient* par grant humilité
    Et en lour cuers en ont tant souspiré
    Et de lor iex tante larme plouré   [113r]
    Et ont as povres tant garniment doné
50 Que Nostre Sires, par la soie bonté,
    En regarda la leur grant charité;
    En le moullier proumist fecondité;
    Un fil leur donent,* si l'en seurent bon gré.
    De saint baptesme l'ont tost rengeneré;
55 Bel nom li donent sur le crestïenté.

6

Quant a le foy font l'e[n]fant apeler*
Li gentiex hons qui Diex le vaut doner
Et la dansele qui tant le pot amer,
Mout bien le fait nourir et alever
60 Tant qu'il fu teus* ke il puet bien aler.
Adonc le fisent a l'escole mener
Et l'escriture ensignier et moustrer;
En poi de tans sot bien lire et chanter
Et en latin mout sagement parler.

7

65 Quant l'enfes fu des ars mout bien letré[s]
Et des autours mout sagement fondés,
De mout chiers dras s'est mout bien acesmés.
Droit a le cour le roy s'en est alés;
Tant le servi par se humilité
70 Ki li a armes et garnemens dounés,
Et les hounours dont ses péres est casés
Li a rendues et des autres asés.   [*113v*]

8

Dont voit li péres jamais n'ara enfant*
Fors que chu seul que il par amoit tant,
75 Dont se pourpense del siecle a en avant;
Or veut qu'il pregne moullier a son vivant.
Si l'en a quise une mout avenant,
Fille a .i. conte redouté et poissant;
Cieus li otrie et mil livre d'argent
80 Et .i. castel asasé et manant.
Noument le terme de cel assemblement;*
Quant vint au terme,* se le font richement.
Mout en sont liet d'anbes part li parent
Et li maisnie ki a aus d'eus apent.
85 Sains* Alesins l'espousa vraiement,
Mais de cel plait ne vausist il noient;
Del tout en tout a a Dieu son talent;

Se lui loisist, il vesquist castement,
Mais li siens péres l'en coureche forment
90 Ki de cest siecle li quiert enconbrement.

9

Quant ses boins péres ot fait si aprester
Et ses barons venir et aüner
Et son palais mout ricement parer
Et fait des noces le premerain souper,
95 Li jours s'en va, si prent a avesprer;
Traient les napes, si vont tables oster   [*114r*]
Et le relief quellir et asanbler,
As pouvres gens departir et douner.

10

Ce dist li péres, "Biaus fieus, va toi coucier
100 Avec t'espeuse, Diex te doinst iretier."
Ne vaut li enfes son pére courecier,
Sus se drecha qu'il ne l'osa lassier;
Vint en la cambre, si se fist descaucier.
Li pére i fu et se femme au cochier*
105 La chambre font encenser et jonchier;
Tantost s'en issent,* si l'ont faite widier.
Sains Alesins regarda son moullier.

11

Quant li sains hons a le dame veüe,
Qui tant par est courtoise et bien creüe
110 Et couvoitouse et blance la cha[r] nue,
Et voit la chambre que si est pourtendue,
Dont li ramenbre de la celeste drue,
Le sainte eglise ke tant a maintenue;
A il cele amie* qui del ciel est venue
115 Pour coucier aveuc femme relenquist ne remue*

[LACUNA]

Dont crïent il mout s'ame se soit perdue
Et al juïse devant Dieu confondue.

12

"Ha Diex," dist il, "ki pour nous a sauver,
Ki en la virge te dignas aonbrer
120   Et en la crois te laissas tourmenter   [*114v*]
Pour nous kaitis pecheours racater,
Fai nous, chiers, tes commans si garder
Ke diables ne s'en puissent gaber.
Bien me cuida mes péres adouber
125   Quant il me fist ceste femme espouser;
S'or ne m'en fui, tout me veut afoler
Et en infer ou plus parfont geter."

13

Sains Alesins souspire mout forment
Et prie Dieu de cuer parfondement;
130   Il l'aime plus que nul sien tenement.
Se franche espouse apele tenrement,
Les escritures li despont saintement
Et si li blasme ceste vie forment
Et l'autre voie de glore li aprent.
135   Tant vaut parler o li tout belement
Ke tout soient couchiet communalement,
Et puis s'en fuira s'il peut tout coiement.

14

[T]ant le castie que le nuis est moiié*
Et le gaite est endormie et couchié
140   Et la pucele durement anuié,
Puis prent l'anel dont il l'ot engagié;
Deus pars en fait al espee fourbié.*
La dame en a la moitie baillié,
Et puis a l'autre desour lui estoiié;   [*115r*]
145   Se jamais a tant Romme aprochié
K'il resoit en la sale vautié
Qu'il recounoisse se femme et sa maisnié.

15

Dist la pucele, "Or sui mout esgarée.
La me reporte dont tu m'as aportée; *
150 Pour coi me laisses quant tu m'as esposée?
Demain serai de ta chambre jetée,
Puis m'en vai comme maleurée;
Tel honte arai, jamais n'iére honerée."
"Bele," dist il, "tu n'es mie senée.
155 Ceste grant joie tanra courte durée; *
T'arme ert el ciel de glore courounée,
Avec les angeles asise et alosée.*

16

"Franche pucele, par l'amor Dieu merchi,
Lai m'ent aler car tout sont endormi."
160 "Alés a Dieu," la bele respondi;
"Cil ert dolans qui t'a engenui,
Si ert la mére ki soef te nouri,
Et jou meïme qui t'avoie a mari; *
Hui verra[i] plait a grant deul departi,
165 Et comment quides que li miens cors t'oublit?
Se ne vous voi, je morai tout de fi.*

17

"Or t'en va, sire, ne te puis retourner; *
Hui verrai noces a grant duel desevrer; *   [*115v*]
Se ne te voi, n'arai mais mon cuer cler.
170 S'en ton consel le peusse trover
K'avekes* toi me laissaises aler,
Ja me veroies rikement aprester,
Tondre mes crins et chinces affubler
Et prendre eskerpe et bourdon acater.
175 Si servirai de ces dras relaver,*
Ensi que ja toi ne quier adeser,
Ne carnelment dalés toi converser."

18

Cil se depart, li cors Dieu le conduie.*
Al departir ensi la araisnie:
180   "Je te laïs, bele, Jesus te beneie;
Si te kemant a la virge Marie,
Ki des diables te port el garantie
Que mais ne puisse par lui estre honie."
A tant s'en torne, se fuite cuellie,
185   A vois chantant a s'onour deguerpie.*
De toute Rome k'il ot en sa baillie;
Mais Damedieu, le roy de ciel, merchi
De la pucele qu'il a si conversie
K'ele li doigne poesté et baillie
190   De Dieu servir tant que s'ame ait garie.
De tout cest plait ne set ses péres mie,
La soie mére qui doit bien estre fie   [*116r*]
K'il en sa cambre gesist dalés s'amie;
Quant il saront que il la deguerpie,
195   Si durement en ert Rome estourmie
K'ainc mais n'i fu si grans dolours oïe.

19

Sains Alesins vint a le mer fuiant;
As lices troeve une barge flotant
Que de passer se va apareillant;
200   Done son pris, au tref si tres courant.
Drechent lor voiles li maistre maritant;
Par le mer vont aforche najant.
Droit a le Lice quidant venir siglant,
Mais Dieu ne pleut ne le sien chier commant;
205   Uns vens lor vient sour destre costiant
Ki les enpoint .iii. C lieues avant,
Si qu'il aprocent de Jerusalem tant
Que de cel port ou il vienent najant;
I va on bien, ce trovons nos lisant,
210   En .i. seul jour sor .i. mulet anblant.
Savoir devés qu'ensi plot Dieu le grant.

20

Es vous a port saint Al[esin] venu,
Et de li barge fors a tere issu;
Vint au sepulcre ou Nostre Sire fu;
215 Fist ses prieres, si est confés rendus.
Un jour entir et deus [nuits] i estu[t],*   *[116v]*
Et au tierch jour vers flum Jordain s'esmut;
Si abaigniet sen propre cors tout nu,
Puis prent les paumes et le bourdon agu;
220 Si s'en repaire a Dieu rendant salu.
Droit a le Lice vint le cemin batu,
Mais je ne sai combien si arestu;
Ou k'il alast, servi Dieu et connut,
Et Nostre Sire li presta grant vertu,
225 Si le garda si comme le sien dru.

21

Quant li sires d'iluec se remua,
Droit a Assix la cité s'en ala
Pour une imaige c'on illuec li loa
Que li sains angles illuec figura
230 Ki a la virge le mesage nuncha
A icel tans ke il le salua;
Fist si l'imaige que bien le resanbla;*
Par .i. devenres* en Alsix le porta.
Li boins preudons que Damedieu ama
235 Tantost com il ens el moster entra,
L'imaige enclina, puis si s'age[noill]a,
De ses pechiés pardon requis li a;
Puis prist l'avoir que de Roume jeta,
As povres gens le parti et douna
240 Que onques maille sour lui n'en n'estoia.   *[117r]*

22

Quant li sires ot departi son avoir,
Avec les povres se vait ou renc seoir.
Rechoit l'aumosne quant il le peut avoir;

Si en erra vers Dieu par tel savoir
245 Q'ains ne retient de disner point au soir
Ne de souper ne vaut tant rechevoir
Dont el demain peüst repas avoir.
Tant a juné que tout a le vis noir;
Ne fait le char gaires de son voloir.
250 A Dieu servir met paine tout pour voir,
Et Nostre Sires l'en dona tel pooir
C'onques diables ne le pot dechevoir.

23

Or revenrai a chiaus de la contrée
Ki tel dolour ont pour lui demenée.
255 Li dame crie com femme foursenée:
"Fieus Alesin, douche rose honerée,
Dont te vient cuers de guerpir t'espousée
Ke je t'avoie si courtoise donnée?
Tel deul me fais ja serai foursenée."
260 Court en la chanbre, si la descourtinée;
Oste les pailles et le courtine lée.
Sa grande joie* est en dolour tornée;
Jamais n'en ert par homme comfortée.
"Canbre," dist ele, "mal fustes estorée;*   [*117v*]
265 Mout t'avoie ore gentement aornée;
Ja mais liece n'ert e[n] toi demenée."
De deul que l'a, ciet a tere pasmée,*
Mais ses boins sire l'en a bien relevée.

24

La demoisele regrete mout son dru,
270 Et la dame a son paile desvestu;
Andeus s'asient desous le marbre nu,
Si que tapi n'i ot ains estendu.
"Dieus," dist li péres, "chiers fieus com t'ai perdu!"
Respont la mére, "Pechiés le m'a tolu."
275 L'espeuse escrie, "Com petit l'ai eü."
Irie* en est, onques mais si ne fu.

25

Es vous l'espeuse dolante et esmarie;
Si est la dame au pié agenoullie:
La nue boce li a .iii. fois baisie
280 Et de ses larmes arousée et mollie.
"Dame," fait ele, "quant tes fiex m'a lasie,*
Or me retien en la toie baillie.
Pour soie amour que tant men a proie.
Damedieu ai caästé voukie
285 Que mais d'autre homme ne weul estre baillie."
O [l]e* la mére, contre li est drecie;
Tante fois l'a de pité enbrachie
Que toute en fu lassée et travellie.   [*118r*]

26

Li péres crie, "Que vous deceveroit
290 Dieu en la face jamais voi[t] ne veroit.
Quant mon enfant veus porter si grant foi
Dont est raisons, certes, que mieus t'en soit;
Or te serrai ou mes fieus se seoit
Et si tenras l'ounour que il tenoit.
295 Si te tenrai vers tous mout bien a droit
Ke s'il ert hons ki te moustrant destroit,
Jamais mes cuers nul jour ne l'ameroit."
Quant ele oï que li péres disoit
Al cordoan s'en vaut aler tout droit,
300 Mais li frans hons en ses bras le rechoit
Et se li baise andeus les iex destroit.

27

Dont prent li péres ses mesages courans;
Par maintes teres fait querre son enfant.
Droit* en Ausis s'en vinrent doi courant.
305 Sains Al[esins] a mué son samblant
Que ne le porent raviser li serjant,
Mais leur aumosnes leur va il demandant;

Il en dounérent, il le prent doucement,
Et s'en aoure Damedieu le poissant.

28

310 Li sers Dieu prent l'aumosne a messagiers;*
Si en aure Damedieu volentiers
De cel sien sers cui il est aumosniers;   [*118v*]
Ains fu lor sires, ore est lor prouvendiers;*
Tel joie en a que tous en est legiers.
315 Li serjant cerkent tous les jors les mostiers
Et les grans rues et les palais pleniers;
Il les poursieut d'encoste et par deriers,
Se lui fera de fuir nus mestiers.

29

Li serjant sont anuiiet de baer
320 Et de cherkier et de lui demander;
Chiés .i. bourjois sont torné pour disner,
Que hons ki va peut petit juner.
Il les poursieut ou qu'il les puist trouver;
Pour l'ocoison de l'aumosne rouver
325 Ala a l'uis loi raison escouter.
"Signeurs," dist il, "mout vous voi dementer."*
Et chil respondent, "Ne faisons a blasmer.
Perdu avons un gentil baceler,
Le fil au conte ki Roume ot a garder;
330 N'ot plus d'effans, si le pot bien amer,*
Tant qui li fist une femme espouser;
Mais il n'ot cure de tel vie mener,
Fuis en est en eschil outre mer.
Li pére en quide esragier et desver,
335 Li mére ausi nel peut entre oublier,
Ne le pucele ki mout le pot amer.   [*119r*]
Sous ciel n'a homme si li ot regreter
Ne li conviegne des iex du chief plourer.*
Or le cuidames chi aluec encontrer,
340 Mais ne le trovons ne n'en oüns parler.
Avoirs nous faut, nous estuet restourner."*

Dist li sains hons,* "Ne faites a blasmer."
A icel mot font la nape lever;
Prendent congiet, si pen[sent] du raler.

30

345 Quant Alesins les sent bien eslongiés
Lors set il bien qu'il est quites de l'en cergier.*
Ne vous sai deviser com il en est tres liés.
Tantost court en le glise, si ciet l'imaige au pié*

[LACUNA]

Que se loial espouse pardonne ses pechiés
350 Et que ses cors ne soit nul jour mais vergoniés,
Ne part ait de diable souduis ni engigniés,*
Ne d'omme carnel adesés ne touchiés.
Es vous atant a Romme les serjans repairiés;
Sel vont nonchier au pére qui jamais n'en ert liés.
355 Or poés bien savoir qu'il fu grains et iriés.

31

Li Dieus sers en Ausi est tot droit remanus;*
.xii. ans tous plains est si ensi maintenus
Que tout adés jeüt, sachiés, les piés tos nus,
Ne nus yviers n'i est si frois keus
360 K'il au mostier ne soit anchois venus   [*119v*]
Ke li prestres soit hors de son lit issus
Ne des matines li premiers caus ferus.
Ne se fait pas enparlés ni agus,
Souvent se taist com s'il fust trestous mus,
365 Et du diable s'est si esconbatus
C'onques ne peut par lui estre vencus
Tant c'uns maus mos* soit de sa boce issus.

32

Sains Al[esins] a sa car relenkie
Et en cest siecle itant forment honnie
370 Ke en sa bouche ne n'entre de pain mie

Se chascun jour par les wys ne le prie,
Et la cité par a si convoitie
Que mais n'estra * si peut pour lui guerpie,
Tout pour l'imaige k'est de sainte Marie
375 A cui il sert et par nuit et par die.
Grant paine met a deservir la vie
Qu'il aime plus que nule mainadie.

33

Quant li sains [a] * le bourc si enamé,
N'en istra mais qu'il puist en son aé;
380 Le saint ymaige dont je vous ai conté
Le coutre del moustier en a araisonné:
"Frere," dist ele, "je t'ai chi apelé
Pour .i. signour de grant nobilité
K'en cest vile a pour moi sejourné,   [120r]
385 .xii. ans esté en mout grant povreté.
Le biau service qui'l m'a presenté
A Nostre Sires mout keulli en gré.
Or va sel quier tant que l'aiés trouvé,
Car bien est drois ke cil de la cité
390 Cestui connoissent et sacent sa bonte."
Es vous le clerc forment espoenté;
Le marchié cerke et de lonc et de lé;
Saint Al[esin] a trois fois e[n]contré,
Mais vraiement nel quide ne ne set
395 Que teus hons soit de si grant dignité.
Maintes fois l'a lendengiet et bouté,
Fors du mostier sakiet et deskiré,
Et souduitour et pautonnier clamé.

34

Li clers revient a l'imaige courant:
400 "Dame," dist il, "par Dieu le tout poussant, *
Je l'ai mout quis et ariere et avant,
Mais n'en truïs nul qui soit de tel sanblant
Ki si soit dignes com vous m'alés contant."
Ele respont, "Tel peus trouver seant

405 Derier cel wys en son sautier lisant."
    O le li clers, cele part vient courant;
    Tout droit as piés li est keüs plorant:
    "Sire," dist il, "merchi pour Dieu le grant,   [*120v*]
    Ta sainte vie nous as celée tant
410 Que tout en sommes envers toi meserrant."
    Sains Al[esins] s'en vaut torner fuiant,
    Ne mais li clers la ert tout maintenant
    Et les canoines va illuec apelant;
    Si lor raconte sa raison en tranblant
415 De cel imaige ki li fist le commant
    Ke cel saint homme lor amenast avant
    Et ses bontés lor fesist entendant.

35

    Quant cil ouïrent le conte raconter
    Que Nostre Sires fist l'imaige parler
420 Par cel saint home counoistre et demoustrer,
    Communalement le corent aourer,
    Et si le veulent a enveske sacrer, *
    Mais il ne vaut soufrir et endurer.
    Or voit il bien com le veut honerer.
425 Et de grant fais del siecle recombrer:
    "Certes," * dist il, "chi ne veul mais ester,
    Car de rikeche ne d'orgeul demener
    Ne peut nus hom paradis acater."
    A mienuit lor escape li bers
430 Et vient fuiant droitement a le mer.
    Prete est li barje qu'il doit outre passer;
    Donne son pris, si se fait a louer.   [*121r*]
    Droit vers Corsaut * s'en quidiérent sigler,
    Mais Nostre Sires ne li laissa aler;
435 Vers son païs fist le barge tourner
    Et a .vii. lieues pres de Romme arester.

36

    Quant li sains hons voit Romme le majour
    Ou il fu quens desous l'empereour,

Dont set il bien et s'en a grant paour
440 Sel voit ses péres et li grant vavasor,
La soie mére qui mainte grant tristour,
Et la pucele o le gente colour, *
I[l] le prendront par grant force d'amor
Et l'enbatront en terriene honour. *
445 A orisons s'est couchiés de paour,
Si en apele Jhesu son creatour.

37

"He Dieus, Dieus", dist il, * "li fieus sainte Marie,
Se toi pleüst, je ne vausisse mie
Qu'en cest païs fust la barge vertie.
450 S'or me voit mes péres qui Romme a en baillie,
La moie mére qui pour moi est marie,
Et la pucele ke jou ai deguerpie, *
Et la maisnie ki si est envoisie,
Ke jou avoie si doucement nourrie,
455 Il m'enbateroient en ceste mortel vie,
Si me tauront la toie compagnie.   [121v]

38

"He Dieus," dist il, "biau Péres precieus,
Hui me deffen du diable engineus
Que de mal faire est adés si voiseus
460 K'il ne m'en bache en nul lieu perilleus
Dont vers toi soie coupaubes ne honteus.
Ce sai je bien, biaus Péres glorieus,
Ke mi parent sont forment corechous,
De moi veïr mervelles desirous.
465 A aus irai parler .i. mot ou dous;
Il ne[m] saront car tous sui povellous
Et mal baillis et desfais et hidous.

39

"Conduis me, sire, par un tel devisse
Ke ne soit m'ame perdue ne malmise

470 Ne en infer el fu ardent esprise.
　　Se je pooïe lor amosne avoir prise
　　Et la lor cose deveüe et esquise,
　　Lors m'en rirai faire le tien service
　　Tant que j'arai si ta grasse conquise,
475 Qu'ens en tien regne en sera m'ame mise."

40

　　[S]ains Al[esins] est issus de le mer;
　　Or se commenche par lui a pourpenser
　　K'a Romme ira son pére arasonner,
　　Que par griois le vaura apeler,
480 K'en son rommant ne le puist raviser,
　　Et sa prouvende li vaura demander.　　　　　　[*122r*]
　　Se Dieu plaisoit k'il le vausist donner,
　　Jamais de lui ne vauroit rennier,
　　Nis en sa sale une fois entrer,
485 Mais cha defors en un petit angler
　　La fera il, s'il peut, le sien lit estorer *
　　Si qu'il vera chascun jour au disner
　　Les grans dentiés par devant lui passer,
　　Non pas pour chou qu'il en veulle gouster,
490 Ains le fera sa bouche desirer.
　　En icel sicle veut le cors si pener
　　Et des pechiés si pourgier et munder
　　Ke ja diables ni sache que clamer.
　　Adont s'adoube pour lui atapiner,
495 Si va a Romme a son pére parler;
　　Tres or ira ses aumosnes rouver
　　Car ne si veut des autrui enconbrer.

41

　　Sains Al[esins] se met en abandon.
　　Et vient a Romme apoiant d'un baston.
500 Or pleust a Dieu ki vint a passion
　　Ke il son pére encontrast li preudon *
　　[Et] la soie mére droit devant le dongnon
　　De saint Piére l'apostre de predication. *

A messe i furent et a pourcession; *
505 De lor enfant mainent grant marison.
Il les salue * belement sans tenchon: [*122v*]
"Eufemiien, escoute me raison.
L'ostel te quier, pour Dieu et pour son non,
Et pour ton fil Alesin le baron,
510 Ke Damedieus ki gari Aaron
Et Moÿsen de le mer Pharäon
Et suscitas le cors saint Lasaron,
Te rende encore ton fil en sa maison."

42

Quant ot li péres le reclain d'Alesin, *
515 Tant forment pleure del biaus iex de son vis *
Que tous en fu moulliés li chiers samis.
Vers lui s'en tourne, si l'a a raison mis:
"Ostel auras, biaus frere pelerins,
Tout pour l'enfant pour cui le m'as requis; *
520 Ne te faura ne pains ne chars ne vins. *
Ke Dieus li mire tous chiaus en paradis
Ki le herbergent par estranges païs!
Or a esté .xvii. ans, kaitis,
Dolans pechiéres, ne sai s'est mors ou vis."

43

525 Es vous illuec dant Constentin errant,
Un per de Romme mout proisie et manant; *
Vers li s'aproche, se le va consellant:
"Biaus pelerins, c'onques n'alés avant.
O moi herberges, si feras con sachant;
530 Ne te faurai en trestout mon vivant."
Sains Al[esins] respondi maintenant: [*123r*]
"Sire," dist il, "je n'en ferai noient,
Car pelerins qui va par terre errant
Ne doit ostel pour riens aler c[hang]ant; *
535 Si herbeioit ciés cascun mendiant,
Ne doit guerpir pour autre mieus vaillant."

44

Or voit li mére ke chieus lor veut tolir;
Tant est dolente plus ne peut souffrir.
A ses deus mains le courut dont saisir:
540 "Sire," dist ele, "tu nous veus mal baillir;
Pour mon enfant que jou forment desir
T'ai herbegiet et tu nous veus guerpir."
"Ma douche dame, de chou n'ai nul desir;
Dieus herbert t'ame quant tu devras fenir
545 Et icelui que t'a a maintenir; *
Et a l'enfant pour cui me veus servir
Doinst Diex corage qu'il veulle revenir." *
O le li péres, * si geta un soupir.

45

Sains Al[esins] se gaita mout forment;
550 Le sien chier pére rapele doucement:
"Sire," dist il, "un petitet m'enten.
Je te priai l'ostel premierement
Pour l'amour Dieu, le Pére omnipotent,
Et pour l'[enfant] * dont je te voi dolent;
555 Sel m'otrias mout deboinarement.
Malades sui et enfers durement,   [*123v*]
Si ne puis mie monter el pavement;
Mais or me fai un poi d'abitement
Sous le degré ki du palais descent
560 Ou je puisse estre un poi pasivlement,
Et si me pais de chu menu forment
Ki du maingier remaint devant ta gent;
Ke Damedeus par son kemandement
Te rent encore ton fil en ton present."

46

565 Quant ot li péres du fil araisonner,
De ses biaus ix commenche a souspirer.
"Boins hons," dist il, "Dieus te puist respasser!
Tout pour l'enfant que je t'och chi noumer

Je te ferai et pain et char * livrer
570 Et .i. boin lit en ta chanbre * estorer.
Ke Dieus le veulle tous chiaus gueredouner
Ki bien li font et livrent a disner.
N'est mie vis quant ne veut retorner."
Ot le le mére, si commenche a plourer.

47

575 La mére pasme trois fois en .i. tenant.
Li pére va si ses mains detorjant *
Ke a la tere li sont keü si * gant;
Sains Al[esins] li rendi maintenant.
Quant il les vit si aler souspirant,
580 Irés en est mais il n'en fait sanblant, *
Car il se doute ne le voisent connissant.   [*124r*]
Del tout en tout a a Dieu son talent.
"Jhesus," dist il, "li Péres tous poissans, *
Quele amistés est de pére * et d'enfant!
585 Aide, Dieus, s'or me vont connissant,
Tel joie aront c'onques n'orent plus grant."
"Dieus," dist li péres, "s'or avoie .i. serjant
Ki me gardast cest pelerin vaillant,
Jel franchiroie son cors tout maintenant."
590 Un en i a ke se presente atant: *
"Jel garderai, sire, par ton commant, *
Mais nel ferai, certes, ne tant ne quant, *
Pour le francise ke me vas presentant,
Mais pour l'amour a ton gentil enfant
595 Le servirai a trestout mon vivant."

48

Atant en est li rices hons alés,
S'en a se femme et ses enfans * menés,
Et li sires est en la place remés.
Li boins serjans qui * il fu delivrés
600 L'en a mené tout droit sur les degrés;
De l'iaue caude li a ses piés lavés. *
"Sire," dist il, "un petit atendés

Tant k'uns li[t] vous soit chi aprestés
Et de blans dras bel et bien acesmés."

605 Dist li sains hons, "Amis, ne vous penés;
Jamais sur lit ne gera mes costés,   [*124v*]
Mais une nate, s'il vous plaist, m'aportés."
"Volentiers, sire, quant vous le kemandés."
Il li a quise, puis s'en est retournés;

610 Del tout en tout li fait ses volentés.
Vers son signour ne veut estre blamés
Ne envers Dieu pechieres ne danpnés.
Boin vit le jour que il fu commandés,
Car il en fu en glore courounés.

49

615 Puis a li péres souvent son fil veü,
Et cele mére en qui costés il fu,
Et le pucele ki tant l'a atendu;
C'onques nus d'aus ne le reconneü
Ne li ont [il] demandé ne querru

620 Ques hons il est ne de quel terre i[l] fu, *
Et li cors saint voirement n'en calu.
Son pére voit durement irascu;
A Dieu si tient par si tres grant vertu
Ke lu[i] ne cait de parent ne de d[r]u.

50

625 Signour, mout fait cis cors sains a prisier
Ki toute Romme avoit a justicier
Et ki pooit mener tant chevalier
Et converser o se gente moullier,
Et si s'ala sous le degré couchier

630 Pour l'amor Dieu a loi de pautonnier.
Ki vous vauroit tout son estre a cointier,   [*125r*]
Ja vous porroit molt durement annuiier.
Quant li serjant ki lui ot a garder *
Li porte fors du palais principel *

635 [D]e cel relief qui remaint du disner,
Un poi en prent pour son fain reposer

Et l'autre rent a chiaus qui·n ont mestier.
Chascuns .viii. jours * se fait communiier;
Tout si deduit repairent au sautier.
640 De Dieu servir ne reveut efforchier, *
Que li sains [hons] ne vaut entrouvliier,
Ains en fait tant com se peut mervellier.

51

Sains Al[esins] vint desous le degré;
Sa franche espouse l'a souvent revidé
645 Et de bien faire son consel demandé,
Mais voirement ne quide ne ne set
Que chou soit chieus pour cui a tant plouré.
Si felon serf li font mainte vieuté;
Il prendent l'iaue quant leur mains ont lavé,
650 Se li reversent par desous le costé,
Mais li sains a si son cueur afremé
Qu'il tout chou seffre par mout grant carité;
Jhesu en prie par grant humilité
Qui lor pardoinst par sa sainte bonté.

52

655 Tout l'eskernissent, sel tienent pour bricon;
De laveure li moillent son plichon,   [125v]
Et li Dieus sers se couche a abandon.
S'en proie Dieu par boine entension
Qu'il lor en face et mande et pardon,
660 Car il ne sevent s'il font ou mal ou non. *
Par une feste de saint Rouvison
S'estut li péres cha sus de son doingnon
Et voit son fil ki gist el grabeton.
Cele part vient, si l'a mis a raison:
665 "Biaus crestiiens, * ne savons mes ton non,
Et car nous di se de riens as besoin."

53

"Certes, biaus sire, bien a droit me noumés;
Chrestiiens sui vraiement apelés.

En saint baptesme me fu cis nons donnés;
670 Se tant sui boins que par moi soit gardés.
Mais jel crien perdre par mes grans ordeés; *
Trop ai errour, cis en soit aourés
Pour qui amor il m'est si aprestés;
Et si li rende l'enfant que tant amés."
675 "Boins ons," dist il, "quel me ramentevés?
N'est mie vis quant il n'est retournés."
Vait s'en li péres dolans et effreés;
Li fieus demeure par desous les degrés.

54

Es vous le mére fors de la sale issue
680 Et en la place devant son fil venue, *
Et li espeuse ki mout [est] irascue;   [*126r*]
Quant il les voit, tous li sans li remue;
Paour a que se mére ne soit apercheüe
Et par pechiet nel connoisse se drue;
685 De paour qu'il a tous li frons l'en tressue.

55

Souvent les voit venir devant lui et aler
Et par deseure lui et descendre et monter, *
Et de lor iex souvent mout tenrement plorer.
N'est tant hardis que il les ost arasonner
690 Pour chou que ne le puissent connoistre au parler. *
La dame prent l'espouse a apeler:
"Certes, pucele, forment me peut peser;
Cis hons n'a mie envers moi le cuer cler.
Tant ne me vit onques par devant lui passer
695 Que nule riens me vausist demander.
Ne vivra gaires, par le mien aësmer, *
Car mout le voi souvent coulour muer.
Dist la pucele, "Alons a lui parler,
Et de son non enquerre et demander.
700 S'or le laissons entre nous devier
Ke par son non nel sachomes noumer,
Trestous li siecles nous en porroit gaber." *

56

"Certes, pucele, jou i vois trop envis; *
Quant je le voi, menbre moi d'Alesin; *
705 Pour un petit nel resanble del vis.
Li deus de lui m'ochirra ains mes dis."   [*126v*]
Passa avant, si l'a a raison mis:
"Comment as non, biau frere pelerin?" *
"Crestiens, dame, ensi le vous plevis."
710 Tant s'aproicha que le pié li a pris.
Si li pria, "Merchi, li Dieu amis."

57

"Sire," fait ele, "de coi me vas priant?"
"Jel te ferai, bele dame, entendant.
Quant primes ving en ta grant court manant,
715 Si te priai l'ostel pour Dieu le grant
[Et] pour l'amour Alesin ton enfant.
Ains puis cel eure n'eus le cuer riant,
Ne ne venis par devant nu passant;
Se me veïs, n'en ralaisses plourant
720 De ton chier fil que vas ramentevant;
Mesfait vers Dieu, jel sai tout vraiement.
Pres est ma fins, car mout vois agrevant;
Sel me pardone pour l'amor Dieu le grant."

58

Tant a li freres et proiiet et rouvé
725 K'eles li ont et bonement pardonné
Ire et descorde et male volenté.
A tant s'en tornent, ni ont plus demouré,
Et il remaint tous liés sur le degré.
Dis et .vii. ans i a si conversé
730 Que autretant en Ausis la cité;
Ne but de vin ne de car n'a gousté;
N'onques nus hons ne devit sa bonté   [*127r*]
Ki li sera mout guerredoné.

Son boin serjant a lui a apelé
735 Et son talent li a dit et conté.

59

"Freres serjant, je morrai le martin;
Ne te lairai ne argent ne or fin, *
Car je n'ai mais fors que cest seul tapi,
Mais Dieus de glo[re], ki de l'iaue fist vin
740 Quant sit as noces le saint Archedeclin,
Il le te mire au jour que prendras fin.
Or me quier, frere, enque et parkemin;
Si escrirai un petit de latin." *
"Volentiers, frere, * biaus frere pelerin."

60

745 Tres itel eure qu'il ot en mainburnie *
Li a si bien se volenté sievie,
C'onques n'i ot mal talent ni envie
Et quant entent qu'il doit partir de vie
Et qu'il perdra sa sainte compaignie,
750 Quant chou entent, ne le veut courchier mie.
L'enke aporta et si li a baillie
Et si li a la chartre aparellie.
Li sains homs a escrite se vie,
Puis l'a esconsé em soie baillie
755 Que ne puist estre veüe et ouïe
Tres que li ame soit del cors partie.

61

Quant li sires a escrit et enbrievé,
Sa coupe dite et son pechiet plouré,   [*127v*]
Et pris le cors dont nous sommes sauvé,
760 Dont li tramist li Dieus de maisté
Li vois du ciel qui l'a reconforté:
"Vien ent, chier frere, li Sires t'a mandé *
Pour cui tu as le tiens cors si pené;
Si l'as servi selonc sa volenté
765 Qu'en paradis as ton lit estoré."

62

Puis i revint une autre vois huchant
Ke tout ouïrent, nis li petit enfant. *
Che dist la vois, "Pecheour nunsachant,
Car alés querre le Damedieu serjant
770 Ki gist a Romme entre vous languissant
Et doit del siecle partir maintenant. *
Si s'en ira o les angeles cantant,
Lassus el ciel el regne permanant.
Sous uns degrés le trouverés gisant
775 Sour une nate a loi de mendiant.
Se li proiés pour Damedieu le grant
Qu'il prist pour vous hui ceste jour en avant."
Cil ki l'entendent en vont tout soupirant
Et l'un a l'autre s'en revont demandant
780 Ou cil cors sains peut estre celés tant
Dont cele vois va par Romme nunchant.

63

Sains Innocens estoit donc apostoles,
Et dans Acaires * et ses freres Honores   [*128r*]
Estoient roy adont en cel tempore.
785 Si ont mandé de Romme tout l'estore
Et tout le pule, les riches et les povres, *
Si leur requiérent consel de cele cose.

64

Sains Innocens est mout espoentés.
O son clergie est a la tere alés;
790 Lisent lor saumes, si ont lor cans levés,
Et li doi roy ke je vous ai nommés
Et tous li pules ki leuc fu asamblés,
Et proient Dieu par grant humilités
Ki lor demoustre par les soies bontés
795 Ou cil sains cors porra estre trouvés.
Illuec ont tant de grant soupirs getés
Que Nostre Sires par les soies bontés

Les a tres bien par sa vois confortés.
Che dist la vois, "Par foi trop i estés; *
800 Sempres sera li cors sains deviés.
A le maison Eufemiien alés;
La est li sires dont vous ouï avés.
Par lui sera chu regnes gouvernés
Et tous li pules de Romme honerés.

65

805 Li apostoles fu mout saintismes hon;
De le vois Dieu entent bien la raison
Ke Eufemiiens, li quens de Pré Noiron,
Icel Dieu serf avoit en sa maison.   [*128v*]
En piés se dreche, se fine s'araison,
810 Et vient au cont[e], si l'a keut a tenchon.
"Certes," dist il, "fait as grant mesproison
Ke tant nous as celé cest saint baron
Dont Dieus nous fait si gente anontion.
Moustre le nous, si le deproierons;
815 De nos pechiés nous en petre pardon."

66

Eufemiiens a mout grant paour,
Car li apostoles et li enpereour
Et li abbé et li riche contour
Crient sur lui et mainent grant tabour:
820 "Moustrés nous tout le serf au creatour!"
"Baron," dist il, "merchi pour Dieu amor;
Je [vous] jurai sour la fierté majour
K'ains mais n'ouï parler de tel signour." *

67

Mais or ne caut de quanques il a juré
825 Ne fisent tant qu'il aient escouté;
En son palais en sont trestout entré.
Li apostoles et saintismes abbé
Courent devant, si ont bien encensé;

Et li doi roy e lor riche barné
830 Vienent avant iré et tres pensé. *
Si l'asisient as bans ki sont paré,
Et li frans cuens ki le cuer ot sené
Prent se maisnie a un consel privé;   [129r]
Ses conjura sour leur crestienté
835 Ke del cors saint li dient verité.
Il jurent tout ke nus d'aus ne le set,
Ne quident pas, li fol, li meserré,
Ke ce soit [il] qui gist sur le degré,
Ke tante fois ont mouilliet et gabé.

68

840 Li baron sont par le palais assis,
Et l'espousée ert a Saint Alexis.
"Sire," fait elle, "mout vous trouble li vis."
"Certes, pucele, cor * aproche ma fins;
Grant paour ai, pour voir le vous plevis.
845 Veés que chi a de ces noirs anemis;
Dolant celui ki en lor mains ert mis.
Dieus je·n ai jou de mes deus piés requis
Le saint sepulcre ou Dieus fu mors et vis.
Encore est chi li palme et li espis;
850 A mon cavech, quant en tere sui mis,
Le me plantés, si sera leus repris.
Diex te mire les biens que tu m'as fait toudis;
Enforche toi d'entrer en paradis.

69

"Franche pucele, pense de l'ensevelir;
855 Main[t] bien m'as fait, Dieus le te puist merir.
Tout mi parent erent a l'enfouir.
Mes péres i ert, ja n'i porra fallir;
Ma boine mére ki bien me fist nourir   [129v]
Et une dame ke je deuch mainburnir.
860 Mout fu dolante quant vint au departir."
Ot lui le bele, si jeta un soupir.

70

"Sire," fait ele, "ou sont cil tien parent?
Quant il veront a ton definement
Dont sont il chi voisin pr[o]cenement?"
865 Ne pot parler ne respondre noient,
Car l'ame en est alée douchement.
Com boin fu nés qui a celui se prent,
Ki a siens sers itel merite rent,
Li angele sont illeuc tout present
870 Ke l'ame enportent vers le ciel liément.
Li saint de Romme sonnent communaument,
Si que nus hons ni sace ne n'i tent,
Mais de lor gré sonent tant doucement
K'ains mais ne furent oï tant belement.
875 Cant la bele ot cel miracle tant gent,
Ens en son cuer se plaist mout et repent
K'ele ne l'ot revidé plus souvent,
Et li serjans ki tant l'amoit forment
S'en keurt au pére, se li dit coiement.

71

880 Li boins serjans qui li pére ot tan chier *
Le court au pére, sovanet consellier: *
"Damedieus a rekeulli ton paumier;
.x.vii. ans sont passé tout entier   [130r]
Ki le m'a fait sous un degré gaitier;
885 Ains une fois nel pauch faire bainier,
N'ains puis ne vaut autre chose au couchier
Fors une nate et un poi d'estramier.
N'onques nul jour nel seuch tant anuiier
C'onques vausist fors une foys mongier;
890 O le sien Dieu toudis a graciier." *

[LACUNA]

Belement ist de son palais plenier
Si qu'il n'i maine serjant ne escuiier;
Devant son fil se vait agenoullier

Cui vaut le brief estraindre et enpunier.
895 Il tent le main, s'il vaut a lui sacier,
Mais li cors sains ne li vaut pas lassier.

72

Es vous le pére dolent et esgaré.
Laisse son fil si com il l'a trouvé;
Si remonta sus el palais listé;
900 A haute vois lor a sour tous crié:
"Uns pelerins gist mors sous mon degré;
.x.vii. ans a o nous conversé,
Mais si nous a tant son estre celé
Ke nus de nous ne devit sa bonté,
905 Et tient un brief en sen puing enfermé;
Je le vaul prendre mai[s] il le m'a veé.
Certes, bien sai qu'il m'a keulli en hé, *
Car malement ai envers lui esré
Quant plus ne l'ai veü et revidé.
910 Sire apostoles, vien cha pour l'amour Dé,   [*130v*]
Et si me donne consel de verité."

73

Li apostoles fu mout saintismes hon;
Si escouta del pére la raison
Et des angeles entendi l'araison
915 Ki enportent l'ame a grant porcession.
Vers le degré en corut de randon
Et apres lui tout chil autre baron.
Il ne le noument car ne sevent son non; *
Par devant lui chient a orison
920 Et si se misent en grant affliction.

74

A vois s'escrient li doi roy par vigour:
"Merchi, chiers freres, par le toie dochor, *
[C]i devant toi sommes doi pecheour; *
En icel siecle nous fait Dieus tele honor

925   Ke desous lui sommes gouverneor,
       Mais l'apostole traions nous a signour
       Et sour tous autres et maistre et doctor.' *

75

       Quant l'apostole ot l'orison oïe
       Ke li doi roi ort pour lui †oubliet,*
930   En piés se dreche, s'a la soie fenie,
       Sour le cors saint s'a baissé et humielie.
       Si a le chartre de sa main rekeullie*
       Et il li a doucement consentie.
       Il le desploie, si va lire se vie,
935   Mais ne plaist Dieu ne se mére Marie :
       Hors de ses mains li est esvanuie
       Et en el saim la pucele lanchie.*   [131r]

76

       Chi peut on bien veoir et escouter
       Ke mariaiges fait forment a garder.
940   Quant a le mére ne vaut la chartre aler
       Ne a son pére caoir ni arester,
       Mais sour l'espouse le fist Dieus a voler,
       Pour chou k'il vaut ensignier et mostrer
       Ke cascuns doit se femme honerer
945   Et les dames lor signours bien garder,
       Et k'il ne fait tres bien se peut fier
       Ke ens infer les convenra aler.

77

       Or fu li chartre sour l'espouse arestée ;
       A l'apostole en est tantost alée.
950   "Sire," fait* ele, "je sui mout esgaré[e]."
       "Bele," dist il, "beur fustiés onques née.*
       Toi est la chartre, car Dieus* le t'a donnée,
       Et li cors sains ki le t'a presentée.
       O le fai lire quant a toi est alée
955   Ou qu'il te plaist doit estre livrée.

Ele esgarde les clers de la contrée;
Un cardounal a la chartre livrée.
Cis lit le lettre et il l'ont escoutée
De cel ymage q'en Auxis ot trouvée;*
960 Lors a le vie de chief en chief contée,
Et son pére a et sa mére nommée
Et la pucele ke il ot espousée,*
Et le moitiet de l'anel ont trouvée
Ens en la chartre mout bien envolepée,   [*131v*]
965 K'il departi au trenchant de s'espée,*
Dont se moitie li ot rekemandée.
On li demande, ele l'a aportée
Et l'une part a a l'autre ajoustée,
Et Nostre Sires l'a mout tost resaudée.
970 Illeuques eut tante larme plourée
Et tante barbe desachie et tirée,
Ains puis que Romme fu primes estorée
N'i ot il mais si grant dolour menée.

78

Quant ses chiers péres ot le brief et entent*
975 Ke c'est ses fieus qui leuc gist si viement,
Sa blanche barbe detire fort et tent,*
Et puis s'escrie mout angusseusement:
"Fieus Alesins, mout me fais or dolent;
Jamais .vii. jours ne vivrai longuement!"

79

980 Ce dist li péres, "Ahi, fieus Alesin,
Encore wy [main] t'atendoie pensis;
Cuidoie que deusses a moi repairier vis*
Pour conforter les tiens dolans amis.
Mout m'esmervel ou tu tel cuer fesis
985 K'ains une fois servis ne te fesis."

80

A haute vois a li pére escrié:
"Fieus Al[esins], quel deul m'as demoustré!

Com male garde eus desous mon degré;
Dolans pecieres, com euc le sens desvé
990 Quant en tant jours n'a[i] mon fil ravisé.

81

"Fieus Alesin, com dolerous mesage*   [*132r*]
A quel tourment as usé ton aage?
Comment eüs si viel ton haut lignaige
Et t'espousée et ton riche barnaige*
995 Que tant jours as esté a tel hontaige?
Tel deul me fais, a poi d'ire n'esrage.

82

"Fieus, ki tenra tes larges iretés
Et mes aleus et mes grans fremetés
Et les palais dont jou avoie assés?
1000 Pour toie amour m'en estoie penés
Qu'apres ma mort en fusses honerés."*

83

Quant la mére a le dolour entendue,*

[LACUNA]

"Mout m'esmervel comment li cuers me dure,
Ke il ne part de deul et de rancure.
1005 Cant chi voi mort toute ma porteure,
Jamais n'aurai, certes, de joie cure."

84

Par mi le presse estes vous la pucele.
Ses crins sachant et tirant se maistele.*
Par mi le cors fust keüe la bele,
1010 Quant l'apostoles le retient et rapele.

85

L'espouse escrie com femme foursenée:*
"Sire Alesin, com longe demorée!
T'ai atendu en ma cambre celée
Ou me laissas* dolente et esgarée.

86

1015 "Sire Al[esin], maint jour* t'ai esgardé
Et tante larme pour le tien cors ploré.
Se te seüsste cha sus sous le degré
O[u] as jeü en si grant povreté,*   [*132v*]
Je ne laisse pour trestout cest regné
1020 K'ensanla o toi n'eusse conversé."

87

Dist la pucele au gent cors precious:
"Ou trouvas tu le cuer si mervellous*
Que me veïs devant toi par tant jors
P[o]r le tien cors mener si grant dolours
1025 K'ains ne t'en prist ne secours ne amours?

88

"Or par sui, sire, ceüe en vevé.
Jamais n'arai, certes, autre espousé,
Ains servirai le roy de maïsté
K'en l'autre siecle en la vraie clarté
1030 Puissent nos ames avoir societé."

89

Mout le regrete cieus ki lui engenra,
Sa boine mére ausi ki le porta,
Et la pucele ki tant forment l'ama;
Ains puis cel eure ke seule le laissa
1035 A homme nul fors a lui ne pensa.

90

Endementiers que chu troi le criérent,
Li apostoles et li roy ki la érent
Mout belement le serf Dieu aprestérent.
Boineuré* tout cil qui l'ounerérent.

91

1040   Dist l'apostoles, "Signour ke ichi sommes,
Chou est folie ke tel deul demenommes,
Dont en avant si grant joie atendommes;
Levés le sus et si nous en alommes
Dusque au moustier ou poser le devommes.

92

1045   Atant le prendent, si ont laissiet le cri;   [*133r*]
Cantant l'enportent car bien l'a deservi,
Et si li prient qu'il ait d'aus tous merchi.
N'estut semonre chiaus ki l'eurent oï:
Tout i coururent, nis li enfant petit.

93

1050   Nus hons n'i ose estoussir ne esgondre,
Mais trestout penssent a lire et a respondre:
Par mi ces places leur vienent a l'encontre.
Ne dus ne quens ne set par [mi] deronpre,
Ne de quel part il puissent passer outre.

94

1055   Dist l'apostoles, "Tout sommes enconbré.
Pour cest cors saint que Dieus nous a moustré,
Liés est li pules ki tant l'a desiré;*
Or en vient tant s'il ne sont retourné
Ke nous serons estaint et afolé."

95

1060 Entr'eus en prendent un mout grant parlement;*
De lor tresor* prendent l'or et l'argent,
Si l'ont geté devant le povre gent,
Car pour chou quident avoir desconbrement.*
Ke caut de chou quant ne leur vaut noient,*
1065 Mais au saint cors ont trestout lor talent.*

96

Onques a Romme ne fu tel joie ouïe*
A icel jour a povre ni a riche
Pour cel cors saint ki l'ont en lor baillie.
Che lor est vis que ce soit Dieus meïsme;
1070 Tel joie en font ke nus nel porroit dire.

97

Sours ne contrais, awles ne liepprous,*
Ensourketout ne li palasineus,*   [*133v*]
K'ains nul n'i ot tant portant grant dolour*
N'en soit garis au saint cors glorious.

98

1075 Auquant i vont, aucant si font mener;*
Si vraie espesce lor vaut Dieus demostrer;*
Ki vint plorant, cantant l'en fist aler.*
N'i a enferm de cel enfremeté*
S'il vient a lui, n'en revoist tous sanés.
1080 Grant joie mainent cel ki la sont sané.*

99

Sains Bonifasces, qui martir on apele,*

[LACUNA]

Illeuc enportent* saint Al[esin] en tere.
Mout gentement le servent et governent.*
Boineuré ki tel signour herberguent.*

100

1085   Aiiés,* signour, cel saint homme en memore,
       Se li proiiés pour ki nous assole*
       Et que·n cest sicle nous i otroit si grant joie
       Et ens en l'autre del regne Dieu le glore.

101

       Et de celui ki le romant escrit.*
1090   A Dieu proions que il en ait merchi*
       Et la soie ame en meche en paradis*
       Avec le nostre et de tous nos amis,
1093   Pour la proiiere au boin saint Alesin. Amen.*

11. il; Dieus *M¹ (LAPS)*.
23. morant / En lounour dieu le glorieus poissant / En lonor Dieu.
26. .conter.
28. dus.
34. auques siens *M¹M²*.
38. bos. *G. P.*, bors.
56. efant.
65. letre.
92. aunes, s *erased and* r *written above*.
110. cha.
138. Cant, *M¹*, tant.
155. tanras.
164. verra.
216. deus i estu; .ii. nuis i estut, *SM¹*.
236. ageloigna; lla *written in above*.
243. avoirr.
247. pas; re *written in above*.
266. e toi.
286. O de.
287. la *de* pite, de *written above*.
290. voir.
309. dame dieu dou le.
311. deme, a *written in above*.
312. cel sien seus.
344. pent, *G. P. emend*.
347. Ne vous vous sai.
370. pain, de *written in above*.
378. li sains le.
393. e tre.
443. I le.
466. ne saront.
476. Mains.

502. La soie mere; *M¹*, et puis sa mere.
534. cachant.
545. tas.
554. amour.
603. li vous.
609. Il li q'se, a *written in above* li.
619. ont demande.
620. i fu.
624. Ke lu; de deu.
635. Que cel.
641. sains ne.
645. demander.
681. mout irascue.
714. primes voit ving.
716. Que.
739. de glo.
792. Et li tous li pules.
807. quens prenoiron, de *written in above*.
810. aucont.
822. je jurai; *M¹*, je vous jurai.
838. soit qui.
840. le paisale palais.
855. Main bien.
864. prcenement.
906. mail.
923. Ki; *M¹ missing, S*, ci.
928. lorison fenie oie.
950. esgare.
981. Encore wy tatendoie.
990. na mon.
1014. laissas en ma canbre dolete.
1024. Par.
1053. par V deronpre.

ALEXIS M^2

NOTES

5. G. P. reads *tens*; *u* and *n* are usually indistinguishable in M^2, but here the *u* is unmistakable; *teus* is supported by M^1 as well as by *LAP, tel.* Lacking in *S*.

9. M^1 reads, "Cis siecles est malvais, tornés est al desos." M^2 here is closer to *S*, "Fraisle est la vie, ne duërra lons jours" (19). The reading of M^2, avoiding the repetition of *tornés*, seems preferable.

17. The phrase *ne tant ne quant*, not found in M^1 in this laisse, occurs in *S* (Laisse 2), "Qui de mencoigne n'i a ne tant ne quant."

23. Lacking in M^1; compare *S* 22, "S'est empierés et li biens va morant." Of the other MSS, only P^1 also reads *morant*, the rest having *remanant*.

27. An alexandrine.

29. The scribe begins laisse 3 at this line with a capital *Q*.

34. Both M^1 and M^2 read *auques siens*; *Q*, however, has the correct reading, *anciens*.

35. No indication of a new laisse, although M^1 does begin one here, but *S* does not.

45. The reading of M^1, *nous*, is preferable to M^2, *me. LAPS* read *amfant nus done*.

46. $LAPSM^2$, *prient*; M^1 *deproient (depriérent, Q)*.

53. *donent:* here a singular form; see the note on *S* 1256.

56. M^2 here fails to give the saint's name, and as a result the saint is not named in until 107. M^1 54 reads, "Dant Alexins ont le fil apielé."

60. G. P. transcribes *tens* for *teus* (see note on l. 5). M^2 consistently spells the word for 'time' or 'world' *tans*, and in the MS the *u* is clear.

73. *LAP* also begin a new laisse here but *S* does not.

81. $LAPSM^1$ all begin a new laisse, but the scribe of M^2 does not indicate a change, rhyming *-ant* and *-ent* interchangeably.

82. *Terme* is also the reading of the fragment P^2.

85. *S* also reads *Sains*; M^1, *Mais*, emended (silently) by G. P. to *Dans*. Gatto-Pyko also emends to *Dans*, giving the MS reading in her notes.

104. M^2 is here closer to *S* than is M^1; *S* 117, "Li pére i fu et la mére au coucier" (M^1 101, "la mere au vis fier").

106. M^1 is here closer to *S*, reading, "Et quant (*S* 120, quant) s'en issent" (103).

114. A mistake? M^1 reads "S'il cele amie."

115. There appears to be a lacuna in both M^1 and M^2.

138. M^1, *tant*, a better reading. The mistake might have arisen if the scribe's exemplar had had a lower case letter here, since lower-case *c* and *t* are easily confused. *moiié* (and the rhyme words of the subsequent lines) are feminine; see introduction: Phonology.

142. M^2 is closer to the tradition of other versions than is M^1 which omits all mention of the sword ("II. pars en fist par merveille boidie," 138).

149. After this line M^2 omits a line contained in both S and M^1: "Que querras ore in estrainge contree? / Pour coi me lais quant tu m'as espousee?" (M^1 147-48). The order is reversed in S.

155. After this line S (174) and M^1 (154) read, "A Diu te tien, si devien s'espousée."

157. Here M^2 omits 150 lines contained in M^1, including the *planctus* addressed by the soul to the body. The lines are lacking in Q (and S), suggesting that they may be original to M^1.

163. M^2 here agrees with S ("qui t'avoie a mari," 292); cf. M^1, "qui soëf te chieri" (312).

166. Missing from M^1, the line paraphrases S 296, "S'encor ne [t'] voi, de duel m'estuet morir."

167. M^1 omits the first three lines of laisse 17. In S these lines are part of *laisses similaires*; M^2 recapitulates the last three verses of laisse 16 in the first three of laisse 17. "Or t'en va sire" forms the first half of S 297, "ne te puis retorner," the second hemistich of S 298.

168. Equals S 302.

171. M^1, *ensamble*, is closer to S than M^2, *avekes*. Q follows M^2: "car me lessiez aller: / Sil vous plest, avec vous..." (32b).

175. *relaver* = S 312; cf. M^1, *a laver*. MS D of the Q-family reads *relavery*, the others *luvery* (33c).

178. M^2 here inserts two lines before Alexis' response, which directly follows the bride's offer in M^1 and in S.

185. In S Alexis is happy to have slipped away unnoticed but weeps at the pain he knows he is causing his family (see the discussion in the introduction). Lines 185-88 are not found in M^1 and G. P. indicates a lacuna. Q here (35a) paraphrases 185.

216. After this line, M^2 omits a line found in both S and M^1, "Qu'il ne manja ne sa bouce ne but" (S 347, M^1 359). Q also mentions Alexis' fasting.

232. M^2 omits the name of the statue *(Mariien)*, given by M^1 in the following line and by S 374-75 *(Marie)*.

233. "Par .i. devenres" = S 377; for a discussion of the breakup of a potential formula in M^1 at this point, see Elliott, 1981. From here through 277, M^1 and M^2 diverge significantly. The details contained in M^1 do not come from S.

262. With M^2's reading of *joie*, compare S 415, *ricoise, LAP, honur*. The line lacks in M^1; cf. Q 31c, where, in the interview between Alexis and his bride, the girl says, "la joie d'ier tourna a grant misere!"

264. M^1 omits the mother's speech to the bedroom (264-66; S 417-19), as does Q.

267. M^2 is closer to S than is M^1; S 420, "Tel duel en ot"; M^1 413, "Ha icest duel."

276. *Irié* is feminine, *-iée* being rare in Picard; here the word means "sad."

281. In *S*, the wife's request to remain with Alexis' family precedes the brief laments.

286. This line, not in *M*[1], is necessary for the sense and fills the lacuna signaled there by G. P. and Gatto-Pyko. For *O de* G. P. conjectured *Ot li*, but for O *[l]e*, cf. 406, "O le li clers," where *le* refers to the feminine statue. *O* is 3 pf., *oïr;* cf. *Huon de Bordeaux*, 346n.; in *Huon* the verb form is used exclusively in the expression, *O le*. Ruelle writes: "Le graphie *o* pour *ot* ne m'est connue que par les nombreux passages de *Huon* où elle figure" (p. 397). *Huon* is also in Picard.

304. *Droit:* the only earlier MS containing this preposition is *A; L* reads *jusque an, P, desque en,* and *S dedens* (*M*[1] 449, "Droit en Alis").

310ff. *M*[1] omits 310-11, while 312 becomes the last line of the preceding laisse. The effect in *M*[1] is to eliminate the narrative repetition (and linking of laisses) contained in *LAPSM*[2].

313. See the note to *S* 474.

326. In *S* the messengers, overheard by Alexis, tell their story to the innkeeper and his wife. *M** eliminates these characters, having the messengers speak to Alexis himself, an alteration which heightens the pathos and dramatic tension of the scene. *M** could be used to fill in the lacuna in *S. Q* retains the host (73a).

330. *M*[2] is closer to *S* than is *M*[1]; cf. *S* 486, "sel pooit mout amer," *M*[1] 476, "molt le doivent amer."

338. In the first hemistich *M*[1] is closer to *S* than is *M*[2] (*S* 488, "esteuce," *M*[1] 448, "esteuve"); in the second, *M*[2] = *S*, while *M*[1] reads "d'ans .II. les ieus plorer."

341. Cf. *S* 489, *M*[1] 487, "Avoirs nous faut, n'avons mais que donner."

342. *M** reads "Dist li sains hons," although both G. P. and Gatto-Pyko emend to "Dist li borgois" (*cf. S* 491, " 'Dius,' dist li ostes"); the attribution of these lines to Alexis, however, is defensible since, in *M*[2] and *M*[1], unlike *S*, the host plays no further role.

346. The next thirteen lines (all of laisse 30 and two of the first three lines of 31) are alexandrines, with the exception of 352 and 357. 357 has eleven syllables, ten if *si* and *ensi* are elided.

348. There appears to be a lacuna following this line in *M**.

351-52. The order of these lines is reversed in *M*[1]

356ff. *M** is more informative about this stage of Alexis' career than is *S*. In *S* the poet, following *LAP*, declares (509-10): "Dis et .vii. ans ainc rien n'en fu a dire; / Pena son cors en Damedieu service." The epic phrase used here by *M*[2], ".xii. ans tous plains," can be paralleled in *S* 637, ".vii. ans tous plains." *M*[2]'s .xii. appears to be an error (but see 385); *A* also makes a mistake in numbering at this point, reading "dix ans" in its equivalent for line 357.

367. *M*[1] 514 reads "Que uns seus mos"; *Q* 81d; "Nul mauvais mot," reveals its filiation with *M*[2].

373. *estra:* a future formed on the inf. *estre;* cf. Fouché, 1967, p. 424.

378. Emended on the basis of *M*[1] 524, "Quant li sains a le borch si enamé"; the auxiliary verb is needed, and without it the first hemistich contains only three syllables.

400. *Q* here follows *M*[2]: "Dame, par Dieu le tout puissant" (87a); cf. *M*[1] 546, "Dame, dist il, par tout vois espiant."

422. *sacrer:* cf. *Q* 90d, "Il le vourent evesque beneir et sacrer"; *M¹* 567, "evesque alever."

426. *Certes,* the reading of *M**, reflects *L* not *S* (which has "E Dieus," 575). The second hemistich of *M²*, on the other hand, reproduces *S; M¹* substitutes *quier* for *voel.*

433. There is little agreement among the *Alexis* manuscripts as to the saint's hoped-for destination; *LA* read *Tarsun* (the location given in the *vita*), *P*, *Romme* (a mistake), *S*, *Troholt*, and *M** *Corsant*, *Q*, *Coursant.* Gatto-Pyko explains *Corsant* (<CORPU SANCTU) as "relique = Jérusalem?" (p. 100).

442. *M²* omits this line: the poem makes better sense with it.

444. *Q* here follows *M²*, "en terrien onnour" (94d); cf. *M¹* 588, "en la terre a honor."

447. For the first hemistich, see *S* 602, " 'E Dius,' dist il"; *M¹* reads "Haï, dist il" (591); *SM²* are preferable. The line in *M²* is an alexandrine.

452. Cf. *S* 619, "que je lor ai guerpi" (also *LAP*); *M¹, delaisie;* cf. *S* 1012, "que jou ai deguerpi."

486. In *M¹* this passage is put into the mouth of Alexis himself; it expands even more than the rendition in *M²* on the details of Alexis' self-inflicted temptation (see the introduction). The line in *M²* is another alexandrine.

501. *Q* 98c follows *M²:* "Il encontra son pére qui estoit mout proudon"; *M¹* 648, "encontrast li frans hom."

503. *M¹* here closer to *S* than *M²:* *M¹* 650, "Del mostier viennent saint Piere el Pré Noiron"; *S* 662, "Del mostier vienent saint Piére le baron."

504. This line (= *S* 663) omitted from *M¹*.

506. *M²* appears to paraphrase *S* 665a, "Il l'apela," while *M¹* 652 substitutes a new idea, "Il vint avant."

514. *le reclain d'Alesin:* cf. *Q* 100a, *le reclain Alexis; M¹* 659, *d'Alesin le sien fis.*

515. *vis:* cf. *Q* 100b, *vis; M¹ fron* (like the preceding line, rhyming in *-on*).

519. *requis:* cf. *Q* 100d, "puisque l'avez requis"; *M¹* 665, "cui j'ai souef norri."

520. In *S* this line forms part of Constentin's invitation to Alexis.

526. *S* offers a somewhat similar identification of Constantine, "Uns rices hom iert la, [dans] Constentins" (681); cf. *Q* 104a, "Li uns des pers de Romme c'on nommoit Contantin"; *M¹* omits the line.

534. *riens:* nom. for obj.; see Foulet 1930, 398. *M¹, cangant* makes better sense than *cachant; S* assigns a different speech to Alexis, and there is probably a lacuna in that MS at this point.

545. *S maintenir, M¹ mainburnir.*

547. *S* and *M¹* both read "Doinst tel coraige que il puist revenir" (*S* 713). *Q* appears to reflect this line in one given to the mother (106d), "Doint a mon fiex courage qu'il puisse revenir." MS *P* of the *Q*-family, however, reads "quil veulle revenir."

548. *S* and *M¹* both contain *mére; péres* may be a mistake (confusion between the two is not uncommon).

554. *enfant,* MS *amour: M¹*'s "pour l'enfant" is better; cf. *S* 721, "pour cel enfant." The scribe's eye may have strayed up to 553, "Pour l'amour Dieu."

569. *char:* M^1Q unite here against M^2, as Eufemien offers Alexis "et pain et vin"; *S* 726-27: "Herberc aras et pain et car assés, / Et puis del vin quant vous boire en vaurés."

570. M^2Q, *chanbre;* M^1, *angle.*

576. M^2 closer to *S* 733, "Li pére en va ses mains si detorjant"; M^1 728, "Li peres va aussi ses mains torgant." *Q* omits the episode of the gloves.

577. *S, si;* M^1, *li.*

580. $M^2 = S$ 745; cf. M^1 732; "mais n'en fait nul samblant."

583. Cf. *S* 736, "vrais pére tous poissans"; M^1 735, "qui mains en Orient."

584. *S* 737 here also reads *pére,* but M^1 and Q (wrongly) give *mére* (see note on 548). The following two lines in M^1, missing from M^2, paraphrase the subsequent lines in *S.*

590. M^2's reading, *atant,* is unique; other MSS give *avant.*

591. Here M^1 contains a unique reading, *talant,* the other MSS having *commant.*

592-95. The servant's disinterested reason for caring for Alexis is (apparently) an invention of M^*; not in *S. Q* develops this idea even more explicitly (113b-c): "Je le garderai bien, non pas pour vostre argent; / Mez pour vostre chier fils que j'amoie forment."

597. *enfans* makes little sense since we are told that Eufemien had no other children, but cf. *Q,* "son fiex" (114b). M^1, *barons* is better. The error might have been caused by a poet having access to the *vita* at some point; the Latin texts refers on a number of occasions (e.g. 44, 52) to Eufemien's *pueri* — his servants.

599. *qui = cui.*

601ff. These details of the servant's care of Alexis are an apparent invention of M^*. At 604, *Q* follows M^2, *blans dras* (115d); cf. M^1 761, *uns linceus.*

620. The reading of M^*, "et (M^1 ne) de quel terre il fu" (M^1 tere fu), reflects *L* alone. "ne de quel terre il eret" (240); cf. *P,* "ne de quel regne il ere," and *AS,* "ne (*S* et) de quele cuntree."

633-37. These four lines are in assonance rather than strict rhyme; M^1 preserves rhyme almost entirely (but see note to 1065). Rhyming *-ier* with *-er* is perhaps an allowable licence (for *garder,* 634, M^1 has *baillier,* 739), but *principel* is a clear instance of assonance, a carryover from an earlier, assonanced version? The phrase "du palais principel" is popular in the *chansons de geste* (e.g. *Les Enfances Guillaume* 2395, "Grans fu la joie el palais principel").

634-35. M^1 combines these two lines into one (795) ("Li aportoient le grant relief entier"). *Q* follows M^2, MS *F* reading "le relief quil avoit du grant palais plenier" (120a).

638. The reading of M^1 799, "Caschune feste," reflects *LP;* the line is missing from *S* (although restored by G. P.), the entire strophe missing from *A.*

640. A line which shows the complexity of the MS tradition: the first hemistich of $M^2 = PS$; LM^1 read "del Deu servise." The verb of the second hemistich in M^1 is closer to that of *PS* (*P, rove, SM^1, rueve*), while M^2 (*reveut*) seems to reflect *L* (*volt*).

660. M^1 omits this line, a paraphrase of *S* 790 (*L* 270), "mais ne

sevent qu'il font"; its inclusion makes Alexis' *imitatio Christi* more explicit (cf. Luke 23:34).

665-66. M^1 is defective here; Alexis is addressed as "Biaus pelerins," which renders pointless his reply, "Bien a droit me noumés"; it also omits 664, contained in S as well as M^2. Q follows M^2, addressing the saint as "Chrestien frere" (126c). On the other hand, in M^1 the second half of Alexis' reply, "Crestïens ai jou a non" (827), = S 797, "Crestïens ai a non." The *amplificatio* which follows in M^1 (828-31, esp. 828-29) is close to the equivalent lines in *S;* M^2 omits these lines, as does Q.

671. An alexandrine.

680. Compare M^1 845, "Et les degrés contre val descendue," and S 817, "E vous le mére qui descent al degré." M^2 abbreviates this laisse (7 lines compared to 11 in M^1), omitting the courtly details of the wife's dress contained in S as well.

687. Omitted by M^1; = S 826.

690. An alexandrine. M^1 substitutes for this line, "Que en roumanch nel puisent raviser / Et ne le fache del siecle rencombrer" (859-860), which paraphrases S 827-28.

696-97. The treatment of these two lines in M^2 more closely resembles S than does that in M^1, which offers no explanation of Alexis' changing color. "Ne vivra gaires" = S 835. Once again Q aligns with SM^2; cf. 131d, "Il ne vivra mes guerez" (*F*, "vivera gaires"). On the other hand, M^2 omits the line which follows in SM^1 (in Q it precedes 696), the offer to wash Alexis' clothes, perhaps because nothing more is said about the subject in the ensuing conversation. A number of omissions in M^2 appear not to be due to carelessness or to a desire to abbreviate but seem rather to reflect a conscious impulse to polish the narrative by omitting superfluous details, elements which remained undeveloped in S. (Strophe 131 indicates that Q is following a version similar to, but not identical with, S for it mentions the mother's fear that Alexis hates her (131b), contained in S [831] but not in M^*.)

702. *gaber:* M^1 reads *blasmer,* an interesting difference in reasoning. The lines are original to M^*.

703. For the second hemistich, cf. S 841, "Jou i vois mout envis" (Q 133a, "J'y vois envis"); M^1 873, "l'aime [jou] mieus que pis."

704. S also reads "membre moi" (842), while M^1Q paraphrase, "moi souvient." *Alesin* preserves an assonance, as does 708 (*pelerins* is also the assonance word in *S*).

708. *biau frere pelerin:* obj. for nom. (compare 518); Foulet, 1930, p. 45. In S the women ask Alexis where he is from, but the poet does not repeat the business about the name. The development of this scene, through line 722 (slightly more developed in M^1 than in M^2), appears original to M^*. It is reproduced in Q.

737. M^* amplifies the idea in S 901, "Povres hom sui, ne t'ai que departir."

743. S makes no mention of the language of the letter, if, indeed, the word *latin* here refers to a specific language and not to speech in general.

744. The reading of M^1 916, "Volontiers, certes," is preferable, avoiding the repetition of "frere."

745. In M^1 the order of the lines is 748, 747, 745, 746. The order in M^2 makes better sense. S does not mention the servant's reaction to the

news; he merely does as he is told. Instead *S* devotes 7 lines to the contents of the letter, recapitulating Alexis' life, an account which will be repeated *verbatim* when the letter is read.

762. The account of the heavenly voices is much amplified in *M** from that given in *S*.

767. Here MS *D* of *Q* (144b) follows *M²* ("neis les petis enfans"), while the others follow *M¹* ("li petit et li grant").

771. Cf. *M¹* 946, "Qui doit transir de che siecle dolant"; *Q* 145a, "Qui maintenant sera de ce siecle partis."

783. *dans Acaires:* the title *dans*, normally reserved for ranks inferior to count, is a little humble for Arcadius, elder son of Theodosius and emperor of the Eastern Empire. *M¹* reads "sains Acayres," an emendation of desperation; the lines caused trouble in *Q* as well, where consensus lacks.

786. The second hemistich, not in *M¹*, = *S* 935. *M¹* reads "les malvais et les per" (963).

799. *M¹* begins a new laisse rhyming in *-oit*. *S*, like *M²*, continues in the same assonance *(É)*.

823. *M¹* here links laisse 83 to 84 ("Ainc mais n'oï de sa valor," 1000; "Ainc mais n'oï parler de sa bonté," 1002). *M²* has eliminated the link.

830. *M¹* gives no description of the emotional state of the Pope and two kings. *M²* paraphrases *S* 962, "pensif et ploureos (cf. *LA* 327; *P* reads "pensis et corocous").

838. A pronoun is missing; *M¹* 1016 reads "Que chou soit chius."

843. *Cor:* introduces a wish (see *T. L.* II. 838); the conjunction is typical of northern dialects.

880. *M¹* omits the first two lines of laisse 71, thereby eliminating the close link between laisses; *S* here closely links laisses.

881. *sovanet consellier:* this appears to have been suggested by *S* 1025, "Souef l'apele, se li a consillié."

890. At least one line appears to be missing which contains the subject of the verb in 891. Following 886, *M¹* reads (1067-70):

> C'est li Deu sers, bien le t'os afichier,
> Dont cil signor te voelent enplaidier,
> Que Deus nous fait par sa vois anonchier."
> Od le li peres, Diu prent a grasiier.

Q reads for 1070, "Quant le conte l'oy, si i vint sans targier" (159d).

907. MS *P* of the *Q*-family reflects *M²* here: "cueilly ma en he" (162c); *Q*, "bien m'a prise en grant hé"; cf. *M¹* 1085, "molt forment me hé."

918. An interesting line: *S* reads, "N'en apelérent car ne sorent son non" (1053); *M¹* uses the same verb *(apieler)*, but by putting the statement in positive form, appears to contradict itself, "Apielé l'ont, mais ne sevent son non" (1095). *M²* reflects the meaning of *S* if not the wording.

922. The spelling *dochor* was occasioned by the fact that the scribe ran out of space on the line; the *r* extends into the right-hand margin (as does the *r* of *honor* in 924).

923. *M¹* omits this line contained in *S* (1060).

927. *M¹* does not contain this *amplificatio*, substituting the emperor's request that the Pope read the letter. This request, omitted from *M²*, is found also in *S*.

929. *oublie:* a mistake; M¹ reads *obeïe*, which is no better. Lines 927-29 are unparalleled in *S* or *Q.*

932. This section in *Q* is closer to M¹ than M²: M¹ 1108, "Le cartre a prise"; *Q* 165b, "Il a prise la lestre."

937. M²Q here follow *S* (1077) in having the letter fly into the wife's bosom; in M¹ it goes to her hand. In *Q*, however, the verb (*saly*, 166b) is that of M¹.

950. *SM¹, dist.*

951. Cf. *S* 1108, "buer fuisses tu ains née"; M¹ 1127, "a bien fusiiés nee."

952. *SM², Dieus;* M¹, *Jhesus.*

959. *SM¹* lack this line; the detail, however, about the statue at Alsis is given in *S* when the letter is written (911-12).

962. M¹ lacks this essential line; cf. *S* 1118, "Et de celi que il ot espousée."

965. Unique to M², followed by *Q; SM¹* go from 964 to 966.

974-76. An amplification on the part of M*; *S* reads (1137-38): "Quant ot li pére ke on troeve en la cartre, / A ses .ii. mains desront sa blance barbe." M², *si viement; Q, si vilment* (177b); M¹, *si forment.*

976. M¹ omits this detail; cf. *S* 1138 (quoted above).

982. M² is here closer to *LAPS* in structure; cf. *S* 1140, "Jou aesmoie que tu"; *L* 389, "io atendi." M¹ 1155 reads "Que tu deüsses" (*Q* 178d, "Je te cuidoie fere tenir mon heritage," but also cf. 179b, "Encore t'atendroie au jour d'uy par ma foy").

991ff. M² considerably shortens the father's *planctus*, omitting the epic line, "Blanc ai le cief e le barbe kenue (*S* 1158; cf. *Rol.* 117) as well as an account of the father's hopes concerning his son's chivalric career (given in *S* laisse 101, *L* strophe 83).

994. M² is better than M¹: "Et ton espeuse et ton ruiste corage" (1167)

1001. M² here appears to reflect most closely *P*, "Puis mun deces en fussiez honorez" (st. 81); cf. *S* 1157, "Se tu vesquisses, t'en fusses hounerés"; M¹ 1174, "Qu'apriés ma mort en fusses yretés."

1002. A lacuna in M². The scribe rhymed -*ue* and -*ure* (a remnant from a version in assonance?). Two MSS of the *Q*-family, *A* and *F*, also have a lacuna, omitting strophe 180. M¹ devotes 11 lines (and *S* 12) to a description of the mother's grief. *Q* appears here to go back to *LAP;* the mother rushes in "com femme forsenée" (180b); cf. *L*, "cum femme forsenede" (423); *S* "comme femme dervée" (1175). The equivalent line is missing from M¹.

1008. *maistele:* in *S* (1179-80, 1183), it is the mother who tears her hair and beats her breast. M¹ reads (1192), "batant sa forciele," followed by *Q*, MS *A*, (183b), "bastant sa forcele," while MSS *BCP* read *mamelles.*

1011. The phrase "com femme foursenée" does not appear in *S;* in *LAP* (423) it describes the mother (see note above); in *Q* the lines are jumbled, those belonging to the mother given to the wife and *vice versa.*

1014. M² here reproduces exactly the reading only of *A*, "U me laissas"; M¹ 1199, "Quant me laissastes"; *S* 1215, "Tu m'i laissas."

1015. *SM¹, tant jour.*

1018. M² is closer to *S* 1225, "U as geü de longe enfremeté"; M¹

1203, "U tu as giut de si longhe enfreté." However, M^2's adjective, *grant*, is the reading of *AP* (St. 90).

1022ff. This accusation by the bride of hard-heartedness does not occur in *S*.

1039. *Boineuré* is also found in *A; LP* have *felix*. *S* lacks the line, and M^1 reads "Et ki le jor de bon cuer l'ounererent" (1225).

1049. The second hemistich represents the reading of *P* (lacking in *A;* *L* 510, "li grand et li petit"; *S* "et l. e. p."; M^1, "nes l. e. p."). M^1 reads *tant* in the first hemistich. The line order has reverted to that of *LAP; S* has the lines in the order 1048, 1049, 1047.

1050-54. M^1 has preserved only one line (approximating 1053) of this laisse.

1057. *S* (1251) also gives the verb in the singular, "qui tant l'a desiré"; M^1 1239 has the plural ("l'ont desiré").

1060. M^1 1242 gives ".I. hastiu parlement," a nicer reading.

1061. *tresor:* the line reveals the complexity of the MS tradition; *tresor* is the reading of *LAP; S*, however, has *avoir* — perhaps a mistake, perhaps a sign of independence. The hemistich "de lor avoir" is formulaic in *S* (387, 514, 1262, 1264).

1063. M^2 preserves the reading of *LAPS*, "avoir descombrement"; M^1 1254, "venir a sauvement."

1064. Lacking in M^1; M^2 is a paraphrase of *S* 1261, "Que lor ajue? Il nen veulent nient."

1065. The reading of M^* is essentially that of *L* 530, "A cel saint hume trestut est lur talent." *APS* read, "A cel saint cors ont torné lor talent" (*S* 1262). In all other manuscripts another laisse or strophe follows this line (e.g. M^1 1247-1251):

> A un vois crient la gente menue:
> "De cest avoir, sachiés, n'avons nous cure.
> Fors ce cors saint ne querons chose nule
> Car par cestui n'aron chose ki nuise.
> Deus, quel grant joie nous est ore venue.

Note that this strophe from M^1 is in assonance.

1066. In M^1 this line is the last of the preceding laisse, "Onques Romme n'en ont tele veüe" (1252). What would constitute the subsequent laisse in M^1 consists of only one line, an approximation of M^2 1070. From 1066 to the end of M^2, all lines are in assonance, not rhyme. This laisse approximates strophe 108, found only in *L* and here (missing, therefore, in *APVSM^1*). This is evidence for another version similar to *L* in laisses in assonance.

1071. The equivalent strophe (111) is lacking in *A* (which concludes with st. 110), and in *PQ; LVS* read, "Sours, n'avulés, ne contrais, ne lepreus" (*S* 1267). *S* then adds a line (1268) for which there is no parallel in any other MS. M^1 reads "Ne nus liepreus ne malades ne sours" (1254).

1072. M^1 1257, "Ne nus enfers ne nus palasinous"; *L* 552, "Ne mus ne orbs ne neuls palazinus"; *S* 1269, "Ensorquetout nus hom palasinex" (cf. *L* 553, "Ensur tut ne nuls languerus").

1073-74. Consensus is utterly lacking (see note on *S* 1270).

> *L*:   Nuls n'en i at ki n'alget malendus
>   Cel n'en n'i at ki'n report sa dolur.

V: Cil n'en i unt k'il m'aportast languor.
    Ne cil n'i vint k'il n'en alhe repous.
M^1:   N'i est alés ken portast ses langurs ...
S: Icil n'i vint qui·n n'alast refuses,
    Ne nus n'i vient qui report sa dolour.

Therefore M^2 1073 approximates L 555 (the last line of strophe 111), but there is no parallel for 1074. On the other hand, the equivalent line in M^1 (1255) in the second hemistich resembles the reading found only in V ("kil naportast languor").

1075. M^* omits the lines which form the first two (three in V) lines of the subsequent strophe, beginning with the third. M^2's *mener* is unique, $LVSM^1$ reading *porter*.

1076. Lacking in M^1. The first hemistich, "Si vraie espesce," occurs in SV; cf. L, "Si voirs miracles."

1077. $M^2 = S$ 1276; M^1 1258, "Ki plourant vint cantant s'en est alés."

1078-79. These lines form the first two of a strophe or laisse in versions other than M^*. The exact filiation is again confused. Essentially M^1 appears to resemble LV while M^2 is slightly closer to S.

L: Ni vint amferm de nul amfermetet
    Quant il l'apelet sempres n'en ait sanctet (556-57)
M^1:   N'i a enfert de si grant enfreté
    S'il vint a lui ki n'en porte santé.   (1259-60)
S: N'i vient enfers de cele enfremeté
    A cel saint cors, lués ne soit rasenés.   (1272-73)

1080. Lacking in M^1.

1081. A line must be lacking after 1081; cf. M^1, 1262 "Il ot a Romme une eglise molt biele" (S, "Avoit a Romme"). The end of M^2 is particularly fragmentary. Line 1081 is equivalent to the first line of strophe 114; strophe 113 is lacking in M^*, as it is in PQ.

1082. *enportent*: the verb of $LPVS$: M^1, *enfeuent*.

1083. The second hemistich of M^2 is unique (M^1 and M^2 agree on the first); M^1 preserves the common reading, "l'ont posé en la terre." The line is lacking in S.

1084. LP reads "Felix le liu," V "riche"; SM^1 lacking. In place of this line, M^1 substitutes "Vai[t] s'ent li peules, li peres et li mere" (1265), the equivalent of S 1310. Before line 1085 M^1 inserts four lines. Line 1266 should not begin a separate laisse (120), for it follows directly in S (1312), the scribe not having bothered to alter the original assonance *(desevrent; S, desevrérent)* to rhyme. The next two lines (1267-68) = S 1315-16 (and approximate L 611-12). 1269 is unique to M^1.

In omitting strophes L 115 and following, M^2 is closer to the tradition of A. M^1 contains three more lines before the conclusion.

1085. M^* here is closer to LPV than is S, which reads *Tenons*.

1086. The last line of S.

1089. This strophe is unique to M^*. M^1 reads "le vie en escrist." For the distinction between author and performer, see the introduction.

1090. M^1, "Devés proier que Deus en ait merchi."

1091. M^1, "meche en saint paradys."

1093. After this line, omitting the *Amen*, M^1 adds the Explicit, "Chi define li romans de saint Alesin."

PROPER NAMES: S

ABRAHAM, 19, *Biblical patriarch.*

ACAIRE, 940, *Arcadius, Roman emperor of the east, 395-408 A. D.*

ALESSINS, Alessis, Allessis *(saint)*, 2, 69, 97, 122, 123, 139, 211, 212, 227, 267, 342, 343, 358, 382, 390, 399, 424, 463, 472, 492, 506, 517, 553, 566, 570, 628, 670, 735, 777, 967, 985, 997, 1071, 1147, 1193, 1216, 1219, 1239, 1284, 1307.

AMBROSE *(saint)*, 1114, *bishop who reads* Alexis' *deathbed letter aloud.*

ARCEDECLIN, 555, *steward at the feast of Cana.*

AUSIS, Ausi, Aussis, 362, 385, 462, 498, 506, 574, 878, 911, 1131, *Alsis (for the possible derivation, see the introduction).*

BELLIANT, 145, *Bethlehem.*

BOINE EURÉE, Bone Eurée, 55, 56, *mother of* Alexis.

BONIFACES *(saint)*, 981a, 1282, *martyr in whose church* Alexis *is buried.*

CONSTENTINS *(Dans)*, 681, *Roman citizen who offers to shelter* Alexis.

DAMEDÉ, Damedieu, Damediu, 27, 41, 113, 182, 199, 239, 256, 323, 341, 367, 446, 449, 459, 510, 523, 531, 577, 647, 650, 677, 718, 724, 908, 986, 990, 998, 1083, 1095, *God.*

DAVI, 21 *King David.*

DÉ, Dieu, Diu, 4, 7, 21, 35, 37, 39, 47, 60, 100, 101, 109, 174, 180, 186, 194, 207, 224, 228, 233, 235, 236, 237 242, 257, 259, 260, 263, 265, 266, 288, 303, 305, 315, 333, 360, 364, 371, 373, 375, 379, 391, 439, 442, 455, 457, 472, 491, 517, 524, 527, 529, 533, 542, 545, 560, 575, 584, 593, 597, 602 607, 614, 622, 644, 666, 667, 668, 674, 689, 691, 692, 694, 698, 700, 703, 710, 722, 728, 736, 743, 748, 749, 764, 769, 776, 789, 813, 814, 848, 868, 888, 889, 891, 893, 900, 906, 912, 923, 927, 930, 932, 942, 964, 976, 979, 984, 1007, 1014, 1030, 1040, 1061, 1069, 1074, 1100, 1109, 1132, 1141, 1167, 1205, 1250, 1275, 1312, 1315, 1319, *God.*

ERMENER, 525, *cleric at* Alsis.

EUFEMIEN, 52, 717, 947, 949, 1024, 1031, 1037, *father of* Alexis.

FLOURENS, 55, 56, *father of* Bone Eurée, Eufemien's *wife.*

FRANC, 87, *Frank.*

INNOCENS *(saint)*, 934, 1044, 1081, 1084, 1105, *Pope (401-417 A. D.).*

JEHAN *(saint J. de Latran)*, 96, *Church in Rome where* Alexis *is married.*

JHERUSALEM, Jhersalem, 28, 341, 1003, *Jerusalem.*

JHESU, 330, 747, *Jesus.*

JORDANS, 146, *the Jordan river.*

JUIS, 353, *Jews.*

LATRAN *(saint Jehan de L.)*, 96, *see* Jehan.

LESIGNE, 90, Alexis' *wife*

LE LICE, 356, 357, *Laodicea, city visited by* Alexis.

MARIE, 374, 375, *the statue at* Alsis.

PROPER NAMES: M

AARON, 510, *the prophet.*

ACAIRES, 783, *the Roman emperor Arcadius.*

ALESINS, Alexis, *(saint)*, 85, 107, 128, 197, 212, 256, 305, 345, 368, 393, 411, 476, 498, 509, 514, 531, 549, 578, 643, 704, 716, 841, 978, 980, 987, 991, 1012, 1015, 1082, 1093.

ALSIX, Assix, Ausi, Ausis, Auxis, 227, 233, 304, 356, 730, 959, *city where* Alexis *spends 17 years in exile; for the name, see the introduction.*

ARCHEDECLIN, 740, *steward at the wedding at Cana.*

BONIFASCES *(Saint B. qui martir on apele)*, 1081, *the church where* Alexis *is buried.*

CONSTENTIN *(Dant)*, 525, *citizen of Rome.*

CORSAUT, 433, *unknown city, perhaps Jerusalem* (< CORPU SANCTU); *see textual note ad loc.*

CRESTÏENS, 709, *the name* Alexis *claims as his in Rome.*

DAMEDEUS, Damedieus, 187, 234, 284, 309, 311, 510, 563, 769, 776, 882, *God.*

DAVY, 11, *King David.*

DÉ, 910, *God.*

DIEU, 16, 24, 43, 87, 117, 129, 158, 160, 178, 190, 204, 211, 220, 223, 244, 250, 290, 310, 400, 408, 482, 500, 508, 553, 582, 612, 623, 630, 640, 658, 711, 715, 721, 723, 793, 806, 808, 821, 890, 935, 1038, 1088, 1090. Dieus, 11, 273, 356, 447, 457, 521, 544, 567, 571, 585, 587, 656, 739, 760, 813, 847, 848, 855, 924, 942, 952, 1056, 1069, 1076. Diex, 57, 100, 118, 547, 852. Dius, 28, *God.*

EUFEMIIENS, 28, 801, 807, 816, Alexis' *father.*

HONORÉS, 783, *Honorius, brother of* Arcadius, *Roman emperor of the West.*

INNOCENS *(saint)*, 782, 788, *Pope of Rome.*

JERUSALEM, 207, *Jerusalem.*

JESUS, Jhesu, 180, 446, 653.

JOURDAIN *(flum)*, 217, *the Jordan river.*

LASARON *(le cors saint L.)*, 512, *Lazarus.*

LE LICE, 203, 221, *Laodicea, city to which* Alexis *intended to escape.*

MARIE *(sainte)*, 181, 447, 935, *the Virgin.*

MOŸSEN, Moÿset, 10, 511, *Moses.*

NOÉ, 10, *Noah.*

NOSTRE SIRES, 50, 214, 224, 251, 387, 419, 434, 797, 969, *God.*

PHARAON, 511, *Pharaoh.*

PRÉ NOIRON, 807, *Roman place name, the* pratum, prata Neronis, *site of the Vatican.*

ROME, Romme, Ronme, Roume, 29, 145, 186, 195, 238, 329, 353, 436, 437, 450, 478, 495, 499, 526, 626, 781, 785, 804, 871, 972, 1066, *Rome.*

ROUVISON *(une feste de saint R.)*, 661, *Rogations.*

WORKS CITED

Adenet le Roi. *Buevon de Conmarchis.* Ed. Albert Henry. In *Les Œuvres d'Adenet le Roi,* vol. II. Brugge: De Tempel, 1953.

Adenet le Roi. *Les Enfances Ogier.* Ed. Albert Henry. In *Les Œuvres d'Adenet le Roi,* vol. III. Brugge: De Tempel, 1953.

Aspland, C. W. 1970. *A Syntactical Study of Epic Formulas and Formulaic Expressions Containing the -ant Forms in Twelfth-Century French Verse.* St. Lucia, Queensland: University of Queensland.

Aston, S. C. 1970. "The Saint in Medieval Literature." *Modern Language Review* 65, xxv-xlii.

Auerbach, Erich. 1958; rpt. 1964. *Literary Language and its Public in Late Latin Antiquity and in the Middle Ages.* Trans. Ralph Mannheim. Princeton: Bollingen Series, 74.

Axton, Richard. 1974. *European Drama of the Early Middle Ages.* London: Hutchinson University Library.

Batiouchkof, Th. 1891. "Le Débat de l'âme et du corps." *Romania,* 20, 1 55.

Beattie, Bruce A. 1977. "Saint Katharine of Alexandria: Traditional Themes and the Development of a Medieval German Hagiographic Narrative." *Speculum,* 52, 785-800.

Bonnard, Jean. 1884. *Les Traductions de la Bible en vers français au moyen âge.* Paris: Imprimerie nationale.

Bossy, Michel-André. 1976. "Medieval Debates of Body and Soul." *Comparative Literature,* 28, 144-63.

Boucherie, A. 1874. "La Vie de saint Alexis, Poëme du XIe siècle (Edition de M. Gaston Paris)." *Revue des Langues Romanes,* 5, 5-37.

Carr, Gerald F. 1976. "On the *Vie de saint Alexis.*" *Romance Notes,* 17, 204-207.

Chaytor, H. J. 1945; rpt. 1966. *From Script to Print.* London: Sidgwich and Jackson.

Chenu, M. D. 1969. *L'Eveil de la conscience dans la civilisation médiévale.* Montréal: Inst. d'études médiévales.

Contini, Gianfranco. 1968. "Scavi alessiani." *Linguistica e Filologia: Omaggio a Benvenuto Terracini.* Ed. Cesare Segre. Milan: Il Saggiatore. Pp. 57-95.

———. 1970. "La 'Vita' francese 'di Sant'Alessio' e l'arte di publicare i testi antichi." *Un Augurio a Raffaele Mattioli.* Florence: Sansoni. Pp. 343-74.

Contini, Gianfranco. 1971. "La Critica testuale come studio di strutture." *Atti del il Congresso Internazionale della Società Italiana di Storia del Diritto*. Florence: L. S. Olschki. Pp. 11-23.

———. 1977. "Una Scheda curiosa." *Studi filologici, letterari e storici in memoria de Guido Favati*. Padua: Antenore. Pp. 225-31.

Crosland, Jessie. 1956. *Medieval French Literature*. Oxford: Blackwell.

Curschmann, Michael. 1967. "Oral Poetry in Mediaeval English, French, and German Literature: Some Notes on Recent Research." *Speculum*, 42, 36-52.

Curtius, E. R. 1937. "Zur Interpretation des Alexiusliedes." *Zeitschrift für romanische Philologie*, 56, 85-93.

Delisle, L. 1891. *Manuscrits latins et français ajoutés aux fonds des nouvelles acquisitions pendant les annés 1875-1891*. Vol. II. Paris: H. Champion.

Dembowski, Peter F. 1976. "Literary Problems of Hagiography in Old French." *Medievalia et Humanistica*, 7, 117-30.

Detienne, Marcel. 1967. *Les Maîtres de verité dans la Grèce archaïque*. Paris: Flammarion.

Duggan, Hoyt N. 1976. "The Role of Formulas in the Dissemination of a Middle English Alliterative Romance." *Studies in Bibliography*, 19, 265-88.

Duggan, Joseph J. 1966. "Formulas in the *Couronnement de Louis*." *Romania*, 87, 315-44.

———. 1973. *The Song of Roland; Formulaic Style and Poetic Craft*. Berkeley and Los Angeles: University of California.

Elioxe. Ed. Emmanuel J. Mickel, Jr. In *The Old French Crusade Cycle*. Vol. I. University of Alabama Press, 1977.

Elliott, Alison Goddard. 1977. "Saints and Heroes: Latin and Old French Hagiographic Poetry." Dissertation, University of California, Berkeley.

———. 1979. "The *Triumphus sancti Remacli*: Latin Evidence for Oral Composition." *Romance Philology*, 32, 292-98.

———. 1980. "The Ashburnham *Alexis* Again." *Romance Notes*, 21, 254-58.

———. 1981. "The *Vie de saint Alexis*: Oral *versus* Written Style." *VIII Congreso de la Société Rencesvals*. Pamplona: Príncipe de Viana. Pp. 137-48.

Les Enfances Guillaume. Ed. J.-L. Perrier. New York: Columbia University, 1933.

Les Enfances Guillaume. Ed. Patrice Henry. Paris: S. A. T. F., 1935.

Ewert, Alfred. 1933; rpt. 1966. *The French Language*. London: Faber and Faber.

Faral, Edmond. 1910. *Les Jongleurs en France au moyen âge*. Bibl. de l'Ecole des Hautes Etudes, 187. Paris: H. Champion. Rpt. 1964.

———. 1924. *Les Arts poétiques du XIIe et du XIIIe siècle*. Paris: E. Champion.

Fawtier, R. and E. C. Fawtier Jones. 1923. "Notice du manuscrit *French 6* de la John Rylands Library, Manchester." *Romania*, 49, 321-42.

———. 1924. "Note sur un légendier français conservé dans la bibliothèque du Chapitre de Carlisle." *Romania*, 50, 100-10.

Fawtier-Jones, E. C. 1932. "Les Vies de sainte Catherine d'Alexandrie en ancien français. Deuxième et dernier article." *Romania*, 58, 206-17.

Floovent. Ed. F. Guessard and H. Michelant. Paris: F. Vieweg, 1859.

Foerster, W. and E. Koschwitz. 1911: rpt. 1921. *Altfranzösiches Übungs-buch.* 6th Edition. Leipzig: O. R. Reisland.

Foley, John Miles. 1976. "Formula and Theme in Old English Poetry." *Oral Literature and the Formula.* Ed. Stolz and Shannon. Ann Arbor: University of Michigan. Pp. 207-32.

Fouché, Pierre. 1967. *Le Verbe français: étude morphologique.* Paris: Klincksieck.

Foulet, Alfred and Mary Blakely Speer. 1979. *On Editing Old French Texts.* Lawrence, Kansas: Regents Press of Kansas.

Foulet, Lucien. 1920. "De *icest* a *cest* et l'origine de l'article." *Romania,* 46, 571-77.

——. 1930. *Petite syntaxe de l'ancien français.* Paris: H. Champion.

Fox, John. 1974. *A Literary History of France: The Middle Ages.* London: Benn.

Fry, Donald. 1975. "Caedmon as a Formulaic Poet." *Oral Literature: Seven Essays.* Ed. Joseph J. Duggan. Edinburgh: Barnes and Noble. Pp. 41-61

Gaiffier, B. de. 1946. "Intactam sponsam relinquens. A propos de la vie de S. Alexis." *Analecta Bollandiana,* 65, 157-95.

Gatto-Pyko, Danièle. 1973. "*La Vie de saint Alexis,* version *M* —édition critique." Dissertation, Florida State University.

Gaydon. Ed. F. Guessard and S. Luce. Paris: A. Franck, 1862.

Gieysztor, Alexander. 1974. "*Pauper sum et peregrinus.* La légende de saint Alexis en occident: un idéal de pauvreté. In *Etudes sur l'histoire de la pauvreté.* Ed. M. Mollat. Paris: Vol. I, pp. 126-39.

Girart de Vienne par Bertrand de Bar-sur-Aube. Ed. Wolfgang van Emden. Paris: S. A. T. F., 1977.

Goose, A. 1960. "La 'Vie de saint Alexis.'" *Lettres Romanes,* 14, 62-65.

Gossen, Charles Théodore. 1970. *Grammaire de l'ancien picard.* Paris: Klincksieck.

Gsteiger, Manfred. 1959. "Note sur les préambles des chansons de geste." *Cahiers de Civilisation Médiévale,* 2, 213-20.

Gui de Bourgogne. Ed. F. Guessard and H. Michelant. Paris: F. Vieweg. 1859.

Gui de Nanteuil. Ed. James R. McCormack. Geneva: Droz, 1970.

Harris, Roy. 1966. "Gallo-Romance Third Declension Plurals." *Revue de Linguistique Romane,* 30, 57-70.

Hatcher, Anna Granville. 1952. "The Old-French Poem St. Alexis: A Mathematical Demonstration." *Traditio,* 8, 111-58.

Hemming, Timothy D. 1968. "Restrictions lexicales dans la chanson de geste." *Romania,* 89, 96-105.

——. 1974. "La Forme de la laisse épique et le problème des origines." Société Rencesvals. *Actes du VIe Congrès International.* Aix-en-Provence: Université de Provence. Pp. 223-39.

Holmes, Urban Tigner. 1947. Review of E. B. Ham, *Textual Criticism and Jehan le Venelais. Speculum,* 22, 468-70.

Hunt, Tony. 1973. "The Structure of Medieval Narrative." *Journal of European Studies,* 3, 295-328.

Huon de Bordeaux. Ed. Pierre Ruelle. Brussels and Paris: Presses Universitaires, 1960.

Jauss, Hans Robert. 1970. *La Littérature didactique, allégorique et satirique. Grundriss der romanischen Literaturen des Mittelalters,* VI:2. Heidelberg: C. Winter.

Jauss, Hans Robert. 1973-74. "Levels of Identification of Hero and Audience." *New Literary History*, 5, 283-317.

Johnson, Phyllis and Brigitte Cazelles. 1979. *Le vain siecle guerpir: A Literary Approach to Sainthood through Old French Hagiography of the Twelfth Century.* North Carolina Studies in the Romance Languages and Literatures, 205. Chapel Hill, N. C.: University of North Carolina.

Jourdain de Blaye. Ed. Peter F. Dembowski. Chicago and London: University of Chicago, 1969.

Labriolle, Pierre de. 1921. "Le 'Mariage Spirituel' dans l'antiquité chrétienne." *Revue Historique*, 37, 204-25.

LeBras, Gabriel. 1968. "Le mariage dans la théologie et le droit de l'Église du XIe au XIIIe siècle" *Cahiers de Civilisation Médiévale*, 11, 191-202.

The Life of Christina of Markyate: A Twelfth Century Recluse. Ed. and trans. C. H. Talbot. Oxford: Clarendon, 1959.

Maddox, Donald. 1973. "Pilgrimage Narrative and Meaning in Manuscripts L and A of the *Vie de saint Alexis.*" *Romance Philology*, 27, 143-57.

McCulloch, Florence. 1977. "Saint Euphrosine,' Saint Alexis, and the Turtledove." *Romania*, 98, 168-85.

Meyer, Paul. 1901. "Notice du MS. 10295-304 de la Bibliothèque Royale de Belgique (Légendes en prose et en vers)." *Romania*, 30, 295-315.

Miletich, John S. 1976-77. "The Quest for the 'Formula': A Comparative Reappraisal." *Modern Philology*, 74, 111-23.

Molin, J.-B. and P. Mutembe. 1973. *Le Rituel de mariage en France du XIIe au XVIe siècle.* Paris: Beauchesne.

Mölk, Ulrich. 1978. "La *Chanson de saint Alexis* et le culte du saint en France aux XIe et XIIe siècles." *Cahiers de Civilisation Médiévale*, 21, 339-55.

Morris, Colin. 1972. *The Discovery of the Individual, 1050-1200.* New York: Harper Torchbooks.

Nichols, Stephen G. 1969. "The Interaction of Life and Literature in the *Peregrinationes ad Loca Sancta* and the *Chansons de geste.*" *Speculum*, 44, 51-77.

―――. 1970. "The Spirit of Truth: Epic Modes in Medieval Literature." *New Literary History*, 1, 365-86.

Odenkirchen, Carl J. 1978. *The Life of Saint Alexius: In the Old French Version of the Hildesheim Manuscript.* Brookline, Mass. and Leyden: Classical Folia Editions.

Olsen, B. Munk. 1963. "Problèmes d'attribution. La version de la Vie de saint Alexis en alexandrins monorimés (XIVe siècle)." *Etudes romanes dediés à Andreas Blinkenberg. Orbis Litterarum.* Supplément 3, 144-65.

Pächt, Otto, C. R. Dodwell, and F. Wormald. 1960. *The St. Albans Psalter.* Studies of the Warburg Institute, 25. London: University of London.

Paris, Gaston, and Léopold Pannier. 1872. *La Vie de saint Alexis: Poème du XIe siècle et renouvellements des XIIe, XIIIe et XIVe siècles.* Bibliothèque de l'Ecole des Hautes Etudes, 7. Paris: A Franck.

Paris, Gaston. 1879. "La Vie de saint Alexis en vers octosyllabiques." *Romania*, 8, 163-80.

―――. 1888. "Un second manuscrit de la rédaction rimée (M) de la *Vie de saint Alexis.*" *Romania*, 17, 106-20.

Payen, Jean-Charles. 1970. *Littérature française: Le Moyen âge: des origines à 1300.* Paris: Arthaud.

Perrot, Jean-Pierre. 1978. "Le cœur dur d'un saint: un motif hagiographique (A propos du v. 446 de la *Vie de saint Alexis*)." *Romania,* 99, 238-46.

Pope, M. K. 1934; rpt. 1973. *From Latin to Modern French.* Manchester: Manchester University.

The Prise d'Orenge according to MS A 1. Ed. Blanche Katz. Morningside Heights, New York: King's Crown, 1947.

Raby, F. J. E. 1934. *A History of Secular Latin Poetry in the Middle Ages.* 2 vols. Oxford: Clarendon.

Rajna, Pio. 1929. "Un nuovo testo parziale del 'Saint Alexis' primitivo." *Archivum Romanicum,* 13, 1-86.

Les Rédactions en vers de la Prise d'Orange. Ed. Claude Régnier. Paris: Klincksieck, 1966.

Richter, Elise. 1932. "Alexius 95e 'Pur felunie nient ne pur lastet." *Zeitschrift für französische Sprache und Literatur,* 56, 65-67.

———. 1933. "Studien zum altfranzösischen Alexiusliede." *Zeitschrift für französische Sprache und Literatur,* 57, 80-88.

Riquer, Martín de. 1956. *Les Chansons de geste françaises.* Trans. Irenée Cluzel. Paris: Nizet.

Robertson, Howard S. 1970. *"La Vie de saint Alexis:* Meaning and Manuscript A." *Studies in Philology,* 67, 419-38.

Rohlfs, Gerhard. 1963. *Sankt Alexius. Altfranzösische Legendendichtung des 11. Jahrhunderts.* Sammlung romanischer Übungstexte, XV, 4th rev. ed. Tübingen: Niemeyer.

Roncaglia, Aurelio. 1971. *La Lingua d'oïl.* Rome: Ateneo.

Rutebeuf. *Les Œuvres complètes de Rutebeuf.* Ed. Edmond Faral and Julia Bastin. 2 vols., 1977. Paris: Picard.

Rychner, Jean. 1955. *La Chanson de geste: Essai sur l'art épique des jongleurs.* Geneva: Droz.

———. 1959. "Observations sur la versification du *Couronnement de Louis.*" In *La Technique littéraire des chansons de geste: Actes du Colloque de Liège.* Bibliothèque de la Faculté de Philosophie et Lettres de l'Université de Liège, CL. Paris: "Les Belles Lettres." Pp. 161-78.

———. 1977. "La *Vie de saint Alexis* et le poème latin *Pater Deus ingenite.*" *Vox Romanica,* 36. 67-83.

Scholes, Robert, and Robert Kellogg. 1966; rpt. 1975. *The Nature of Narrative.* Oxford: Oxford University.

Sckommodau, Hans. 1954. "Zum Altfranzösichen Alexiuslied." *Zeitschrift für romanische Philologie,* 70, 161-203.

———. 1963. "Das Alexiuslied: Die Datierungsfrage und das Problem der Askese." *Medium Aevum Romanicum: Festschrift für Hans Rheinfelder.* Ed. H. Bihler. Munich: Hüber. Pp. 298-324.

Segre, Cesare. 1974. "Des vies des saints aux chansons de geste: techniques et centres culturels." Société Rencesvals. *Actes du VIe Congrès International.* Aix-en-Provence: Université de Provence. Pp. 305-13.

Smeets, J. R. 1963. *"Alexis* et la *Bible* de Herman de Valenciennes: Le problème de l'origine de la laisse." *Cahiers de Civilisation Médiévale,* 6, 315-25.

Spitzer, Leo. 1932. "Die Erhellung des 'Polyeucte' durch das Alexiuslied." *Archivum Romanicum,* 16, 473-500.

Sprissler, Manfred. 1966. "Das rhythmische Gedicht 'Pater deus ingenite' (11. Jh.) und das altfranzösiche Alexiuslied." *Forschungen zur romanischen Philologie*, 18.

Stebbins, Charles E. 1974. *A Critical Edition of the 13th and 14th Centuries Old French Poem Versions of the "Vie de saint Alexis."* *Beihefte zur ZRPh*, 145. Tübingen: M. Niemeyer.

————. 1978. "Une Etude comparative des trois grandes versions en vers de la *Vie de saint Alexis* conservées en vieux français." *Revue des Langues Romanes*, 83, 379-403.

Stimm, H. 1963. "Zur Sprache der Handscrift V des ,Alexiusliedes," *Medium Aevum Romanicum, Festschrift für Hans Rheinfelder.* Munich: M. Hüber.

Storey, Christopher. 1968. *La Vie de saint Alexis: Texte du manuscrit de Hildesheim (L).* Geneva: Droz.

Thomas of Chobham. *Thomae de Chobham Summa Confessorum.* Ed. Rev. P. Broomfield. Analecta Medievalia Namurcensia, 25. 1968.

Tyssens, Madeleine. 1967. *La Geste de Guillaume d'Orange dans les manuscrits cycliques.* Bibliothèque de la Faculté de Philosophie et Lettres de l'Université de Liège, Fasc. CLXXVIII. Paris: "Les Belles Lettres."

Uitti, Karl. 1966-67. "The Old French *Vie de saint Alexis:* Paradigm, Legend, Meaning," *Romance Philology*, 20, 263-95.

————. 1970. "Recent *Alexis* Studies from Germany." *Romance Philology*, 24, 128-37.

————. 1973. *Story, Myth, and Celebration in Old French Narrative Poetry, 1050-1200.* Princeton: Princeton University.

Vincent, Patrick R. 1963. "The Dramatic Aspect of the Old-French *Vie de saint Alexis.*" *Studies in Philology*, 60, 525-41.

Wagner, Fritz, 1964. "Die Verslegende vom hl. Alexius: "Duxit Romanus vir nobilis Eufemianus." *Mittellateinisches Jahrbuch*, 1, 78-99.

————. 1965. "Die metrische Alexius-vita "Eufemianus erat, ceu lectio sacra revelat." *Mittellateinisches Jahrbuch*, 2, 145-64.

Walther, Hans. 1920. *Die Streitgedicht in der lateinischen Literatur des Mittelalters.* Munich: O. Beck.

Waters, E. G. R. 1928. *The Anglo-Norman Voyage of St. Brendan by Benedeit: A Poem of the Early Twelfth Century.* Oxford: Clarendon.

Windelberg, Marjorie L. 1978. "Theoretical Questions About Metrical Irregularities in the *Chanson de Roland.*" *Olifant*, 6, 6-19.

Winkler, Emil. 1927. "Von der Kunst des Alexius-dichters." *Zeitschrift für romanische Philologie*, 47, 588-97

Wolf, Carol Jean. 1970. "Christ as Hero in *The Dream of the Rood.*" *Neuphilologische Mitteilungen*, 71, 202-10.

NORTH CAROLINA STUDIES IN THE ROMANCE LANGUAGES AND LITERATURES

I.S.B.N. Prefix 0-8078-

Recent Titles

MEDIEVAL MANUSCRIPTS AND TEXTUAL CRITICISM, edited by Christopher Kleinhenz. 1976. (Symposia, No. 4). *-954-5.*

SAMUEL BECKETT. THE ART OF RHETORIC. edited by Edouard Morot-Sir, Howard Harper, and Dougald McMillan III. 1976. (Symposia, No. 5). *-955-3.*

DELIE. CONCORDANCE, by Jerry Nash. 1976. 2 Volumes. (No. 174).

FIGURES OF REPETITION IN THE OLD PROVENÇAL LYRIC: A STUDY IN THE STYLE OF THE TROUBADOURS, by Nathaniel B. Smith. 1976. (No. 176). *-9176-2.*

A CRITICAL EDITION OF LE REGIME TRESUTILE ET TRESPROUFITABLE POUR CON-SERVER ET GARDER LA SANTE DU CORPS HUMAIN, by Patricia Willett Cummins. 1977. (No. 177).

THE DRAMA OF SELF IN GUILLAUME APOLLINAIRE'S "ALCOOLS", by Richard Howard Stamelman. 1976. (No. 178). *-9178-9.*

A CRITICAL EDITION OF "LA PASSION NOSTRE SEIGNEUR" FROM MANUSCRIPT 1131 FROM THE BIBLIOTHEQUE SAINTE-GENEVIEVE, PARIS, by Edward J. Gallagher. 1976. (No. 179). *-9179-7.*

A QUANTITATIVE AND COMPARATIVE STUDY OF THE VOCALISM OF THE LATIN INSCRIPTIONS OF NORTH AFRICA, BRITAIN, DALMATIA, AND THE BALKANS, by Stephen William Omeltchenko. 1977. (No. 180). *-9180-0.*

OCTAVIEN DE SAINT-GELAIS "LE SEJOUR D'HONNEUR", edited by Joseph A. James. 1977. (No. 181). *-9181-9.*

A STUDY OF NOMINAL INFLECTION IN LATIN INSCRIPTIONS, by Paul A. Gaeng. 1977. (No. 182). *-9182-7.*

THE LIFE AND WORKS OF LUIS CARLOS LÓPEZ, by Martha S. Bazik. 1977. (No. 183). *-9183-5.*

"THE CORT D'AMOR". A THIRTEENTH-CENTURY ALLEGORICAL ART OF LOVE, by Lowanne E. Jones. 1977. (No. 185). *-9185-1.*

PHYTONYMIC DERIVATIONAL SYSTEMS IN THE ROMANCE LANGUAGES: STUDIES IN THEIR ORIGIN AND DEVELOPMENT, by Walter E. Geiger 1978. (No. 187). *-918/-8.*

LANGUAGE IN GIOVANNI VERGA'S EARLY NOVELS, by Nicholas Patruno. 1977. (No. 188). *-9188-6.*

BLAS DE OTERO EN SU POESÍA, by Moraima de Semprún Donahue. 1977. (No. 189). *-9189-4.*

LA ANATOMÍA DE "EL DIABLO COJUELO": DESLINDES DEL GÉNERO ANATOMÍSTICO, por C. George Peale. 1977. (No. 191). *-9191-6.*

RICHARD SANS PEUR, EDITED FROM "LE ROMANT DE RICHART" AND FROM GILLES CORROZET'S "RICHART SANS PAOUR", by Denis Joseph Conlon. 1977. (No. 192). *-9192-4.*

MARCEL PROUST'S GRASSET PROOFS. *Commentary and Variants,* by Douglas Alden. 1978. (No. 193). *-9193-2.*

MONTAIGNE AND FEMINISM, by Cecile Insdorf. 1977. (No. 194). *-9194-0.*

SANTIAGO F. PUGLIA, AN EARLY PHILADELPHIA PROPAGANDIST FOR SPANISH AMERICAN INDEPENDENCE, by Merle S. Simmons. 1977. (No. 195). *-9195-9.*

BAROQUE FICTION-MAKING. A STUDY OF GOMBERVILLE'S "POLEXANDRE", by Edward Baron Turk. 1978. (No. 196). *-9196-7.*

THE TRAGIC FALL: DON ÁLVARO DE LUNA AND OTHER FAVORITES IN SPANISH GOLDEN AGE DRAMA, by Raymond R. MacCurdy. 1978. (No. 197). *-9197-5.*

A BAHIAN HERITAGE. An Ethnolinguistic Study of African Influences on Bahian Portuguese, by William W. Megenney. 1978. (No. 198). *-9198-3.*

When ordering please cite the *ISBN Prefix* plus the last four digits for each title.

Send orders to: University of North Carolina Press
Chapel Hill
North Carolina 27514
U. S. A.

NORTH CAROLINA STUDIES IN THE ROMANCE LANGUAGES AND LITERATURES

I.S.B.N. Prefix 0-8078-

Recent Titles

"LA QUERELLE DE LA ROSE: Letters and Documents", by Joseph L. Baird and John R. Kane. 1978. (No. 199). *-9199-1.*

TWO AGAINST TIME. *A Study of the Very Present Worlds of Paul Claudel and Charles Péguy,* by Joy Nachod Humes. 1978. (No. 200). *-9200-9.*

TECHNIQUES OF IRONY IN ANATOLE FRANCE. Essay on *Les Sept Femmes de la Barbe-Bleue,* by Diane Wolfe Levy. 1978. (No. 201). *-9201-7.*

THE PERIPHRASTIC FUTURES FORMED BY THE ROMANCE REFLEXES OF "VADO (AD)" "PLUS INFINITIVE, by James Joseph Champion. 1978 (No. 202). *-9202-5.*

THE EVOLUTION OF THE LATIN /b/-/ṷ/ MERGER: A Quantitative and Comparative Analysis of the *B-V* Alternation in Latin Inscriptions, by Joseph Louis Barbarino. 1978 (No. 203). *-9203-3.*

METAPHORIC NARRATION: THE STRUCTURE AND FUNCTION OF METAPHORS IN "A LA RECHERCHE DU TEMPS PERDU", by Inge Karalus Crosman. 1978 (No. 204). *-9204-1.*

LE VAIN SIECLE GUERPIR. A Literary Approach to Sainthood through Old French Hagiography of the Twelfth Century, by Phyllis Johnson and Brigitte Cazelles. 1979. (No. 205). *-9205-X.*

THE POETRY OF CHANGE: A STUDY OF THE SURREALIST WORKS OF BENJAMIN PÉRET, by Julia Field Costich. 1979. (No. 206). *-9206-8.*

NARRATIVE PERSPECTIVE IN THE POST-CIVIL WAR NOVELS OF FRANCISCO AYALA "MUERTES DE PERRO" AND "EL FONDO DEL VASO", by Maryellen Bieder. 1979. (No. 207). *-9207-6.*

RABELAIS: HOMO LOGOS, by Alice Fiola Berry. 1979. (No. 208). *-9208-4.*

"DUEÑAS" AND "DONCELLAS": A STUDY OF THE "DOÑA RODRÍGUEZ" EPISODE IN "DON QUIJOTE", by Conchita Herdman Marianella. 1979. (No. 209). *-9209-2.*

PIERRE BOAISTUAU'S "HISTOIRES TRAGIQUES": A STUDY OF NARRATIVE FORM AND TRAGIC VISION, by Richard A. Carr. 1979. (No. 210). *-9210-6.*

REALITY AND EXPRESSION IN THE POETRY OF CARLOS PELLICER, by George Melnykovich. 1979. (No. 211). *-9211-4.*

MEDIEVAL MAN, HIS UNDERSTANDING OF HIMSELF, HIS SOCIETY, AND THE WORLD, by Urban T. Holmes, Jr. 1980. (No. 212). *-9212-2.*

MÉMOIRES SUR LA LIBRAIRIE ET SUR LA LIBERTÉ DE LA PRESSE, introduction and notes by Graham E. Rodmell. 1979. (No. 213). *-9213-0.*

THE FICTIONS OF THE SELF. THE EARLY WORKS OF MAURICE BARRES, by Gordon Shenton. 1979. (No. 214). *-9214-9.*

CECCO ANGIOLIERI. A STUDY, by Gifford P. Orwen. 1979. (No. 215). *-9215-7.*

THE INSTRUCTIONS OF SAINT LOUIS: A CRITICAL TEXT, by David O'Connell. 1979. (No. 216). *-9216-5.*

ARTFUL ELOQUENCE, JEAN LEMAIRE DE BELGES AND THE RHETORICAL TRADITION, by Michael F. O. Jenkins. 1980 (No. 217). *-9217-3.*

A CONCORDANCE TO MARIVAUX'S COMEDIES IN PROSE, edited by Donald C. Spinelli. 1979 (No. 218). 4 volumes, *-9218-1* (set); *-9219-X* (v. 1); *-9220-3* (v. 2); *-9221-1* (v. 3); *-9222-X* (v. 4.)

ABYSMAL GAMES IN THE NOVELS OF SAMUEL BECKETT, by Angela B. Moorjani. 1982 (No. 219). *-9223-8.*

GERMAIN NOUVEAU DIT HUMILIS: ÉTUDE BIOGRAPHIQUE, par Alexandre L. Amprimoz. 1983 (No. 220). *-9224-6.*

When ordering please cite the *ISBN Prefix* plus the last four digits for each title.

Send orders to: University of North Carolina Press
Chapel Hill
North Carolina 27514
U. S. A.

The Department of Romance Studies Digital Arts and Collaboration Lab at the University of North Carolina at Chapel Hill is proud to support the digitization of the North Carolina Studies in the Romance Languages and Literatures series.

DEPARTMENT OF
Romance Studies
Digital Arts and Collaboration Lab

CPSIA information can be obtained
at www.ICGtesting.com
Printed in the USA
LVHW110355031121
702252LV00008B/1317

9 780807 892251